Proceedings of the
Energy & Mineral Law Institute 2023

Forty-Fourth Annual
Energy & Mineral Law Institute

June 18-20, 2023
Charleston, South Carolina

Anna Girard Fletcher
Editor-in-Chief

Published By
The Energy & Mineral Law Foundation
2365 Harrodsburg Road, Ste B215
Lexington, KY 40504
2024

Questions about this publication?
For assistance with shipments, billing
or other customer service matters,
please call 859.231.0271.

For editorial assistance,
please call Anna Girard Fletcher
at 859.231.0271.

Disclaimer: The views expressed in this volume are solely those of the authors and should not be taken to reflect the views of the Energy & Mineral Law Foundation. This publication is presented with the understanding that neither the Foundation nor the authors are engaged in rendering legal, accounting, or other professional services. In no event, including negligence on the part of the authors, the reviewers, or the Foundation, will the authors, reviewers, or the Foundation be liable for any direct, indirect, or consequential damages resulting from the use of this material.

Copyright © 2024 by the Energy & Mineral Law Foundation
All Rights Reserved
Printed in the United States of America

When published as issued, works of the federal and state governments, including all statutes and decisions of the courts, as well as all legislative and administrative histories, studies, and reports, are matters in the public domain. As compiled, arranged, and edited, however, these works and all other materials in this publication are subject to the foregoing copyright notice.

CITE AS
44 *Energy & Min. L. Inst.* __ (2024)

Table of Contents

Preface v
President's Remarks — Clay Larkin

Chapter 1 3
Appalachian Energy Law Case Update 2023
Whitney R. Kerns

§ 1.01. Introduction 3
§ 1.02. Nationally Impactful Litigation 3
§ 1.03. Case Developments in the Ohio Marketable Title Act 7
§ 1.04. Recent Royalty Disputes 10
§ 1.05. New Coal Lease Litigation 12

Chapter 2 15
Devil's Advocate: Crossing the Line of Zealous Advocacy
Katrina Bowers, Austin D. Rogers and Joshua Snyder

§ 2.01. Introduction 15
§ 2.02. The Law of Extortion and Model Rules of Professional Conduct 16
§ 2.03. Case Illustrations 20
§ 2.04. Conclusion 23

Chapter 3 25
Fair Labor Standards Act Compliance Update
Michael C. Griffaton

§ 3.01. Summary 26
§ 3.02. Why Wage-Hour Compliance Matters 27
§ 3.03. Overtime Requirements Under the Fair Labor Standards Act 31
§ 3.04. Day-Rate Compensation Plan 33
§ 3.05. Misclassification of Employees as Independent Contractors 38
§ 3.06 Compensation for Travel Time 52
§ 3.07. State Law Protections 57
§ 3.08. Minimizing Liability by Auditing Payroll Practices 59

Chapter 4 67
Protecting Your Brand with Trademarks
Joshua A. Claybourn

§ 4.01. Introduction 68
§ 4.02. Understanding Trademarks 68
§ 4.03. Trademark Selection Process 70
§ 4.04. Trademark Registration Process 72

§ 4.05. Trademark Maintenance and Renewal 74
§ 4.06. Trademark Enforcement and Dispute Resolution 75
§ 4.07. Trademark Protection in Mergers in Acquisitions 77
§ 4.08. Trademark Best Practices 79
§ 4.09. Conclusion 80

Chapter 5 .... **83**
AAPL Joint Operating Agreements: Standards of Operator Conduct, Exculpatory Provisions, and Jury Charges

Michael K. Reer

§ 5.01. Joint Development of Oil and Gas Resources: Unique Problems and Opportunities 84
§ 5.02. Why Use a Joint Operating Agreement? 84
§ 5.03. Operator Standards of Conduct 90
§ 5.04. Exculpatory Provisions 96
§ 5.05. Lawsuits: Allocating Cost and Risk 118
§ 5.06. Conclusion 121

Chapter 6 .... **123**
PHMSA/LDAR Rulemaking: What's Proposed and What's Next

Keith J. Coyle and Abigail M. Reecer

§ 6.01. Introduction 123
§ 6.02. Background on PHMSA Rulemaking 124
§ 6.03. 2020 PIPES Act Congressional Mandate 128
§ 6.04. May 2023 Proposed Rule on LDAR 128

Chapter 7 .... **137**
Who Owns the Pore Space? A State-by-State Overview of Pore Space Ownership for Geological Carbon Capture, Utilization, and Storage

Ryan Haddad, Lucas Liben and Simone Senior

§ 7.01. Introduction 137
§ 7.02. The "American Rule" 138
§ 7.03. The "English Rule" 141
§ 7.04. Undecided Jurisdictions 141
§ 7.05. Conclusion 146

Chapter 8 149
MSHA and OSHA Safety Enforcement in the Biden Administration: What's Changing and Where Are We Headed in Enforcement
Mark E. Heath and Chris Petersen
§ 8.01. Introduction 151
§ 8.02. What to Expect from MSHA in 2023: An Employer's Guide to Developments in Workplace Safety 151
§ 8.03. What to Expect from OSHA in 2023: An Employer's Guide 165

Officers and Executive Committee 181
Foundation Membership 186
Table of Reported Cases .... I-i
Major Topic Index .... I-vi

Preface

Dear EMLF Members, Patrons, and Friends,

Thank you for attending the 44th Annual Institute in Charleston, South Carolina. The important work of EMLF was on strong display during this event, and throughout the year. As a direct result of your active support and participation, EMLF continues to distinguish itself as a national leader in the fields of energy and mineral law.

The 2023 Annual Institute Programming Committee, led by Co-Chairs Alexandria Lay and Todd Myers, put together an impressive program which highlighted both EMLF's traditional core strengths in coal, oil & gas and related energy issues, as well as our innovative scholarship in areas such as renewable resources and critical minerals. Through thoughtful, diverse, and balanced programming, EMLF members enhanced their existing practices and are prepared to address new and emerging issues.

I want to thank everyone who planned the agenda, spoke, drafted, edited, asked a question about, or otherwise contributed to any of our scholarship this year. Your contributions help us all advance in the understanding of these important legal issues.

But EMLF is about more than just scholarship. Our members are friends and colleagues, and the fun and fellowship of events like the Annual Institute distinguish EMLF from other CLE organizations. Through participation in the EMLF, the energy law community builds relationships and makes connections that make the practice of law more enjoyable.

There was much for the EMLF membership to celebrate at the Annual Institute. At the top of the list was the awarding of $30,500 in scholarship funding to eight law students from six of our member law schools. EMLF also provided funding for nineteen students from five law schools to join us, at no cost, in Charleston, thanks to the Russ Schetroma Scholarship Fund.

These students are the future of our profession, and I am particularly proud of the hard work of so many EMLF members in fostering the continued development of these students. To that end, I would like to specifically applaud the efforts of the EMLF Scholarship Committee who, as always, made wise decisions concerning the use of the foundation's resources to further legal education.

EMLF's highest honor — the John L. McClaugherty Award — was given to our friend and colleague Natalie Jefferis. To fully honor all of Natalie's work on behalf of EMLF would require another volume of these proceedings, but to put it succinctly, there simply could not be a more deserving recipient of this award.

As our President, Natalie led this organization through some of its most critical and demanding times, and did so with unmatched skill, dedication, kindness, and enthusiasm. We were lucky to have her as a leader, and are very fortunate to continue to call her a colleague in this organization. We honor and thank Natalie for all of her contributions to EMLF.

We are fortunate to have a great EMLF leadership team comprised of officers, committee members, and trustees. Of particular note, my immediate predecessor, Sheila Nolan Gartland, did a wonderful job of helping me learn this role and she remains an invaluable part of our leadership.

Most of all, I want to thank our incredible Executive Director, Anna Girard Fletcher. Anna possesses an unrivaled mix of judgment, wisdom, intelligence and, perhaps most importantly during my tenure, patience. She works every day to advance our organization's mission, and I am very thankful for her hard work and dedication.

Finally, I was delighted to pass the gavel to our incoming President, Britt Freund. Having worked alongside Britt for several years now, I know he possesses incredible thoughtfulness, kindness, and skill. EMLF will be in good hands under Britt's leadership.

It was truly an honor to serve as the President of this organization. This foundation has meant more to me and my career than I can express, but know that I am very grateful to each of you whom I have met and worked with over the years.

The strength of this organization lies in each of you, and the countless ways in which you have served to make it better. From joining leadership as a trustee or officer, writing a paper, or simply attending our events, you make the foundation better by your presence and participation. Please continue to invest in the next generation of energy and mineral practitioners by

PREFACE

bringing your younger colleagues to our events and encouraging them to actively participate. I know you will, and that our best days remain ahead of us.

Clay Larkin
EMLF President
2022-2023

Chapter 1

Appalachian Energy Law Case Update 2023

Whitney R. Kerns
Bowles Rice
Morgantown, West Virginia

Synopsis

§ 1.01.	Introduction	3
§ 1.02.	Nationally Impactful Litigation	3
	[1] — *Sackett, et ux. v. Environmental Protection Agency, et al.*	4
	[2] — *West Virginia et al. v. Environmental Protection Agency et al.*	5
	[3] — Climate Change Cases Staying in State Courts	7
§ 1.03.	Case Developments in the Ohio Marketable Title Act	7
	[1] — The Marketable Title Act	7
	[2] — *Peppertree Farms, L.L.C., et al. v. Thonen et al.*	8
	[3] — *Chartier et al. v. Rice Drilling D LLC et al.*	9
§ 1.04.	Recent Royalty Disputes	10
	[1] — *Corder v. Antero Resources Corp.*	11
	[2] — *Dressler Family, LP, v. PennEnergy Resources, LLC*	12
§ 1.05.	New Coal Lease Litigation	12
	[1] — *Freeport Gas Coal Trust v. Harrison County Coal Resources, Inc.*	12

§ 1.01. Introduction.

Changing administrations, advances in technology, attention to climate change, and ensuing lease disputes have all contributed to a busy year for energy-related litigation. The Appalachian region, being a relative hot bed for energy development in both renewable and non-renewable sectors, has promulgated much of the new energy case load, and is positioned to be particularly impacted by national policy effectuated through recent opinions from the Supreme Court of the United States. This chapter surveys recent decisions in energy-related cases, focusing primarily on those cases deriving from the Appalachian region, while also surveying national litigation notably significant to the region.

§ 1.02. Nationally Impactful Litigation.

The Clean Water Act and the Clean Air Act stand at the forefront of energy-related cases on the national stage as two key decisions came down from the United States Supreme Court in 2022 and 2023, broadly shaping energy policy under the Acts and limiting the regulatory grasp of the Environmental Protection Agency. Additionally, it appears that the liability for harmful effects of climate change allegedly attributed to carbon emissions will remain a question for state courts.

[1] — *Sackett, et ux. v. Environmental Protection Agency, et al.*

By virtue of its opinion issued in *Sackett v. Environmental Protection Agency*, the Supreme Court of the United States (SCOTUS) scaled back protections of this nation's waters by limiting the definition of "waters of the United States" under the Clean Water Act (CWA), a position supported by the mining and fossil fuel industries.[1]

Factually, in 2004 Michael and Chantell Sackett purchased property near Priest Lake, Idaho, and began backfilling the lot with dirt to prepare for building a home.[2] A few months into the project, the Environmental Protection Agency (EPA) notified the Sacketts that the backfilling violated the CWA, which prohibits discharging pollutants into "the waters of the United States."[3] To that effect, the EPA charged the Sacketts with violating the CWA by contaminating protected wetlands, and the couple faced penalties in excess of forty thousand dollars ($40,000) per day if they failed to comply with EPA orders to restore the property.[4]

The district court entered summary judgment for the EPA, and the Ninth Circuit on appeal agreed, holding that the CWA covers wetlands with an ecologically significant nexus to traditional navigable waterways protected by the CWA, a standard to which the Sackett's wetlands qualified.[5] However,

---

[1] *See* Amy Westervelt, In a Gift to Polluting Industries, Supreme Court Rolls Back Clean Water Act Protections, THE INTERCEPT (May 26, 2023), https://theintercept.com/2023/05/26/supreme-court-sackett-epa-clean-water-act/.

[2] Sackett v. Environmental Protection Agency, No. 21-454 at 1. (hereinafter cited as *Sackett*)

[3] *Id.*; 33 U.S.C. § 1362(7).

[4] *Sackett*, No. 21-454 at 1.

[5] *Id.*

SCOTUS disagreed. In a five to four (5-4) opinion delivered by Justice Alito, the Court held, relying on the plurality opinion issued in *Rapanos v. United States*,[6] that the "waters of the United States" do not include *all* wetlands, but rather includes only those that are, as a practical matter, indistinguishable from the waters of the United States, such that it is difficult to determine where the water ends, and the wetland begins.[7] Further, per the Court, a wetland is indistinguishable from a waterway when the wetland has a continuous surface connection to bodies of water that are waters of the United States in their own right, although temporary interruptions in surface connection may occur because of tides or dry spells.[8]

In other words, for a wetland to now be protected by the CWA one must establish that (1) the wetland is adjacent to a water of the United States and (2) the wetland has a continuous surface connection to that waterway. The decision marks a distinct reduction in the scope of the EPA, which, one could argue, equates with less regulation and restriction for mining operators and fossil fuel recovery.

[2] — *West Virginia et al. v. Environmental Protection Agency et al.*

Of particular importance to the coal and natural gas producing states within the Appalachian region is the 2022 case of *W. Va. et al. v. EPA*, in which nineteen states, led by West Virginia, together with several power companies, challenged carbon dioxide emission standards promulgated by the EPA.[9]

Historically, in 2015, the EPA instituted the Clean Power Plan (the "Plan") which addressed carbon dioxide emissions from existing coal and natural gas fired power plants.[10] Arguably, no existing coal plant would be able to achieve the EPA's emission caps without an entire shift to clean

---

[6] Rapanos v. United States, 547 U.S. 715, 742 (2006).
[7] *Sackett*, No. 21-454 at 22.
[8] *Id.* at 21-22.
[9] *Id.*
[10] *Id.* at 5.

energy sources. The Plan was repealed once the United States presidential administrations changed hands from President Barack Obama to President Donald Trump, but, when the presidency transferred from Trump to President Joe Biden the EPA again asserted its inclination to set stringent emission standards, ripening the case for SCOTUS' consideration.[11]

In evaluating the legality of the EPA's emission standards, SCOTUS employed the "major questions doctrine," which had not before been absorbed into Supreme Court jurisprudence. The doctrine is a principle of statutory interpretation in administrative law which maintains that courts will presume Congress does not delegate to executive agencies issues of major political or economic significance.[12]

Under the purview of the major questions doctrine, SCOTUS ruled that the EPA does not have congressional authority to limit emissions at existing power plants through generation shifting to cleaner sources.[13] Focusing on intent, the Court considered whether the purpose of the EPA's emission limits was to (a) change the electric grid of our nation, or (b) regulate carbon emissions from an individual source, finding that the intent of the EPA with regards to the emission standards fell within the camp of the former.[14] In this regard, the Court struck down the EPA's carbon emission standards for existing coal fired power plants, determining the EPA had exceeded its statutory authority because Congress did not charge the EPA with authority of the makeup of this country's entire power system.[15] Nevertheless, while the EPA may not tell power plant operators that they must shift from fossil fuel energy sources to renewables, the EPA may still develop standards that would require individual facilities to install pollution control measures, such as carbon capture technology.

---

[11] *Id.* at 3-4.
[12] *Id.* at 20.
[13] *Id.*
[14] *Id.* at 20-22.
[15] *Id.*

[3] — Climate Change Cases Staying in State Courts.

In April 2023, SCOTUS denied review to a series of major energy companies seeking to remove certain climate change cases to federal court. Five separate cases were brought by municipalities claiming to have been harmed by the effects of climate change allegedly attributed to certain energy companies' carbon emissions. In summary, SCOTUS found that the involved circuit court rulings did not implicate federal law, meaning such climate change lawsuits may continue in state courts which could, arguably, be more favorable to plaintiffs.[16]

§ 1.03. Case Developments in the Ohio Marketable Title Act.

Within the Appalachian region sits the state of Ohio which offers a statutory measure titled the Ohio Marketable Title Act intended, in theory, to simplify determinations of mineral ownership within the state by clearing up lost severed interests in real property. However, recent decisions from Ohio courts have muddied the operation of this Act.

[1] — The Marketable Title Act.

Pursuant to the Marketable Title Act (the "MTA") a person who has an unbroken chain of title to any interest in land for at least forty (40) years has marketable record title to the interest.[17] Such "marketable record title" means a title of record which operates to extinguish any interests and claims existing prior to the claimant's "root of title,"[18] which said "root of title" is defined as,

> [T]hat conveyance or other title transaction in the chain of title of a person, purporting to create the interest claimed by such person, upon which he relies as a basis for the marketability of his title,

---

[16] Suncor Energy (U.S.A.) Inc., et al. v. Board of County Commissioners of Boulder County, et al., Case No. 21-1550; Mayor and City Council of Baltimore v. BP PLC et al., Case No. 22-361; Chevron Corp. et al. v. San Mateo, California, et al., Case No. 22-495; Shell oil Products Co. LLC, et al. v. State of Rhode Island, Case No. 22-524; Sunoco LP, et al. v. City and Council of Honolulu, et al., Case No. 22-523.
[17] Ohio Rev. Code § 5301.48.
[18] Ohio Rev. Code § 5301.47(A).

§ 1.03

and which was the most recent to be recorded as of a date forty years prior to the time when marketability is being determined.[19]

A "title transaction" is further defined as,

> [A]ny transaction affecting title to an interest in land, including title by will or descent, title by tax deed, or by trustee's, assignee's, guardian's, executor's administrator's, or sheriff's deed, or decree of any court, as well as warranty deed, quitclaim deed, or mortgage.[20]

Effectively, any adverse severed interest or claim that existed prior to the root of title are extinguished and deemed null and void.

[2] — *Peppertree Farms, L.L.C., et al. v. Thonen et al.*

The 2022 decision from the Supreme Court of Ohio in the case of *Peppertree Farms, L.L.C., et al. v. Thonen et al.*[21] provides some qualification as to what constitutes a "title transaction" as it is defined under the MTA.[22] In pertinent part, the court considered whether the recording of a decedent's will that does not specifically distribute the decedent's oil and gas rights was sufficient to prevent those rights from being extinguished by the MTA.[23] The court reasoned that a will that distributes the decedent's oil and gas rights affects title to an interest in land, and when oil and gas rights pass through intestacy, a title transaction also occurs. However, where a will does not transfer, encumber, or otherwise affect title to the oil and gas rights, and the inheritance of those rights was not recorded and does not appear in the record chain of title, neither the recording of the will nor the inheritance is a recorded title transaction preventing the oil and gas rights from being extinguished by the MTA.[24]

---

[19] Ohio Rev. Code § 5301.47(E).
[20] Ohio Rev. Code § 5301.47(F).
[21] Peppertree Farms, L.L.C., et al. v. Thonen et al., 167 Ohio St.3d 52, 2022-Ohio-395.
[22] *Id.*
[23] *Id.* at 62, 1070.
[24] *Id.* at 63, 1071.

[3] — *Chartier et al. v. Rice Drilling D LLC et al.*

In order for an adverse interest in real property to be extinguished under the MTA, it must not be <u>specifically</u> referenced in the requisite unbroken forty-year chain of title of the party claiming superior title to the real estate. As more particularly provided under the MTA, record marketable title is subject to:

> All interests and defects which are inherent in the muniments of which such chain of record title is formed; provided that a general reference in such muniments, or any of them, to easements, use restrictions, or other interests created prior to the root of title shall not be sufficient to preserve them, unless specific identification be made therein of a recorded title transaction which creates such easement, use restriction, or other interest[.][25]

In 2021, the Ohio Supreme Court promulgated that the fundamental question as to whether a reference to an adverse interest is sufficiently specific to preserve the interest under the MTA, or general and therefore not preserved, is whether someone examining the chain of title can determine from the recitation or reference to which interest the recitation or reference is referring.[26] In this regard, the court reasoned that a vague reservation comprised of boilerplate language excepting any and all reservations that may or may not exist is <u>not</u> sufficiently specific to preserve the reserved interest, but found that a reference to a particular mineral reservation recited through a chain of title using the same language as the recorded title transaction that created it was sufficiently specific to preserve the reserved mineral interest.[27]

However, it appears that the court's guidance failed to set a clear standard by which to determine the level of specificity required in a reference or reservation to preserve a severed interest. That is, in the 2023 case of *Chartier et al. v. Rice Drilling LLC et al.*,[28] the Seventh District Court of

---

[25] Ohio Rev. Code § 5301.49.
[26] *See* Erickson et al. v. Morrison et al., 165 Ohio St.3d 76, 176 N.E.3d 1 (2021).
[27] *Id.* at 8, 83.
[28] Chartier v. Rice Drilling D LLC, 2023 Ohio 272, 206 N.E.3d 755 (Ohio Ct. App. 2023). (hereinafter cited as *Chartier*).

Appeals of Ohio, Belmont County, deemed certain reservation language to be general, and therefore insufficient to preserve the reserved interest,[29] while some might argue the reservation language in question fit the bill of specificity required for preservation under the standard previously set by the Ohio Supreme Court.

More specifically, the court in *Chartier* considered reservation language contained in an initial deed which read, "excepting and reserving all the Pittsburgh #8 vein of coal and 1/2 of all oil and gas royalties under said lands together with mining rights and reservations made in the deed conveying said lands from Annie E. Carpenter to Bessie Cook."[30] Two subsequent deeds executed after the initial deed containing the subject reservation contained identical reservation language, and the question presented to the court was, in part, whether the subsequent reference to the reservation constituted specific references sufficient to preserve the reserved one-half (1/2) interest, or general references failing to preserve the same.[31] In answering this question, the court reasoned that the reservation language was ambiguous because the reservation to which the reference referred was open to more than one interpretation - it could effectively apply to mining rights, mining reservations, or any and all other reservations recited in the initial deed. In turn, because the reference in the subsequent deeds was ambiguous, the court found it was also general, and therefore insufficient to preserve the interest reserved in the initial deed.[32]

Further cases will likely follow as Ohio continues to flesh out the operation and effect of the MTA.

§ 1.04.   Recent Royalty Disputes.

A relatively hot topic amidst current energy-related cases is when and what costs or expenses may be deducted from landowner royalty payments

---

[29] *Chartier*, at 763-64.
[30] *Id.* at 763.
[31] *Id.*
[32] *Id.* at 764.

ENERGY LAW CASE UPDATE § 1.04

payable under valid and subsisting oil and gas leases, lending to the following developing cases.

[1] — *Corder v. Antero Resources Corp.*

West Virginia in particular has seen an uptick in litigation revolving around royalty payment disputes. In this state, under the purview that an oil and gas lessee is obligated by an implied covenant to market oil and gas produced from a leased tract and must therefore bear the burden of most post-production costs unless otherwise specifically provided in the lease, six conditions must be met within an oil and gas lease before the lessee may deduct post-production costs from lessor royalties: (1) the lease must expressly provide that the lessor bear some part of the costs incurred between the wellhead and the point of sale; (2) the lease must identify with particularity the specific deductions that the lessee may take; (3) the lease must expressly provide for a method of calculating the amount to be deducted from royalties for post-production costs; (4) the costs, which have been identified with particularity, must be actually incurred; (5) the amount of the costs must be reasonable; and (6) the lessee must prove all costs as it would in an action for accounting.[33]

With these conditions in mind, the United States Court of Appeals for the Fourth Circuit in the case of *Corder v. Antero Resources Corp.*[34] considered the validity of certain post-production cost deductions taken from royalty payments pursuant to market enhancement clauses contained within the respective leases at issue. The subject leases provided that post-productions costs would not be deducted from lessor royalty payments, except as follows:

> However, any such costs which result in enhancing the value of the marketable oil, gas or other products to receive a better price

---

[33] *See* Wellman v. Energy Resources, Inc., 210 W. Va. 200, 557 S.E.2d 254 (2001); Estate of Tawney v. Columbia Natural Resources, L.L.C., 219 W. Va. 266, 633 S.E.2d 22 (2006).
[34] Corder v. Antero Res. Corp. 57 F.4th 384 (4th Cir. 2023). (hereinafter cited as *Corder*).

11

may be deducted...so long as they are based on lessee's actual cost of such enhancement...[35]

The appellate court found that the market enhancement clause contained with the subject leases had an unambiguous meaning and satisfied the requirements for deduction of post-production costs from lessor royalty payments so long as the expenses deducted enhanced the value of the product and were incurred by the lessee after the gas products produced pursuant to the lease became marketable.[36] Although not binding on other state courts, the Fourth Circuit appellate court's decision provides a logical and persuasive framework for interpreting market enhancement clause cases in other states within the fourth circuit.

[2] — *Dressler Family, LP, v. PennEnergy Resources, LLC.*

On February 15, 2023, the Supreme Court of Pennsylvania granted allocator to address the question of whether an oil and gas lease provision setting royalties at one-eighth of "gross proceeds received from the sale of [gas] at the prevailing price for gas sold at the well" permits the lessee to deduct post-production costs from royalties due the lessor.[37] The court is now set to determine if Pennsylvania shall be a jurisdiction permitting post-production cost reductions from "at the well" royalty calculations, a key question to Pennsylvania's oil and gas industry.[38]

§ 1.05. New Coal Lease Litigation.
[1] — *Freeport Gas Coal Trust v. Harrison County Coal Resources, Inc.*

The recent case of *Freeport Gas Coal Trust v. Harrison County Coal Resources, Inc.*[39] reaffirms longstanding lease interpretation principles.

---

[35] *Corder*, at 390.
[36] *Id.* at 399.
[37] Dressler Family, LP v. PennEnergy Res., 2022 Pa. Super. 77 (Pa. Super. Ct. 2022)
[38] *Id.*
[39] Freeport Gas Coal Tr. v. Harrison Cnty. Coal Res., Civil Action 1:21CV123 (N.D.W. Va. Mar. 20, 2023).

In rejecting claims that a coal lessee breached certain implied covenants under an active coal lease, the District Court for the Northern District of West Virginia held in pertinent part that: (i) where a lease expressly places the commencement of mining within the discretion of the lessee, there is no ambiguity within the lease and the recognized implied covenant to commence mining within a reasonable time will not apply; (ii) reformation of a royalty rate contained in a historical lease which remains active requires mutual mistake which is not present where the lessee bore the risk of a rise in the value of coal by accepting a fixed royalty for the production of coal from the leased premises when it could have otherwise anticipated fluctuations in pricing and prepared for the same within the language of the lease.[40] One should take caution, however, in that different lease provisions may take on different meanings, and the construction of any certain coal lease must ultimately be based upon the particular clause at issue within the context of the lease as a whole.

---

[40] *Id.* at 8-9.

Chapter 2

Devil's Advocate: Crossing the Line of Zealous Advocacy

Katrina Bowers
Austin D. Rogers
Babst Calland
Charleston, West Virginia

Joshua Snyder
Babst Calland
Pittsburgh, Pennsylvania

Synopsis

§ 2.01.	Introduction	15
§ 2.02.	The Law of Extortion and Model Rules of Professional Conduct	16
	[1] — Federal Extortion Law	16
	[2] — Model Rules	17
	[a] — Model Rule 3.1—Meritorious Claims and Contentions	17
	[b] — Model Rule 3.6—Trial Publicity	18
	[c] — Model Rule 4.1—Truthfulness in Statements to Others	19
	[d] — Model Rule 4.4—Respect for Rights of Third Persons	19
	[e] — Model Rule 8.4—Misconduct	20
§ 2.03.	Case Illustrations	20
	[1] — Michael Avenatti	20
	[2] — Timothy Litzenburg	21
	[3] — William Dean	22
	[4] — Amy Mousavi	22
§ 2.04.	Conclusion	23

§ 2.01. Introduction.

Settlement negotiations take place in almost every legal dispute. However, several recent high-profile cases have raised the question of when an attorney crosses the line from settlement negotiations to extortion.

This chapter will identify the laws and model rules applicable to this determination and provide context to the issue by analyzing them against cases involving Michael Avenatti, Timothy Litzenburg, William Dean, and Amy Mousavi.

§ 2.02. The Law of Extortion and Model Rules of Professional Conduct.
[1] — Federal Extortion Law.

Federal extortion law is lumped into crimes dealing with interstate communications and includes four subsections. Subsections (a)–(c) address various forms of kidnapping and, most relevant for this paper, subsection (d) codifies the colloquial term "extortion" as:

> [w]hoever, with intent to extort from any person, firm, association, or corporation, any money or other thing of value, transmits in interstate or foreign commerce any communication containing any threat to injure the property or reputation of the addressee or of another or the reputation of a deceased person or any threat to accuse the addressee or any other person of a crime, shall be fined under this title or imprisoned not more than two years, or both.[1]

Pennsylvania,[2] Ohio,[3] West Virginia,[4] Kentucky,[5] Virginia,[6] and Texas[7] each has their own definition of criminal extortion. But each concerns the same principal: a person attempting to obtain something of value by threat of injury to another's reputation.

[2] — Model Rules.

Since 1983 the American Bar Association has propounded The Model Rules of Professional Conduct ("Model Rules"). The Model Rules serve as guideposts for professional and ethical conduct in the legal field. Similarly, all fifty states and the District of Columbia have adopted legal ethical rules

---

[1] 18 U.S.C. § 875(d) (2018).
[2] Pa.C.S. § 3923(a) (2019).
[3] Ohio Rev. Code § 2905.11(5) (2021).
[4] W. Va. Code § 61-2-13(a) (2018).
[5] Ky Rev. Stat. § 514.080(c) (2021).
[6] Va. Code Ann. § 18.2-59(iv) (2010).
[7] Tex. Penal Code § 31.01 (2019)

ETHICS § 2.02

based, in part, on these Model Rules. The Model Rules are divided into sections based on topic. Of particular relevance here are sections 3 and 4. Section 3 is titled "advocate" and addresses ethical responsibilities of lawyers in their roles as advocates. Section 4 is titled "transactions with persons other than clients" and addresses transactions between attorneys and third parties.

As such, the Model Rules show generally accepted rules governing the ethical practice of law and will serve as the standards in this paper. However, at the end of the day, they are just model rules, and each state has its own set of rules, some of which differ. This chapter notes differences in the Pennsylvania, Ohio, West Virginia, Kentucky, Virginia, and Texas rules of professional conduct but does not conduct a fifty-state survey of ethical rules.

[a] — Model Rule 3.1 — Meritorious Claims and Contentions.

As the title suggests, Model Rule 3.1 aims to curb frivolous lawsuits. Specifically, the Rule provides that "[a] lawyer shall not bring or defend a proceeding, or assert or controvert an issue therein, unless there is a basis in law and fact for doing so that is not frivolous, which includes a good faith argument for an extension, modification or reversal of existing law."[8] Pennsylvania,[9] West Virginia,[10] and Virginia[11] have each adopted this rule in its entirety. Ohio[12] and Kentucky[13] have modified the rule slightly, but the substance is very similar. Texas, on the other hand, does not have an equivalent rule in its rules of professional responsibility.

[b] — Model Rule 3.6 — Trial Publicity.

Model Rule 3.6 has four subsections, three of which are relevant here. Subsection "a" prevents a lawyer from making extrajudicial statements they know or should have known would be disseminated and have a substantial

---

[8] MODEL RULES OF PROF'L CONDUCT r. 3.1(a).
[9] Pennsylvania Rules of Prof. Conduct, Rule 3.1 (2023).
[10] W. Va. R. Prof. Conduct 3.1 (2015).
[11] Virginia Rules of Prof. Conduct, Rule 3.1 (2022).
[12] Ohio R. Prof. Conduct, Rule 3.1 (2021).
[13] S. Ct. of Ky. Rules, Rule 3.130(3.1) (2023).

§ 2.02

likelihood of prejudicing a judicial proceeding.[14] Subsection "b" provides seven exceptions to the general rule:

(1) the claim, offense, defense, and (usually) persons involved;
(2) information in a public record;
(3) an investigation is in progress;
(4) scheduling or result of any step in litigation;
(5) a request for assistance obtaining evidence;
(6) likelihood of substantial harm to an individual or public interest; and
(7) in a criminal case.[15]

Finally, subsection "c" provides an eighth exception to the rule to protect a client from "substantial undue prejudicial effect of recent publicity not initiated by the lawyer or the lawyer's client."[16] These exceptions provide carveouts when an attorney may, for example, speak to the press about a pending case.

Pennsylvania,[17] West Virginia,[18] and Kentucky[19] have all adopted this Model Rule in whole. Ohio has modified subsection (b) but has maintained the remainder of the Model Rule.[20] Texas and Virginia do not have a similar rule on the books.

[c] — Model Rule 4.1 — Truthfulness in Statements to Others.

Shifting to the section concerning attorneys' dealings with third parties, Model Rule 4.1 disallows attorneys from making false statements.[21] The Model Rule even goes beyond false statements and requires the disclosure

---

[14] MODEL RULES OF PROF'L CONDUCT r. 3.6(a).
[15] MODEL RULES OF PROF'L CONDUCT r. 3.6(b).
[16] MODEL RULES OF PROF'L CONDUCT r. 3.6(c).
[17] Pennsylvania Rules of Prof. Conduct, Rule 3.6 (2023).
[18] W. Va. R. Prof. Conduct 3.6 (2015).
[19] S. Ct. of Ky. Rules, Rule 3.130(3.6) (2023).
[20] Ohio R. Prof. Conduct, Rule 3.6 (2021).
[21] MODEL RULES OF PROF'L CONDUCT r. 4.1(a).

ETHICS § 2.02

of material facts when necessary to avoid fraudulent acts of a client.[22] This Model Rule does not, however, impose an affirmative duty on the attorney to disclose relevant facts.

West Virginia,[23] Kentucky,[24] and Texas[25] all have a version of this rule in their various rules of professional conduct but have not adopted the Model Rule in whole. Pennsylvania, Ohio, and Virginia have not adopted this Model Rule.

[d] — Model Rule 4.4 — Respect for Rights of Third Persons.

Model Rule 4.4 clarifies that while attorneys owe certain duties to their client, these duties do not allow the attorney to disregard the rights of third parties. The Model Rule prohibits an attorney from doing things that have "no substantial purpose other than to embarrass, delay, or burden a third person, or use methods of obtaining evidence that violate the legal rights of such a person."[26] This responsibility further extends in the event an attorney inadvertently obtains information from an opposing party.[27]

West Virginia has adopted this rule without change.[28] Pennsylvania,[29] Ohio,[30] Kentucky,[31] Virginia,[32] and Texas[33] have all adopted a similar version but modified the Model Rule in some way.

---

22 MODEL RULES OF PROF'L CONDUCT r. 4.1(b).
23 W. Va. R. Prof. Conduct 4.1 (2015).
24 KY Sup. Ct. Rules, Rule 3.130(4.1) (2023).
25 Texas State Bar Rules, V.T.C.A., Government Code Title 2, Subtitle G App., Art. 10, § 9, Rules of Prof. Conduct, Rule 4.01 (2022).
26 MODEL RULES OF PROF'L CONDUCT r. 4.4(a).
27 MODEL RULES OF PROF'L CONDUCT r. 4.4(b).
28 W. Va. R. Prof. Conduct 4.4 (2015).
29 Pennsylvania Rules of Prof. Conduct, Rule 4.4 (2023).
30 Ohio R. Prof. Conduct, Rule 4.4 (2021).
31 S. Ct. of Ky. Rules, Rule 3.130(4.4) (2023).
32 Virginia Rules of Prof. Conduct, Rule 4.4 (2022).
33 Texas State Bar Rules, V.T.C.A., Government Code Title 2, Subtitle G App., Art. 10, § 9, Rules of Prof. Conduct, Rule 4.04 (2022).

[e] — Model Rule 8.4 — Misconduct.

Model Rule 8.4 is found in the "maintaining the integrity of the profession" section and is an attempt at prohibiting any activity that may reflect poorly on the profession. Rule 8.4 identifies: violating the Model Rules,[34] committing a criminal act that reflects on the attorney's trustworthiness,[35] conduct involving dishonesty,[36] conduct that is prejudicial to the administration of justice,[37] improperly influencing a government agency or official,[38] and assisting a judge or judicial officer in violating the Model Rules[39] as actionable offenses. It also includes a catchall at the end geared toward harassment and discrimination.[40]

Pennsylvania,[41] Ohio,[42] West Virginia,[43] Virginia,[44] and Kentucky[45] have adopted some variation of the Model Rule — accepting and rejecting some combination of the prohibited actions. Texas has not adopted a general "misconduct" rule.

§2.03. Case Illustrations.
[1] — Michael Avenatti.[46]

Michael Avenatti was convicted of attempted extortion after attempting to get Nike to hire him as a "consultant" in exchange for withholding bad publicity from the press. Avenatti represented a youth basketball league organizer who was unhappy Nike pulled its sponsorship of the league. Avenatti threatened to link Nike to a bribery scandal in which the families

---

[34] MODEL RULES OF PROF'L CONDUCT r. 8.4(a).
[35] MODEL RULES OF PROF'L CONDUCT r. 8.4(b).
[36] MODEL RULES OF PROF'L CONDUCT r. 8.4(c).
[37] MODEL RULES OF PROF'L CONDUCT r. 8.4(d).
[38] MODEL RULES OF PROF'L CONDUCT r. 8.4 (e).
[39] MODEL RULES OF PROF'L CONDUCT r. 8.4(f).
[40] MODEL RULES OF PROF'L CONDUCT r. 8.4(g).
[41] Pennsylvania Rules of Prof. Conduct, Rule 8.4 (2023).
[42] Ohio R. Prof. Conduct, Rule 8.4 (2021).
[43] W.Va. R. Prof. Conduct 8.4 (2015).
[44] Virginia Rules of Prof. Conduct, Rule 8.4 (2022).
[45] S. Ct. of Ky. Rules, Rule 3.130(8.4) (2023).
[46] United States v. Avenatti, 81 F.4th 171 (2nd Cir. 2023).

of NBA-bound basketball players were paid to steer the players to certain programs. Avenatti said he would not take this information to the press in exchange for $1.5 million for his client and between $15 and $25 million for him and his colleague to conduct an internal audit of the company. In the alternative, Nike could pay him and his colleague $22.5 million to settle his client's claims and to buy Avenatti's silence. The client was not apprised of the threats or the fact that Avenatti was seeking money for himself.

Nike's attorneys recorded phone calls with Avenatti and turned them over to the authorities. In these recordings, Avenatti blatantly threatens Nike, telling them the *New York Times* was waiting on his call. Subsequently, he was convicted of attempted extortion and sentenced to 2.5 years in prison.

An argument can be made that Avenatti broke several of the Model Rules, both those listed in this chapter and otherwise, but this case clearly violates Rule 3.6. Avenatti threatened to publicly accuse Nike of bribery with no basis in fact. To date, Nike has not been accused or even suggested to be a part of the NBA bribery scheme. Avenatti's claim was not based in fact and instead based on bad publicity. Having the *New York Times* ready to publish a story in lieu of simply filing the complaint violates the rule regarding trial publicity.

[2] — Timothy Litzenburg.[47]

Timothy Litzenburg worked at a firm that was involved in some of the initial Round-Up litigation.[48] After leaving his firm, he and Daniel Kincheloe, another attorney, attempted to extort a chemical company under the guise of a $200 million consulting agreement. In exchange for this consulting agreement, Litzenburg would steer clients away from similar litigation.

The chemical company contacted the Department of Justice to investigate Litzenburg for extortion. The chemical company turned over emails and recorded phone calls to the Department of Justice. Both Litzenburg and

---

[47] Press Release, US Dept. of Justice, Virginia Attorneys Sentenced for Attempting to Extort a Multinational Chemicals Company (Sept. 18, 2020) (available at https://www.justice.gov/opa/pr/virginia-attorneys-sentenced-attempting-extort-multinational-chemicals-company).

[48] Round-Up litigation refers to a series of lawsuits against the maker of the pesticide Round-Up and its parent companies alleging the product causes certain cancers.

Kincheloe were charged with extortion and entered guilty pleas. They both served prison sentences and their law licenses were revoked.

[3] — William Dean.

DeAndre Baker was a cornerback for the New York Giants when he went to a cookout with Quinton Dunbar, a cornerback for the Seattle Seahawks, in May of 2020. At the cookout, the pair was accused of robbery and aggravated assault. Four men accused the two of robbing them at gunpoint for over $70,000 in cash and jewelry. Prosecutors brought charges against Baker and Dunbar for armed robbery and aggravated assault.

William Dean was hired as the attorney for the four "victims." He contacted Mr. Baker's attorney in an attempt to get rid of the case, claiming the four men would "do anything . . . so long as the money [was] right." Dean claimed the "victims" would either change their testimony or refuse to cooperate with investigators for $266,000 each.[49]

Through the investigation, prosecutors began finding discrepancies in the "victims'" stories and eventually dropped the charges. Instead, prosecutors charged Dean with extortion. Prosecutors learned that the alleged robbery was fabricated and orchestrated by Dean in an attempt to extort Baker and Dunbar.

Dean squarely violated Model Rule 4.4, by blatantly disregarding the rights of third parties (*i.e.* Baker and Dunbar) in falsely accusing them of armed robbery. The purpose of the claim was to burden Baker and Dunbar enough to have them pay to make the charges go away.

[4] — Amy Mousavi.[50]

Falcon Brands terminated an employee who then retained Amy Mousavi to represent him in his wrongful termination and other employment claims.

---

[49] Michelle Solomon, Local attorney charged with extortion in robbery case involving NFL player, charges dropped against player, Local10, November 16, 2020, https://www.local10.com/news/local/2020/11/16/local-attorney-charged-with-extortion-in-high-profile-robbery-case-involving-2-nfl-players/.

[50] Falcon Brands, Inc. v. Mousavi & Lee, LLP, No. G059477 (Cal. Ct. App. 2022).

Mousavi emailed Falcon Brands' counsel explaining the claims against them and that she intended to file suit. Mousavi then threatened to contact a potential purchaser of Falcon Brands and tell them these claims were outstanding and that, if they purchased the company, they would also be sued. She also informed the potential purchaser about alleged criminal conduct Falcon Brands engaged in that was unrelated to her client's claims against it. The parties could not reach a settlement, so Mousavi made contact with the purchaser about the claims and ultimately caused the purchaser to pull out of the deal.

Mousavi sued based on the employment issues and was countersued by Falcon Brands for extortion and intentional interference with a contract. The court analyzed the series of Mousavi's emails to Falcon Brands. The court found that the first email was "innocent." The court found that her second email was a "closer call" because it contained "at least an implicit threat" by referencing "specified crimes Falcon had allegedly committed, though [Mousavi] never directly linked her settlement demands to them." The court noted that a "skeptical observe might reasonably wonder why Mousavi referenced" the alleged unrelated criminal conduct at all. The court found that Mousavi's next email crossed the line. In that email she threatened to disclose the alleged criminal misconduct to the potential purchaser unless Falcon Brands settled with her client.

Mousavi crossed the line by threatening to disclose criminal activity entirely unrelated to her client's damages claim.

§ 2.04. Conclusion.

In sum, the line for extortion is bright. The best advice is to know and follow the model rules and/or your state specific rules of professional conduct. In particular, to avoid crossing the ethical lines illustrated above, attorneys should ensure that claims are meritorious and not fabricated, use the media appropriately and not in place of the court, make truthful statements to others, respect the rights of third parties over a client's position, and keep clear of the enumerated items in the misconduct section.

Chapter 3

Fair Labor Standards Act Compliance Update

Michael C. Griffaton
Vorys, Sater, Seymour and Pease LLP
Columbus, Ohio

Synopsis

§ 3.01.	Summary	26
§ 3.02.	Why Wage-Hour Compliance Matters	27
§ 3.03.	Overtime Requirements Under the Fair Labor Standards Act	31
§ 3.04.	Day-Rate Compensation Plan	33
	[1] — What It Means to Be Paid a Day Rate	33
	[2] — Some Courts Held Employees Paid a Day Rate Were Exempt from Overtime Pay	33
	[3] — The U.S. Supreme Court Holds that a Day Rate Is Not a Salary	34
	[4] — Day Rate and the Reasonable Relationship Test	36
§ 3.05.	Misclassification of Employees as Independent Contractors	38
	[1] — Misclassification Relating to Overtime Compensation	38
	[a] — The Executive Exemption	39
	[b] — The Administrative Exemption	40
	[c] — The Highly Compensated Employee Exemption	40
	[d] — Illustrative Cases – Exemption Questioned	41
	[i] — *Guyton v. Legacy Pressure Control*	41
	[ii] — *Wimberley v. Beast Energy Servs.*	43
	[iii] — *Ganci v. MBF Insp. Servs.*	44
	[iv] — *Hobbs v. EVO Inc.*	44
	[v] — *Last v. M-I, L.L.C.*	45
	[vi] — *Raptis v. DPS Land Servs., LLC*	45
	[e] — Illustrative Cases – Exemption Found	46
	[i] — *Mondeck v. LineQuest, LLC*	46
	[ii] — *Venable v. Schlumberger Ltd.*	47
	[f] — The Seaman Exemption	48
	[i] — *Adams v. All Coast, L.L.C.*	48
	[ii] — *Hernandez v. Helix Energy Sols. Grp., Inc.*	50

§ 3.01.   ENERGY & MINERAL LAW INSTITUTE

	[2] — Misclassification Relating to Independent Contractors 50
	[a] — Illustrative Cases 51
	[i] — *Bernstein v. Buckeye, Inc.* 51
	[ii] — *Hargrave v. AIM Directional Servs., L.L.C.* 52
§ 3.06	**Compensation for Travel Time.. 52**
	[1] — Whether Travel Time Is Compensated Depends on the Nature of the Travel 52
	[a] — Ordinary Commuting Is Not Compensable 53
	[b] — Travel During the Workday Is Compensable 53
	[c] — Travel Away from Home May Be Compensable 54
	[2] — Illustrative Cases 54
	[a] — *Copley v. Evolution Well Servs. Operating, LLC* 54
	[b] — *Barhight v. Terra Oilfield Servs.* 55
	[c] — *Wimberley v. Beast Energy Servs.* 56
	[d] — *Little v. Technical Specialty Prod.* 57
§ 3.07.	**State Law Protections 57**
§ 3.08.	**Minimizing Liability by Auditing Payroll Practices........... 59**
	[1] — Employer "Good Faith" Reliance on Industry Standards Is Insufficient to Avoid Liability Under the Fair Labor Standards Act................................. 59
	[2] — Employers Can Minimize Potential Liability by Auditing Their Payroll Practices 60
	[3] — Topics to Review When Conducting a Comprehensive Wage-Hour Audit................................... 61

§ 3.01.   Summary.

Employers must contend with an increasingly complex patchwork of federal, state, and local wage-hour requirements. In some states, therefore, compliance with the federal Fair Labor Standards Act does not ensure compliance with state law. Consequently, wage-hour compliance continues to be important because the risk of monetary and business-disruption costs are high.

This update covers recent developments under the Fair Labor Standards Act concerning day-rate compensation plans, employee and independent contractor misclassification, and payments for time employees spend traveling. The United States Supreme Court recently confirmed that being paid a day rate is not the same as being paid on a salaried basis, so those employees would not qualify as overtime-exempt. Employers continue to grapple with the fact-intensive nature of properly classifying their workers as overtime-exempt and/or as independent contractors. Finally, the nature of much oil and gas work requires determining whether employees must be paid for traveling to and from job sites.

To minimize wage-hour liability, employers should conduct internal audits of their payroll processes, policies, and procedures to ensure their employees are being properly paid for all hours worked in accordance with federal law. This will also help minimize exposure under state laws that provide greater employee protection.

§ 3.02. Why Wage-Hour Compliance Matters.

Most employers are covered by the federal Fair Labor Standards Act (FLSA), which sets a minimum wage (currently $7.25 per hour), requires overtime compensation for employees who are not otherwise exempt, and requires that certain employment records be maintained. The FLSA does not preempt state laws that are more protective of employee working conditions, and states may enact their own, higher minimum wage — which a growing number have done.[1] States also may require overtime pay for work on certain days: holidays; regular days of rest; meal and rest breaks, reporting time/call-in pay, and reimbursement for employee business expenses. This means employers must contend with an increasingly complex patchwork of federal, state, and local wage-hour requirements. In some states, therefore, compliance with the FLSA does not ensure compliance with state law.

Of course, "as complexity increases, a system's *understandability* decreases . . . [which] — can be challenging for business leaders, who may struggle to grasp and navigate the system." This lack of understandability, in turn, can lead to unmanageability and unpredictability.[2] Consequently,

---

[1] *See* 29 U.S.C. § 218(a); *see, e.g.,* Thorpe v. Abbott Labs., Inc., 534 F. Supp.2d 1120, 1124 (N.D. Cal. 2008) ("[T]he FLSA clearly indicates that it does not preempt stricter state law claims.").

[2] Reeves, Martin, et al., *Taming Complexity*, HARVARD BUSINESS REVIEW (Jan. – Feb. 2020), https://hbr.org/2020/01/taming-complexity.

employers may fail to properly calculate overtime compensation because they failed to include bonuses in the regular rate of pay or paid employees a day rate without factoring in overtime. Employers may misclassify employees as exempt from overtime or may deem workers to be independent contractors rather than employees. With such errors, comes the very real potential for complaints to administrative agencies like the U.S. Department of Labor (DOL) and to plaintiffs' lawyers.

Generally, there are two broad categories of wage-hour claims under the FLSA: compensable time claims and misclassification claims. With a compensable time claim, employees claim they were not paid for performing duties they claim are compensable (*i.e.*, off-the-clock). These typically arise as:

- Engaging in pre- and post-shift activities, such as donning and doffing uniforms or safety gear; cleaning equipment; attending pre-shift safety briefings or other meetings; or going through security screening.
- Performing work during unpaid meal or rest breaks.
- Attending work-related lectures, meetings, and training programs.
- Working outside of normal work hours, such as working from home after hours and responding to work-related emails or texts after hours.
- Traveling for work, such as between job sites.
- Waiting for available work, such as time spent on call.

In a misclassification claim, employees claim they are misclassified as exempt from overtime when they are classified as an executive, administrative, professional, or highly compensated employees or workers claim they are misclassified as independent contractors when they are actually employees.

Over the past 10 years, the number of FLSA minimum wage and overtime cases has generally ranged between 23,000 and 30,000 each year. The compliance actions the DOL Wage and Hour Division (WHD) used to address these cases primarily involved either on-site investigations or conciliations that seek a resolution between the employer and the worker by phone. Back wages due to workers for FLSA minimum wage and overtime violations increased from $129 million in fiscal year 2010 to $226 million in fiscal year 2019.[3]

United States District Court Fair Labor Standards Act Lawsuits[4]					
Lawsuits	2022	2021	2020	2019	2018
	6,133	5,563	6,663	7,196	7,600

Department of Labor[5]		
Year	Minimum Wage	Overtime
2021	7,287 cases	7,159 cases
	$25,932,824 recovered	$138,674,500 recovered
2022	7,948 cases	5,905 cases
	$17,941,190 recovered	$134,591,521 recovered

According to NERA Economic Consulting, "Overtime violations remain the most common allegation in our settlement data, consistently accounting for about 40 percent of settled cases across the entire 2010–2019 period. On the other hand, the proportion of settled cases, including allegations of minimum wage and off-the clock work violations, has not been as stable, varying from year to year. An increase in the proportion of settlements involving minimum wage allegations occurred in the last five years, with a corresponding relative decrease in settlements with off-the-clock allegations."[6] "In 2019, the average settlement value for a wage and hour case

---

[3] U.S. GOV'T ACCOUNTABILITY OFFICE, GAO-21-13, FAIR LABOR STANDARDS ACT: TRACKING ADDITIONAL COMPLAINT DATA COULD IMPROVE DOL'S ENFORCEMENT, (Dec. 9, 2020) (available at https://www.gao.gov/products/gao-21-13).

[4] U.S. COURTS, TABLE 4.4—U.S. DISTRICT COURTS-CIVIL JUDICIAL FACTS AND FIGURES (Sept. 30, 2022) (available at https://www.uscourts.gov/statistics/table/44/judicial-facts-and-figures/2022/09/30).

[5] *Fair Labor Standards Act | U.S. Department of Labor (Fiscal Year Data for WHD)*, U.S. DEPT. OF LABOR, WAGE AND HOUR DIVISION, https://www.dol.gov/agencies/whd/data/charts/fair-labor-standards-act.

[6] Plancich, Stephanie and McIntosh, Janeen, *Trends in Wage and Hour Settlements: 2019*

increased to $8.2 million, a 64 percent increase from the 2018 average and a 51 percent increase from the 2017 average. Over the last three years, the average settlement value was $6.3 million, higher than the decade average of $5.8 million."[7]

Changes at the DOL and increasing DOL outreach are likely to result in more enforcement actions. In January 2021, the DOL discontinued the Payroll Audit Independent Determination (PAID) program, which the former Trump administration initiated in 2018 to encourage employers to voluntarily correct certain underpayments to employees.[8] And in April 2021, the DOL's Wage and Hour Division returned to pursuing pre-litigation liquidated damages in lieu of litigation "and leveraging this enforcement tool when appropriate," after temporarily halting the practice in 2020 to encourage economic recovery during the pandemic.[9] The DOL answered more than 913,000 calls and conducted 4,000 outreach events reaching 289,000 participants in fiscal year 2022.[10]

Finally, the DOL publicizes it litigation success. For example, a May 2023 press release highlighted the DOL's $22 million jury verdict against East Penn Manufacturing for failing to pay 7,500 employees overtime pay. The DOL will also seek an additional $22 million in liquidated damages (which are all-but mandatory under the FLSA). A 30-day trial ended when the jury found East Penn was required to pay the employees for all of their working time — which included the additional time they needed to put on

---

Update, NERA ECON. CONSULTING, (June 4, 2020), https://www.nera.com/content/dam/nera/publications/2020/PUB_Wage_and_Hour_Settlements_060220.pdf.

[7] *Id*.

[8] *US Department of Labor ends program that allowed employers to self-report federal minimum wage and overtime violations,* U.S. DEPT. OF LABOR, WAGE AND HOUR DIVISION, (Jan. 29, 2021), https://www.dol.gov/newsroom/releases/whd/whd20210129.

[9] *Liquidated Damages in Settlements in Lieu of Litigation*, U.S. DEPARTMENT OF LABOR, WAGE AND HOUR DIVISION, (Apr. 9, 2021), https://blog.dol.gov/2021/04/09/liquidated-damages-in-settlements-in-lieu-of-litigation.

[10] *See WHD by the Numbers 2023*, U.S. DEPARTMENT OF LABOR, WAGE AND HOUR DIVISION, https://www.dol.gov/agencies/whd/data.

and remove protective equipment and to shower to avoid the dangers of lead exposure and other hazards.[11]

In short, compliance matters because the risk of monetary and business-disruption costs are high. The DOL's *East Penn* case shows that even small things (a few minutes of donning and doffing) can add up significantly ($44 million, plus the attorneys' fees East Penn expended). And, because states may have more employee-friendly laws, the exposure and liability and greater (especially in states like California).

§ 3.03. Overtime Requirements Under the Fair Labor Standards Act.

FLSA[12] was enacted to eliminate both "substandard wages" and "oppressive working hours."[13] The FLSA addresses the concern with substandard wages by guaranteeing a minimum wage (currently $7.25 per hour), and the concern with working hours by requiring time-and-a-half pay for each hour worked over 40 hours a week.[14] Unless otherwise exempt from the FLSA's overtime requirements, employees are entitled to overtime compensation even if their regular compensation far exceeds "the statutory minimum."[15] This is because "the overtime provision was designed both to 'compensate [employees] — for the burden' of working extra-long hours and to increase overall employment by incentivizing employers to widen their 'distribution of available work.'"[16] So, employees are not "deprived of the benefits of [overtime compensation] — simply because they are well paid."[17]

---

[11] *Federal jury finds East Penn Manufacturing violated federal law; awards $22M in back wages, among largest wage verdicts in Department of Labor history,* U.S. DEPARTMENT OF LABOR, WAGE AND HOUR DIVISION, (May 10, 2023), https://www.dol.gov/newsroom/releases/whd/whd20230510.
[12] 29 U.S.C. § 201 *et seq.*
[13] Barrentine v. Arkansas-Best Freight System, Inc., 450 U.S. 728, 739 (1981).
[14] *See* 29 U.S.C. § 206 (minimum wage); 29 U.S.C. § 207 (overtime).
[15] Overnight Motor Transp. Co. v. Missel, 316 U.S. 572, 577 (1942); Helix Energy Sols. Grp., Inc. v. Hewitt, 143 S. Ct. 677, 682 (2023) (hereinafter cited as *Helix*).
[16] *Helix*, at 682.
[17] Jewell Ridge Coal Corp. v. Mine Workers, 325 U.S. 161, 167 (1945).

§ 3.03

Not all employees are covered by the FLSA. With respect to overtime, the statutory exemption applies to "any employee employed in a bona fide executive, administrative, or professional capacity . . . (as such terms are defined and delimited from time to time by regulations of the Secretary [of Labor])."[18] Under that provision, the Secretary of Labor sets out a standard for determining when an employee is a "bona fide executive." If that standard is met, the employee has no right to overtime wages.[19]

To be exempt from overtime compensation, (1) the employee must be paid on a salary basis; (2) the employee's salary must meet the salary threshold (currently $684 per week); and (3) the employee must perform exempt duties.[20] Exempt computer employees may be paid at least $684 on a salary basis or on an hourly basis at a rate not less than $27.63 an hour.

Being paid on a "salary basis" means an employee regularly receives a predetermined amount of compensation each pay period on a weekly, or less frequent, basis. The predetermined amount cannot be reduced because of variations in the quality or quantity of the employee's work. Subject to certain exceptions, an exempt employee must receive the full salary for any week in which the employee performs any work, regardless of the number of days or hours worked. Exempt employees do not need to be paid for any workweek in which they perform no work. If the employer makes deductions from an employee's predetermined salary, *i.e.*, because of the operating requirements of the business, that employee is not paid on a "salary basis." If the employee is ready, willing and able to work, deductions may not be made for time when work is not available. Note, simply because an employee is paid a "salary" does not mean that the employee is exempt from overtime. "[C]lassification of employees as exempt solely because they are 'salaried' is overly simplistic and erroneous under the FLSA."[21]

---

[18] 29 U.S.C. § 213(a)(1).
[19] *Helix*, at 682.
[20] *See* 29 C.F.R. § 541.600(a) and § 541.601(b)(1) (minimum compensation requirement to meet the salary exemption); 29 C.F.R. § 541.100(a)(1) (requiring payment on a salary basis); 29 C.F.R. § 541.3 (defining the scope of the exemptions).
[21] Williams v. D'Argent Franchising, L.L.C., 2023 U.S. Dist. LEXIS 71048, at *48-49 (W.D. La. Apr. 21, 2023) (citing *Helix*, at 678).

§ 3.04. Day-Rate Compensation Plans.
[1] — What It Means to Be Paid a Day Rate.

An employee who is paid a flat sum for a day's work without regard to the number of hours worked in that day (*i.e.*, regardless of whether overtime hours are worked) is paid on a day-rate basis.[22]

[2] — Some Courts Held Employees Paid a Day Rate Were Exempt from Overtime Pay.

Before the U.S. Supreme Court ruling in *Helix* (discussed below), there was a split among courts as to whether a day rate satisfied the salary basis test for purposes of the overtime exemption tests. Several courts held that a day rate is not the same as being paid on a salary basis of $455 or $684 per week (depending on when the regulation was in effect).[23] Other courts held to the contrary. In *Scott v. Antero Res. Corp.*, for example, the court held that the salary basis requirement was met where the "Plaintiffs were compensated on a salary basis because their day rate guaranteed them $1,000 for every day that they worked and thus, *perforce*, they would receive more than the minimum of $455 per week for any week in which they performed *any* work."[24] Plaintiffs in *Scott* typically earned $250,000 to $450,000 per year for 26 weeks of work. In *Scott*, and cases like it, the plaintiffs are now

---

[22] *See* Lee v. Vance Exec. Prot., Inc., 7 F. App'x 160, 165 (4th Cir. 2001); Dufrene v. Browning-Ferris, Inc., 207 F.3d 264, 266 (5th Cir. 2000).

[23] *See, e.g.,* Goodly v. Check-6, Inc., 2018 U.S. Dist. LEXIS 179230 (N.D. Okla. Oct. 18, 2018) (noting that courts have taken differing views on the legal merits of whether a sufficiently large day rate can satisfy the salary basis requirement but finding it need not reach the merits of the issue); McQueen v. Chevron Corp., 2018 U.S. Dist. LEXIS 57751 (N.D. Cal. Apr. 3, 2018) (rejecting argument that day rate exceeding $1,000 satisfied salary-basis requirement), *reconsideration denied*, 2018 U.S. Dist. LEXIS 182089 (May 9, 2018); Snead v. EOG Res., Inc., 2018 U.S. Dist. LEXIS 31522 (W.D. Tex. Feb. 13, 2018) (granting employees' summary judgment because employer's day-rate compensation plan did not satisfy the salary basis test); Keen v. DXP Enters., Inc., 2016 U.S. Dist. LEXIS 81069 (W.D. Tex. June 6, 2016) (granting summary judgment because a day-rate "is not pay on a salary basis as is required").

[24] Scott v. Antero Res. Corp., 540 F. Supp. 3d 1039, 1046-47 (D. Colo. 2021), *reversed by, vacated by, remanded by*, 2023 U.S. App. LEXIS 7528 (10th Cir. Mar. 30, 2023).

owed overtime compensation for all hours over 40 in a workweek, and the amount owed can be significant.

In April 2021, the U.S. Department of Labor recovered $3,852,968 in back wages for 1,100 employees who worked as oilfield pipeline inspectors in 40 states for Frontier Integrity Solutions Operations LLC. FIS provides oil and gas pipeline inspection and integrity services. FIS paid these employees a fixed amount per day, regardless of the number of hours worked, and without overtime – in other words, day rate. The employees typically worked between 50 and 60 hours per week. The employer's failure to keep records of the number of hours employees worked also resulted in recordkeeping violations.[25]

[3] — The U.S. Supreme Court Holds that a Day Rate Is Not a Salary.

In February 2023, the U.S. Supreme Court decided *Helix Energy Solutions Group, Inc. v. Hewitt*.[26] Hewitt worked for Helix as a "tool pusher" on an offshore oilrig. Reporting to the captain, he oversaw aspects of the rig's operations and supervised 12 to 14 workers. He usually worked 12 hours a day, seven days a week (84 hours a week) during a 28-day hitch. He then had 28 days off before reporting back to the rig. Hewitt was paid a day rate ranging from $963 to $1,341, with no overtime compensation. He earned over $200,000 annually. Hewitt sued under the FLSA to recover overtime pay. Helix, however, asserted that Hewitt was exempt from overtime because he was an "executive" as defined by the FLSA. To be exempt, an employee must perform exempt duties and be paid on a "salary basis" of at least $455 per week (or $684, as of 2023).

As the Supreme Court explained, under the regulations, an employee falls within the "bona fide executive" exemption only if (among other things)

---

[25] *Wage and Hour Division investigation recovers $3.8M in overtime back wages owed to 1,100 employees of major oil pipeline inspection company in 40 states,* U.S. Department of Labor, Wage and Hour Division, (Apr. 28, 2021), https://www.dol.gov/newsroom/releases/whd/whd20210428-2.
[26] *Helix.*

the employee is paid on a "salary basis." "The question here is whether a high-earning employee is compensated on a "salary basis" when his paycheck is based solely on a daily rate — so that he receives a certain amount if he works one day in a week, twice as much for two days, three times as much for three, and so on. *We hold that such an employee is not paid on a salary basis, and thus is entitled to overtime pay.*"[27] Thus, even highly compensated employees like Hewitt paid on a "day rate" basis do **not** qualify as being paid on a "salary basis" for overtime exemption purposes.

The Court reached this conclusion by looking at the two key DOL regulations that give context to the salary-basis test – 29 C.F.R. § 602(a) and § 602(b). The main salary-basis provision, set out in 602(a), states:

> An employee will be considered to be paid on a 'salary basis' . . . if the employee regularly receives each pay period on a weekly, or less frequent basis, a predetermined amount constituting all or part of the employee's compensation, which amount is not subject to reduction because of variations in the quality or quantity of the work performed. Subject to [certain exceptions], an exempt employee must receive the full salary for any week in which the employee performs any work without regard to the number of days or hours worked.[28]

As the Court explained, "The rule thus ensures that the employee will get at least part of his compensation through a preset weekly (or less frequent) salary, not subject to reduction because of exactly how many days he worked. If, as the rule's second sentence drives home, an employee works any part of a week, he must receive his full salary for that week—or else he is not paid on a salary basis and cannot qualify as a bona fide executive."[29]

Section 541.604(b), on the other hand, focuses on workers whose compensation is "computed on an hourly, a daily or a shift basis," rather than a weekly or less frequent one. That section states that an employer may base an employee's pay on an hourly, daily, or shift rate without "violating the

---

[27] *Helix*, at 682 (emphasis added).
[28] 29 C.F.R. § 541.602(a).
[29] *Helix*, at 684.

salary basis requirement" or "losing the [bona fide executive] — exemption" so long as two conditions are met. First, the employer must "also" guarantee the employee at least $455 each week (the minimum salary level) "regardless of the number of hours, days or shifts worked." And second, that promised amount must bear a "reasonable relationship" to the "amount actually earned" in a typical week — more specifically, must be "roughly equivalent to the employee's usual earnings at the assigned hourly, daily or shift rate for the employee's normal scheduled workweek. Those conditions create a compensation system functioning much like a true salary — a steady stream of pay, which the employer cannot much vary and the employee may thus rely on week after week."[30]

The Court held that day-rate workers are excluded from § 602(a). "That section applies solely to employees paid by the week (or longer); it is not met when an employer pays an employee by the day, as Helix paid Hewitt. *Daily-rate workers, of whatever income level, are paid on a salary basis only through the test set out in § 604(b).*"[31] Again, this means (1) the employee must receive a guaranteed salary, and (2) the guaranteed salary must reasonably relate to the amount *actually* earned.

[4] — Day Rate and the Reasonable Relationship Test.

A recent Fifth Circuit case seeks to further define the contours of § 604(b)'s "reasonable relationship" test. In *Gentry v. Hamilton-Ryker IT Sol., LLC*,[32] Hamilton-Ryker contracted with Freeport LNG Expansion to provide staffing and placement services related to the construction and commissioning of Freeport's natural gas liquefaction and liquified natural gas (LNG) loading facility on Quintana Island near Freeport, Texas. Gentry worked as a senior control system engineer, being paid $123/hour straight time and overtime. He

---

[30] *Id.* (quoting 29 C.F.R. § 541.602(b)).
[31] *Id.* at 685 (emphasis added).
[32] Gentry v. Hamilton-Ryker IT Sol., LLC, No. 3:19-cv-00320, 2022 U.S. Dist. LEXIS 38398 (S.D. Tex. Mar. 4, 2022) (currently on appeal to the Fifth Circuit – appellee brief due June 13, 2023); *see also* Cunningham v. Hamilton-Ryker, No. 3:21-cv-00302, 2022 U.S. Dist. LEXIS 52041 (S.D. Tex. Feb. 16, 2022) (raising identical claims and issues for a piping inspector).

was entitled to a guaranteed weekly salary (for 8 hours of work) of $984, and he would be paid hourly for any work beyond eight hours. The district court found that Gentry's payments failed to satisfy the "reasonable relationship" test under 29 C.F.R. § 541.604(b). The test requires a reasonable relationship between the guaranteed weekly salary and an employee's actual earned pay. This means that the reasonable relationship test will be met if the weekly guarantee is roughly equivalent to the employee's usual earnings for the employee's normal scheduled workweek. Here, however, the court found the test not met because Gentry's average gross hourly earnings ($5,347.66) and the amount purported to be his guaranteed weekly salary ($984.00) had 5.42-to-1 ratio. Thus, the district court found that Gentry was not exempt from overtime compensation. Hamilton-Ryker has appealed to the Fifth Circuit.[33]

In *Martin v. Rush, LLC*,[34] Rush Resources is an industrial services organization offering construction project management, commissioning and startup, and consulting and provides solutions to clients in a variety of industries including oil & gas, power generation, refinery/chemical, and other industries. Martin was offered the position of chief inspector, and his offer letter stated he would be an exempt employee and would be paid weekly at a straight-time rate of $75.00. The court found this failed to satisfy § 604(b)'s salary basis test and granted Martin's motion for summary judgment as to liability. This was because the offer contained "a generic hourly guarantee" but said nothing "about a guaranteed weekly pay generally or specifically as to [him]." The company argued that the court could "extrapolate a guaranteed number of hours from that proposal and multiply it by [Martin's] — hourly rate of $75.00 to conclude that [Martin] — was paid a guaranteed salary of $3,000 per week." The court rejected this argument: "[T]he evidence does not support this inference. Absent from all direct communications to [Martin] — regarding his compensation was any kind of guarantee of

---

[33] A U.S. Department of Labor Opinion Letter notes that a "reasonable relationship" exists when an employee's actual earnings did not exceed approximately 1.2 to 1 to 1.5 to 1. *See* U.S. Dept. of Labor Opinion Letter, FLSA 2018-25 (Nov. 8, 2015) (available at https://www.dol.gov/sites/dolgov/files/whd/legacy/files/2018_11_08_25_flsa.pdf).

[34] Martin v. Rush, LLC, No. 6:20-CV-00005-JDL, 2021 U.S. Dist. LEXIS 12602 (E.D. Tex. Jan. 22, 2021).

minimum weekly pay. For example, [Martin's] — offer letter never stated that he was guaranteed a minimum of $3,000 per week. Rather, his offer letter stated that he would be paid weekly at a 'Straight-Time Rate $75.00'. Importantly, this is consistent with how [Martin] — was *actually* paid."[35] The clear takeaway here is that a payment scheme under § 604(b) requires a guaranteed weekly amount (preferably memorialized in a writing signed by the employee).

§ 3.05. Misclassification of Employees as Independent Contractors.

[1] — Misclassification Relating to Overtime Compensation.

By default, all employees are non-exempt from overtime unless the employer can prove that the employee is properly classified as exempt. The FLSA requires employers to provide overtime compensation for its employees for a workweek longer than 40 hours.[36] In contrast, independent contractors are not entitled to overtime under the FLSA, as the FLSA only covers "employees." Additionally, employers do not have to pay overtime to exempt employees who are employed in a bona fide executive, administrative, or professional capacity or to highly compensated employees.[37] The most common FLSA exemption tests — the white-collar exemptions — require a duties test, a salary-basis test, and a salary-level test. Job titles do not determine exempt status. "If the employer claims that the suing employee is exempt from the overtime requirement, then the employer has the burden of proving that the employee falls within the claimed exempted category."[38] As recently clarified by the Supreme Court, "courts are to give FLSA exemptions a fair reading, as opposed to the narrow interpretation previously espoused by [the Fifth Circuit] — and other circuits."[39]

---

[35] *Id.* at *16-19 (emphasis in original).
[36] 29 U.S.C. § 207(a)(1).
[37] 29 U.S.C. § 213(a)(1); 29 C.F.R. § 541.601.
[38] Johnson v. Heckmann Water Res. (CVR), Inc., 758 F.3d 627, 630 (5th Cir. 2014) (citation omitted).
[39] Carley v. Crest Pumping Techs., L.L.C., 890 F.3d 575, 579 (5th Cir. 2018) (citing Encino Motorcars, LLC v. Navarro, 138 S.Ct. 1134, 1142 (2018)).

Determining whether an employee is exempt can be highly fact-intensive. "[W]orkers in the oil-and-gas industry are particularly difficult to classify."[40] Courts in the Fifth Circuit "have considered whether various types of oil field operators or inspectors qualify as manual or blue collar workers" and "reached different conclusions."[41] The three most common exemptions are described below.

[a] — The Executive Exemption.

To qualify for the executive employee exemption, all of the following must be met:

- The employee must be compensated on a salary basis at a rate not less than $684 per week;
- The employee's primary duty must be managing the enterprise, or managing a customarily recognized department or subdivision of the enterprise;
- The employee must customarily and regularly direct the work of at least two or more other full-time employees or their equivalent; and
- The employee must have the authority to hire or fire other employees, or the employee's suggestions and recommendations as to the hiring, firing, advancement, promotion or any other

---

[40] Wimberley v. Beast Energy Servs., No. 3:19-cv-00096, 2022 U.S. Dist. LEXIS 38392, at *14 (S.D. Tex. Mar. 4, 2022).

[41] Guyton v. Legacy Pressure Control, 5:15-CV-1075-RCL, 2017 U.S. Dist. LEXIS 7836 (W.D. Tex. Jan. 18, 2017). *See, e.g.,* McPherson v. LEAM Drilling Sys., LLC, No. 4:14-CV-02361, 2015 U.S. Dist. LEXIS 40973 (S.D. Tex. Mar. 30, 2015) (discussing conditional class certification of "MWDs [Measuring While Drilling] — and other oilfield service workers *falling on the border* of the executive exemption") (emphasis added); Ferrara v. 4JLJ, LLC, 150 F. Supp. 3d 813 (S.D. Tex. 2016) (denying summary judgment where a Frac Supervisor contended that "primary job duties included a significant amount of manual labor in the field producing the product of the company," but the company argued that he "seldom, if ever, performed manual labor and instead directed others to do so"); Pye v. Oil States Energy Servs., LLC, No. 5:15-cv-678, 2016 U.S. Dist. LEXIS 188039 (W.D. Tex. 2017) (finding a field service operator's primary duties—which included loading equipment, traveling, and setting up, operating, and taking down equipment—were the performance of manual work).

§ 3.05

change of status of other employees must be given particular weight.[42]

[b] — The Administrative Exemption.

To qualify for the administrative employee exemption, all of the following must be met:

- The employee must be compensated on a salary or fee basis at a rate not less than $684 per week;
- The employee's primary duty must be the performance of office or non-manual work directly related to the management or general business operations of the employer or the employer's customers; and
- The employee's primary duty includes the exercise of discretion and independent judgment with respect to matters of sigificance.[43]

[c] — The Highly Compensated Employee Exemption.

The highly compensated employee (HCE) exemption provides that an employee with total annual compensation of at least $107,432 is deemed exempt if the employee customarily and regularly performs any one or more of the exempt duties or responsibilities of an executive, administrative, or professional employee.[44] To perform a duty "customarily and regularly" means to perform it with "a frequency that must be greater than occasional but which, of course, may be less than constant."[45] A highly compensated employee need not perform all of the job duties of an executive or administrative employee; the employee merely needs to perform any one or more of the duties. The DOL's regulations further clarify that the employee's

---

[42] *See* U.S. Dept. of Labor, Wage and Hour Division, Fact Sheet #17A: Exemption for Executive, Administrative, Professional, Computer & Outside Sales Employees Under the Fair Labor Standards Act (FLSA) (rev. Sept. 2019) (available at https://www.dol.gov/agencies/whd/fact-sheets/17a-overtime).
[43] *Id.*
[44] *Id.*
[45] 29 C.F.R. § 541.701.

total annual compensation must include at least $684 per week paid on a salary or fee basis.[46] Thus an employee qualifies for the HCE exemption if they meet the salary threshold and regularly and customarily performs one of the above listed job duties.

The HCE exemption applies only to employees whose primary duty includes performing office or non-manual work. If an employee's primary duty (*i.e.*, the principal, main, or most important duty) is manual labor, the HCE exemption does not apply, regardless of how much they are paid.[47]

[d] — Illustrative Cases – Exemption Questioned.
[i] — *Guyton v. Legacy Pressure Control*.[48]

Legacy Pressure Control (Legacy) is an oilfield services company that provides wireline pressure control, pressure pumping, and test-torque services. Plaintiffs worked as operators who performed their duties on site in the oilfields, standing on an equipment platform known as a skid, and are responsible for maintaining oilfield pressure control. Operators either worked as part of a two-person crew, switching shifts every twelve hours, or as part of a four-person crew where each operator was accompanied by a helper for twelve hour shifts. During the course of these shifts, operators often spent up to several hours of down time on site.

Legacy moved for summary judgment asserting that plaintiffs were exempt from the FLSA overtime regulations under the HCE exemption. Plaintiffs moved for summary judgment, asserting that no FLSA exemptions were applicable. The court denied both parties' motions and explained the fact-intensive nature of the exemption inquiry.

The court found that summary judgment was not appropriate for either party here because genuine disputes of material fact existed with regard to whether plaintiffs qualified as manual laborers as opposed to administratively exempt employees. The company asserted that plaintiffs' primary duty was

---

[46] 29 C.F.R. § 541.601(b)(1).
[47] 29 C.F.R. § 541.601; 29 C.F.R. § 541.700.
[48] Guyton v. Legacy Pressure Control, No. 5:15-cv-1075-RCL, 2017 U.S. Dist. LEXIS 7836, (W.D. Tex. Jan. 18, 2017).

§ 3.05 ENERGY & MINERAL LAW INSTITUTE

controlling and maintaining the pressure of grease injected into the wells so as to prevent blowouts, accomplished by visually monitoring gauges and turning a knob to adjust grease levels. Further, other tasks considered manual labor — "connecting hoses to the skid; filling up the grease unit on a tote; tightening nuts with a wrench, torque wrench, or hammer; moving hoses to keep them from getting tangled on the well head; using hand pumps; torque testing; moving grease around with a forklift or bringing it off the truck; opening and closing the tool trap; and going up in a man lift" — only constituted 10 percent of plaintiffs' job duties. The company argued that the other 90 percent of plaintiffs' jobs duties, including visually monitoring the gauges and turning a knob, did not qualify as manual labor.

Plaintiffs, on the other hand, introduced evidence showing they performed their job duties out in an oilfield, and that their primary duties included operating pressure control equipment, monitoring gauges, supervising the setup of equipment, and rigging jobs up and down. Plaintiffs' evidence showed that they worked outdoors with boots, hard hats, coveralls, and tools, and they contended that the work was "hot, dangerous, and sweaty." With regard to defendant's argument that plaintiffs only spent 10 percent of their time performing manual labor, plaintiffs responded that they spent the rest of their time simply waiting to perform manual tasks (their primary duties), and that waiting cannot be considered a primary duty.

Based on this, the court found that genuine disputes of material fact existed regarding several key issues. First the parties disputed what exactly plaintiffs' primary duties were as *operators*; plaintiffs only conceded that their primary duties during the skid operation process — as opposed to their primary duties as a whole — was monitoring gauges and controlling the amount of grease being injecting into the well to prevent blowouts. Further, the parties disputed whether that duty should be considered "manual labor" at all. In addition, the parties disputed the importance of other tasks performed by plaintiffs, such as connecting and moving hoses, filling up the grease unit, tightening nuts, breaking down the guns and subs, using hand pumps, torque testing, moving grease, opening and closing the tool trap, and going up the man lift. Finally, they disagreed on how much time was spent performing manual labor; defendants said only 10 percent, but plaintiffs claimed that this was a mischaracterization of the testimony and that plaintiffs were engaged to wait for the majority of their time on site.

This case illustrates the highly fact-intensive nature of the administrative overtime exemption.

[ii] — *Wimberley v. Beast Energy Servs.*[49]

Beast Energy Services (Beast Energy) is an oilfield service company that offers a range of downhole drilling tools and techniques and custom engineered products, solutions, and services. Beast Energy employed the plaintiffs as service supervisors for approximately six months. They were generally responsible for loading and transporting oilfield service equipment to clients' well sites in south and west Texas, ensuring the equipment was used in a safe manner, and returning the equipment to Beast Energy's shop in Rosharon, Texas. When not traveling or onsite, they worked at Beast Energy's Rosharon shop, where they prepared, maintained, serviced, and rebuilt tools for upcoming jobs. The plaintiffs, who were classified as exempt from overtime under the administrative exemption, claimed their primary duty was performing manual labor.

Beast Energy admitted that the plaintiffs performed manual work, but contended that doing so was not their primary duty. The court found the plaintiffs worked to produce the services Beast Energy offers — the delivery and operation of oilfield equipment at Beast Energy's customers' well sites. "Simply stated, production employees whose job it is to generate the product or service the business offers to the public will not qualify for the administrative exemption."

The court also found that, even if the plaintiffs were performing non-manual work, there were disputed issues regarding whether the plaintiffs' primary duty included the exercise of discretion and independent judgment. "While some of Plaintiffs' duties suggested that they exercised discretion and

---

[49] Wimberley v. Beast Energy Servs., No. 3:19-cv-00096, 2022 U.S. Dist. LEXIS 38392 (S.D. Tex. Mar. 4, 2022), adopted by, summary judgment denied by, motion denied by, dismissed by, without prejudice, in part *Wimberley v. Beast Energy Servs.*, 2022 U.S. Dist. LEXIS 49374 (S.D. Tex., Mar. 21, 2022).

independent judgment, a fact question remained as to whether they exercised *sufficient* discretion and independent judgment in carrying out their duties to conclude, as a matter of law, that Beast Energy had carried its burden on this factor of the administrative exemption." Consequently, the court denied Beast Energy's motion for summary judgment.

[iii] — *Ganci v. MBF Insp. Servs.*[50]

MBF Inspection. Services (MBF) provides inspection services to customers in the oil and gas industries in various states, and deemed its inspectors exempt and paid a day rate without overtime compensation. The court granted conditional certification and, later, class certification. The company settled for $2,225,000. Generally, inspectors will not qualify for the administrative exemption because they are unlikely to meet the discretion and independent judgment element of the exemption test.

[iv] — *Hobbs v. EVO Inc.*[51]

EVO Incorporated (EVO) offers downhole video camera services to clients in the oil and gas industry. EVO employs proprietary camera technology to enable well owners to identify and diagnose issues that interrupt a well's productivity. The plaintiffs worked for EVO as field engineers. As field engineers, they drove long distances, often on short notice, to provide EVO's camera services at clients' well sites. At the well site, field engineers were often EVO's only representative to the client. While onsite, they interacted with and took direction from the client's representative, the "company man." Field engineers also interacted with wireline operators, who helped to lower the camera into the well. Before filming, field engineers would sample well water from a holding tank and assess its clarity by dropping a coin into a bottle of the fluid to see whether the coin's features remained visible. They would then advise the company man on the quality of the images that could be obtained.

---

[50] Ganci v. MBF Insp. Servs., 323 F.R.D. 249 (S.D. Ohio 2017); Ganci v. MBF Insp. Servs., No. 2:15-cv-2959, 2019 U.S. Dist. LEXIS 207645 (S.D. Ohio Dec. 3, 2019).
[51] Hobbs v. EVO Inc., 7 F.4th 241 (5th Cir. 2021).

The Fifth Circuit found that the field engineers did not qualify for the administrative exemption. The court rejected EVO's contention that field engineers' film preparations, such as decisions regarding the camera's setup and configuration of well equipment based on well conditions, meet this standard. Under the DOL regulations, an employee does not exercise discretion or judgment in the relevant sense if the decisions are essentially "the use of skill in applying well-established techniques, procedures or specific standards described in manuals or other sources." Thus, when filming or preparing to film a well, the field engineers follow guidelines provided by EVO for operating those tools and were also provided with a maintenance schedule and operations manual. Further the field engineers were not consultants or well experts but, rather, experts at operating the camera, and who were onsite not to offer analysis but to obtain usable images for the clients. The court found that the field engineers did not offer recommendations, propose solutions to EVO's clients, or advise them of possible options for remediation. In short, field engineers' work is production related because they provided EVO's service and compile the final video product through their filming and annotating.

[v] — *Last v. M-I, L.L.C.*[52]

Plaintiffs alleged that M-I misclassified its drilling fluid specialists as exempt from overtime. The court granted class certification. The case remains pending.

[vi] — *Raptis v. DPS Land Servs., LLC.*[53]

DPS Land Servs. (DPS) operates a corporate office in Canonsburg, Pennsylvania and describes itself as a full-service land company that is dedicated to the Appalachian Basin. Its work includes obtaining rights-of-way for a gathering system in a complex urban environment and managing

---

[52] Last v. M-I, L.L.C., No. 1:20-cv-01205-ADA-EPG, 2022 U.S. Dist. LEXIS 232167 (E.D. Cal. Dec. 27, 2022).
[53] Raptis v. DPS Land Servs., LLC, No. 2:19-CV-01262-CRE, 2020 U.S. Dist. LEXIS 89407 (W.D. Pa. May 21, 2020).

multifaceted large scale title and land projects. To do this work, DPS employs landmen to assist in acquiring property to expand its network of services and to identify easements, rights-of-way to permit them to operate, and oil and gas leases. Raptis was a landman who DPS classified at various times as an exempt employee and as an independent contractor. Regardless, Raptis was only paid a day rate and never received overtime and performed non-exempt duties. He sued under the FLSA on behalf of himself and similarly situated current and former landmen employed by DPS to recover unpaid overtime wages. The case was voluntarily dismissed in March 2021, presumably because of a settlement between the parties.

[e] — Illustrative Cases – Exemption Found.
[i] — *Mondeck v. LineQuest, LLC.*[54]

LineQuest was a damage prevention company specializing in line locating, mapping, and hydro-excavation that performs work across West Texas and Southeast New Mexico, providing safety, damage prevention, environmental, and regulatory compliance services. The plaintiffs worked at the pipeline and construction sites and alleged they were misclassified as exempt administrative employees under the FLSA. LineQuest moved for summary judgment.

The court found that the employees met the administrative exemption. The primary focus of their job — and the most valuable services provided to LineQuest — was oversight of excavation and backfilling projects on behalf of LineQuest's customers. The performance of other tasks including driving and line locating did not affect this primary function. The employees' oversight was non-manual, without close supervision, related to planning excavation and backfilling projects, not the business of oil and gas transportation, and related to the exempt areas of "safety and health," "legal and regulatory compliance" and loss prevention. All of these are exempt tasks. Further, the court found that the employees used independent judgment and discretion when representing LineQuest customers at a job site that involved safety

---

[54] Mondeck v. LineQuest, LLC, No. MO:19-CV-221-DC, 2021 U.S. Dist. LEXIS 218651 (W.D. Tex. Aug. 28, 2021).

work and plaintiffs were the primary conduit of information concerning backfilling and construction activities between LineQuest and its customers.

[ii] — *Venable v. Schlumberger Ltd.*[55]

The plaintiffs were employed DTR Field Specialists, which was commonly referred to as a "reamer hand" or "reamer." As reamers, their primary duty was to supervise customers' use of the "underreaming" tool. Specifically, reamers supervised the rig crew as they attached and removed the reamer tool to/from the drill string, monitored and oversaw the reaming operation, provided advice and suggestions to the driller on how to operate and use the underreaming tool, and ensured that the driller did not operate the underreaming tool in a manner that would damage the well or the tool. The plaintiffs did not actually operate the underreaming tool; rather the driller was the individual at the controls of and operating the drill string. The plaintiffs were classified as exempt from overtime under the administrative exemption. The court upheld the exemption.

First, the plaintiffs were paid a base salary every week regardless of the number of hours worked. In addition, they were given additional compensation of a day rate paid for any day in which they are present on a customer's rig, which accounted for the majority of their total compensation.[56]

Second, the plaintiffs performed exempt work because they regularly performed "non-manual work directly related to the management or general business operations of the employer or the employer's customers," which includes serving as an advisor and consultant to an employer's customers. As reamers, the plaintiffs provided services to the clients' operations to drill a well that would produce oil and/or natural gas. They supervised the

---

[55] Venable v. Schlumberger Ltd., No. 6:16-CV-00241, 2022 U.S. Dist. LEXIS 55389 (W.D. La. Mar. 24, 2022).

[56] So long as all other aspects of the exemption tests are met, an exempt employee generally may receive additional compensation – in addition to their guaranteed salary – without losing their exempt status. *See* 29 C.F.R. § 541.604(a). However, this additional compensation must bear a "reasonable relationship" to the guaranteed salary. *See* U.S. Dept. of Labor Opinion Letter, FLSA 2018-25 (Nov. 8, 2015) (available at https://www.dol.gov/sites/dolgov/files/whd/legacy/files/2018_11_08_25_flsa.pdf).

customers running of drilling tools offshore, which included monitoring, analyzing, and recording information pertaining to the drilling process. They communicated with and instructed the driller on how to properly operate the underreaming tool, ensuring that the Driller operated the tool within the appropriate parameters, and that the driller did not operate the underreaming tool in a manner that would damage the well. Their main job was assisting clients in drilling operations and ensuring that the driller operated the tool correctly. These primary duties qualify as safety and control and further indicate that the plaintiffs served as advisors and consultants. Finally, supervision of the rig crew as they operated the underreaming tool qualifies as an administrative function.

[f] — The Seaman Exemption.
[i] — *Adams v. All Coast, L.L.C.*[57]

All Coast hired Adams as an able-bodied seaman to work on its fleet of liftboats that service offshore oil and gas platforms in the Gulf of Mexico.[58] All Coast did not pay Adams overtime because a "seaman" is exempt from overtime under the FLSA. Adams asserted that his main duty had nothing to do with maritime work. Instead, Adams spent much of his time operating a hydraulic crane to move personnel and equipment between the liftboat and the dock, offshore worksite platforms, and other vessels, as well as on the liftboat itself. Adams claims that because he was really a crane operator and not a seaman, All Coast owed him unpaid overtime wages under the FLSA. Adams filed a collective action on behalf of himself and other similarly-situated All Coast mates, deckhands, ordinary seamen, and able-bodied

---

[57] Adams v. All Coast, L.L.C., 15 F.4th 365 (5th Cir. 2021). *See also* McKnight v. Helix Energy Sols. Grp., Inc., No. H-19-2852, 2021 U.S. Dist. LEXIS 34712 (S.D. Tex. Feb. 23, 2021), *reversed by, remanded by, McKnight v. Helix Energy Sols. Grp., Inc.*, 2022 U.S. App. LEXIS 20800 (5th Cir. July 27, 2022).

[58] "A liftboat is a self-propelled, self-elevating, offshore supply vessel. Although it functions and navigates much like any other supply vessel, a typical liftboat is equipped with three column-like legs that can be quickly lowered to the seafloor to raise the vessel out of the water and stabilize it for marine operations." Naquin v. Elevating Boats, L.L.C., 744 F.3d 927, 930 n.1 (5th Cir. 2014); *see* 46 C.F.R. § 90.10-20 ("Liftboat means an offshore supply vessel with moveable legs capable of raising its hull above the surface of the sea.").

FLSA UPDATE § 3.05

seamen, claiming their job titles hide their true task: crane operator. They claimed their work servicing offshore oil and gas wells consisted of "the types of things that anyone engaged in oil and gas exploration does regardless of whether drilling onshore or offshore." Along with the crew members, liftboat cooks joined the class, alleging that they too are entitled to overtime pay since they spent their time cooking for third parties and these allegedly non-seamen crew members.

The Fair Labor Standards Act requires that an employee who works more than 40 hours in a workweek be paid overtime wages unless he or she falls within an exemption, including the exemption for "any employee employed as a seaman."[59] The FLSA does not define "seaman." In *Adams*, the Fifth Circuit clarified that an employee is a seaman if: "(1) the employee is subject to the authority, direction, and control of the master; and (2) the employee's service is primarily offered to aid the vessel as a means of transportation, provided that the employee does not perform a substantial amount of different work."[60]

The case revolved around the second prong, particularly whether using a crane aids in a liftboat's operation *as a means of transportation*. The district court concluded it did. The Fifth Circuit, however, disagreed as "contrary to the regulatory language and our decisions interpreting it." The Fifth Circuit held that the employees operating the cranes were not "offered to aid the vessel as a means of transportation." The employees did perform many tasks that satisfied the exemption test. For example, when the boats were underway, they acted as a normal nautical crew. And they remained responsible for their nautical tasks even when the boats were jacked up. They attended safety meetings, cleaned up the liftboats, and performed regular inspections. But, once they finished their duties as the boat's crew, they turned their attention exclusively to operating the cranes. It was as though they were performing two discrete jobs: upkeep of the boat and operation of the crane. Given this,

---

[59] 29 C.F.R. § 213(b)(6).
[60] Adams v. All Coast, L.L.C., 988 F.3d 203, 207 (5th Cir. 2021) (quoting Coffin v. Blessey Marine Servs., Inc., 771 F.3d 276, 281 (5th Cir. 2014)).

§ 3.05   ENERGY & MINERAL LAW INSTITUTE

the Fifth Circuit remanded the case so the lower court could determine how much time was spent performing nautical tasks versus crane operation.[61]

[ii] — *Hernandez v. Helix Energy Sols. Grp., Inc.*[62]

Helix Energy Sols. Grp. (Helix) provides offshore-drilling construction, inspection, maintenance, repair, and salvage services to the oil and gas industry. The plaintiffs worked as electricians for Helix and were classified as exempt seaman (and so were not paid overtime). The plaintiffs argued they are not seamen because their work primarily related to servicing offshore oil and gas wells, not to aiding a vessel in transportation. They claimed they spent over 20 percent of their working time on nonseaman duties. Helix argued that the plaintiffs' work directly related to the transportation of a vessel because, as electricians, the plaintiffs worked on systems that kept the vessel afloat and allowed it to be safely navigated. Further, electricians spend less than 20 percent of their time working on nonmarine equipment, meaning that over 80 percent of the plaintiffs' time was spent working on equipment necessary to keeping the vessel afloat and navigable. Based on this conflicting evidence, the court found genuine factual disputes as to whether the plaintiffs spent such a substantial portion of their working time on non-seaman duties as to fall outside the seaman exemption.

[2] — Misclassification Relating to Independent Contractors.

The Federal Circuits use different (though similar) tests for determining whether a worker is an independent contractor as opposed to an employee. But the tests primarily focus on whether, as a matter of economic reality, the individual is so dependent on the business they provide services to that they are actually an employee. This is a highly fact-intensive inquiry. For

---

[61] Similarly, the lower court was directed to determine how much time the cooks spent preparing food for the crew when they were not performing seamen's work, and how much time they spent preparing food for non-crew members. If that adds up to a "substantial" amount, then they, like the crane-operating crew members, were not doing seamen's work.

[62] Hernandez v. Helix Energy Sols. Grp., Inc., No. H-18-1588, 2021 U.S. Dist. LEXIS 82107 (S.D. Tex. Apr. 29, 2021); Way v. Helix Energy Sols. Grp., Inc., No. H-19-334, 2021 U.S. Dist. LEXIS 82112 (S.D. Tex. Apr. 29, 2021).

example, the Fifth Circuit considers whether, as a matter of economic reality, the individual is so dependent on the business they provide services to that they are an employee and not in business for themself.[63] These "economic realities" factors are: (1) the degree of control exercised by the alleged employer; (2) the extent of the relative investments of the worker and the alleged employer; (3) the degree to which the worker's opportunity for profit or loss is determined by the alleged employer; (4) the skill and initiative required in performing the job; and (5) the permanency of the relationship. Importantly, no single factor is determinative.[64] Indeed, "[t]he determination of whether an individual is an employee or independent contractor is highly dependent on the particular situation presented."[65]

Workers who are misclassified as independent contractors are entitled to unpaid overtime wages. For example, in October 2021, a federal court affirmed Holland Acquisition, Inc.'s liability for $43,276,637 in back wages and liquidated damages owed to 700 workers. The Department of Labor found that from 2012 to 2019, Holland improperly classified abstractors, title examiners, and landmen (whose work included research of land deeds to determine ownership of mineral rights) as independent contractors.[66]

[a] — Illustrative Cases.
[i] — *Bernstein v. Buckeye, Inc.*[67]

Buckeye provides drilling fluid ("mud") and products and services for oil wells. Mud facilitates drilling operations by lubricating the drill bit and stabilizing the well bore among other functions. Mud engineers ensure the mud used at any particular site is chemically compatible with the formation

---

[63] Hobbs v. Petroplex Pipe and Constr., Inc., 946 F.3d 824, 829 (5th Cir. 2020).
[64] *Id.*
[65] Thibault v. Bellsouth Telecomms., Inc., 612 F.3d 843, 848 (5th Cir. 2010).
[66] *Federal court enters judgment affirming US Department of Labor finding oil, energy services employer misclassified 700 Pennsylvania workers,* U.S. DEPARTMENT OF LABOR, WAGE AND HOUR DIVISION, (Oct. 1, 2021) (available at https://www.dol.gov/newsroom/releases/whd/whd20211001).
[67] Bernstein v. Buckeye, Inc., No. MO:18-CV-97-DC, 2020 U.S. Dist. LEXIS 262830 (W.D. Tex. Sep. 23, 2020).

and contains the appropriate additives. Buckeye classified the mud engineers it engaged as independent contractors. The court initially granted conditional certification. After discovery, Buckeye moved to decertify the class, which the court granted. The court concluded, based on the evidence presented, that the nature of the economic-reality inquiry makes collective treatment of the employees' disparate factual situations impractical. The economic reality analysis is fact intensive and the results are context specific, and the divergent factual circumstances of each employee will require individual consideration.

[ii] — *Hargrave v. AIM Directional Servs., L.L.C.*[68]

AIM Directional Services (AIM) provides oil and gas directional drilling, horizontal drilling, mud-motor drilling, and measurement drilling services and tools to various clients. To conduct its drilling operations, AIM employs directional drillers. Directional drillers guide the path of drilling and provide advice on how to most effectively implement the well plan provided by AIM's clients, which functions as the general guideline for drilling operations. AIM uses both employees and independent contractors as directional drillers. Based on the economic realities, and the lack of control AIM exercised over the plaintiff here, the court concluded that he was an independent contractor.

§ 3.06   Compensation for Travel Time.
[1] — Whether Travel Time Is Compensated Depends on the Nature of the Travel.

Employees often travel from job site to job site, and whether that time is compensable has been the subject to litigation. Generally speaking, the FLSA requires employers to pay employees for their work. The U.S. Supreme Court initially explained that compensable time under the FLSA includes employees' activities "controlled or required by the employer and pursued necessarily and primarily for the benefit of the employer and his business," as well as "all time during which an employee is necessarily required to be

---

[68] Hargrave v. AIM Directional Servs., L.L.C., No. 21-40496,(5th Cir. May 11, 2022).

on the employer's premises, on duty or at a prescribed workplace."[69] The Court later recognized that such "expansive definitions provoked a flood of litigation," and "Congress responded swiftly" by passing the Portal-to-Portal Act of 1947, 29 U.S.C. §§ 251- 262.[70] The DOL's regulations note that "whether or not time spent in travel is working time depends upon the kind of travel involved."[71]

The Portal-to-Portal Act provides that employers do not need to compensate employees for:

- walking, riding, or traveling to and from the actual place of performance of the principal activity or activities which [an] — employee is employed to perform, and
- activities which are preliminary to or postliminary to said principal activity or activities, which occur either prior to the time on any particular workday at which such employee commences, or subsequent to the time on any particular workday at which he ceases, such principal activity or activities.[72]

[a] — Ordinary Commuting Is Not Compensable.

Compensable worktime generally does not include time spent commuting to or from work. The DOL's regulations clarify that "[n]ormal travel from home to work is not worktime" regardless of "whether [the employee] — works at a fixed location or at different job sites."[73] Accordingly, ordinary commute time is non-compensable under the FLSA.[74]

[b] — Travel During the Workday Is Compensable.

Unlike ordinary commute time, "travel from job site to job site during the workday, must be counted as hours worked."[75]

---

[69] Anderson v. Mt. Clemens Pottery Co., 328 U.S. 680, 690-92 (1946).
[70] Integrity Staffing Solutions, Inc. v. Busk, 135 S. Ct. 513, 516 (2014).
[71] 29 C.F.R. § 785.33.
[72] 29 U.S.C. § 254(a).
[73] 29 C.F.R. § 785.35.
[74] *See* Aiken v. City of Memphis, Tenn., 190 F.3d 753, 758 (6th Cir. 1999); Johnson v. RGIS Inventory Specialists, 554 F. Supp. 2d 693, 703 (E.D. Tex. 2007).
[75] 29 C.F.R. § 785.38.

§ 3.06 ENERGY & MINERAL LAW INSTITUTE

[c] — Travel Away from Home May Be Compensable.

When employees must travel away from their home communities overnight, such "[t]ravel away from home is clearly worktime when it cuts across the employee's workday. The employee is simply substituting travel for other duties." For example, "if an employee regularly works from 9 a.m. to 5 p.m. from Monday through Friday the travel time during these hours is worktime on Saturday and Sunday as well as on the other days." As an enforcement policy, the Department of Labor's Wage and Hour Division "will not consider as worktime that time spent in travel away from home outside of regular working hours as a passenger on an airplane, train, boat, bus, or automobile."[76] Consequently, travel away from home is compensable "when it cuts across: (1) an employee's workday; and (2) an employee's regular working hours on nonworking days."[77]

However, "[t]ravel time is not compensable when: (1) it occurs outside of the employee's regular working hours, whether on working or nonworking days; or (2) the employee is a passenger on a common carrier and [the] — travel occurs during [the employee's] — regular working hours on nonworking days."[78] Note, state law (*e.g.*, California) may have more restrictive rules relating to travel time.

[2] — Illustrative Cases.
[a] — *Copley v. Evolution Well Servs. Operating, LLC.*[79]

The plaintiffs alleged they were not properly compensated for time spent traveling to remote work locations, where employees would live for 14-day hitches in employer-sponsored housing, and additionally, for time spent traveling from the employer-sponsored housing to daily work sites. The plaintiffs asserted

---

[76] 29 C.F.R. § 785.39.

[77] *See* Bassett v. Tenn. Valley Auth., No. 5:09-CV-00039, 2013 U.S. Dist. LEXIS 83203 (W.D. Ky. June 13, 2013); Espinoza v. Atlas R.R. Constr., *LLC*, 657 F. App'x 101 (3d Cir. 2016); Dieffenbauch v. Rhinehart R.R. Constr., Inc., 2021 U.S. Dist. LEXIS 34907 (N.D.N.Y. Feb. 25, 2021); Lewis v. Sentry Elec. Grp., Inc., No. 1:19-CV-00178, 2020 U.S. Dist. LEXIS 381 (S.D. Ohio Jan. 2, 2020).

[78] *See generally id. See also* Smith v. Aztec Well Servicing Co., 462 F.3d 1274 (10th Cir. 2006) (finding that gas drillers in New Mexico were exempt from compensation for travel time from their central carpooling site to well sites that ranged from 30 minutes to 3.5 hours away).

[79] Copley v. Evolution Well Servs. Operating, LLC, No. 2:20-CV-1442-CCW, 2022 U.S. Dist. LEXIS 17266 (W.D. Pa. Jan. 31, 2022); Copley v. Evolution Well Servs. Operating, LLC, No. 2:20-CV-01442-CCW, 2023 U.S. Dist. LEXIS 23452 (W.D. Pa. Feb. 10, 2023).

that "hitch employees" would arrive at the Evolution Well Services Operating (EWSO)-controlled housing the day before the start of a hitch, that they provided their own transportation to the EWSO-controlled housing, and that, per EWSO policy, such travel time was not compensated. The court found that, EWSO ultimately may be correct that employees' time spent traveling from their homes to the EWSO-controlled housing is not compensable under the FLSA. "But, at this juncture, it is not 'patently clear' that Employees cannot prevail as a matter of law." In ruling on the plaintiffs' motion for conditional certification, the court does not consider the merits of the claim, decide credibility issues, or resolve factual disputes at this stage of the case. The court granted FLSA conditional certification. The parties then settled the case for $2,550,000.

[b] — *Barhight v. Terra Oilfield Se*rvs. [80]

Terra Oilfield provides water to oilfield frac sites in Texas and New Mexico. Operators and frac supervisors working for Terra maintain and operate water lines and pumps to supply water to frac sites. Barhight alleged that Terra Oilfield did not compensate him for hours he spent traveling between his home in Seguin, Texas, and Midland, Texas, before and after a hitch as a frac operator/supervisor.

According to Barhight, the "workday" began at 5:30 p.m. or a.m., depending on the shift; he worked for a set number of days and were off for another set number of days. His commute lasted 5.5 hours and was undertaken on or before the day his hitch was set to start and on the last day of his hitch He also alleged he was required to travel from his home during normal work hours to the remote job site. During the hitch, Barhight was housed at a man camp or a hotel, depending on the location of the job site. Terra Oilfield classified Barhight as exempt and did not pay overtime.

Barhight filed suit under the FLSA, and Terra Oilfield moved to dismiss. The court denied the company's motion: "Taking Plaintiff's allegations as true and drawing all reasonable inferences in Plaintiff's favor, the court rule[d]

---

[80] Barhight v. Terra Oilfield Servs., No. MO:19-CV-00214-DC, 2021 U.S. Dist. LEXIS 111251 (W.D. Tex. Mar. 2, 2021).

§ 3.06

— Plaintiff states a plausible claim for unpaid travel under the FLSA." The case then settled for an undisclosed amount.

[c] — *Wimberley v. Beast Energy Servs.*[81]

Beast Energy moved for summary judgment on the plaintiffs' travel time claim. Specifically, the company asked the court to decide whether the following travel time is compensable under the FLSA — time the employees spent traveling between: (1) Beast Energy's shop in Rosharon and the well site; or (2) their hotel and the well site when working on location.

With respect to the hotel-to-well site-travel, the court held that such time was not compensable.

However, there was a fact question regarding the travel between the shop and the well site. According to the court, "the key takeaway is that, on the days that Plaintiffs drove a company-owned truck or trailer from the shop in Rosharon to a client's well site, Plaintiffs claim that they were tasked with gathering and transporting supplies and equipment necessary to perform their job. If true, Plaintiffs' travel time was likely an integral and indispensable part of their principal responsibilities and, therefore, compensable under the FLSA."[82] And, it was unclear whether time spent traveling home to Rosharon at the conclusion of a project is compensable as an integral and indispensable part of Plaintiffs' principal responsibilities. The Department of Labor opined that "laborers' travel to and from the remote location at

---

[81] Wimberley v. Beast Energy Servs., No. 3:19-cv-00096, 2022 U.S. Dist. LEXIS 38392 (S.D. Tex. Mar. 4, 2022), *adopted by, summary judgment denied by, motion denied by, dismissed by, without prejudice, in part, Wimberley v. Beast Energy Servs.*, 2022 U.S. Dist. LEXIS 49374 (S.D. Tex. Mar. 21, 2022).

[82] *See, e.g.*, Pittard v. Red River Oilfield Servs., LLC, No. 4:15-CV-3753, 2017 U.S. Dist. LEXIS 206956 (S.D. Tex. Dec. 15, 2017) ("The time [Plaintiffs] — spent completing these activities and the drive time from the company shop to the jobsite are compensable under the Portal-to-Portal Act because those hours are integral and indispensable to [Plaintiffs'] — job ... Even though the activities performed at the company shop are not part of Plaintiff's principal responsibilities, without the trailer and the other supplies and equipment, [Plaintiffs] — ... would not be able to perform their duties at the jobsite."); Crenshaw v. Quarles Drilling Corp., 798 F.2d 1345 (10th Cir. 1986) (holding "time spent travelling to and from drill sites" was compensable where workers carried special equipment for servicing oil rigs).

the beginning and end of the job, on the other hand, *may* or *may not* be compensable."[83] Consequently, the court denied Beast Energy's motion for summary judgment on this issue.

[d] — *Little v. Technical Specialty Prod.*[84]

The plaintiff worked as a field service technician based out of his home in McKinney, Texas. He was required to drive to oil rig sites in Texas, Louisiana, New Mexico, and Oklahoma where he installed and serviced video camera systems. Technical Specialty provided him with a company pickup truck, company iPhone, and company credit card for business expenses; it did not pay overtime for the first and last commute of the day, but paid the plaintiff at his regular rate for those hours spent driving. The plaintiff complained to the company about the overtime policy, was soon terminated, and then filed suit for overtime compensation. He also claimed he was terminated in retaliation for complaining about the overtime policy.

The jury found that he was not entitled to overtime compensation for his ordinary home-to-work travel time. However, the jury found that the plaintiff was terminated in retaliation for his complaints. He was awarded $105,366 in back pay and $105,366 in liquidated damages.

This case highlights the danger of retaliation. Even though the employer prevailed on the primary FLSA overtime claim, it was liable for retaliation.

§ 3.07. State Law Protections.

The FLSA does not preempt state laws that are more generous or more protective of employees. Therefore, employers need to be aware of state wage-hour laws and how they affect their local operations, particular as to the statute of limitations, overtime pay requirements, and available damages. For example:

---

[83] U.S. Department of Labor Opinion Letter FLSA2020-16 (Nov. 3, 2020) (available at https://www.dol.gov/sites/dolgov/files/WHD/opinion-letters/FLSA/2020_11_03_16_FLSA.pdf (emphasis added).
[84] Little v. Technical Specialty Prod., No. 4:11-cv-717, 2012 U.S. Dist. LEXIS 152041 (E.D. Tex. Oct. 23, 2013).

§ 3.07   ENERGY & MINERAL LAW INSTITUTE

- The FLSA provides a three-year statute of limitations for wage-hour claims. New York, by contrast, provides a six-year statute of limitations.[85] The FLSA requires overtime at 1.5 times the employee's regular rate for each hour worked over 40.
- California requires overtime pay at: (1) 1.5 times the employee's regular rate of pay for all hours worked in excess of 8 hours up to and including 12 hours in any workday, and for the first 8 hours worked on the seventh consecutive day of work in a workweek; and (2) 2 times employee's regular rate of pay for all hours worked in excess of 12 hours in any workday and for all hours worked in excess of 8 on the seventh consecutive day of work in a workweek.[86]
- The FLSA provides for liquidated (double) damages. Michigan, however, provides for treble damages.[87]

State law may apply even to employees who work off-shore. In *Gulf Offshore Logistics, LLC v. Superior Court*,[88] the Ninth Circuit Court of Appeals reviewed a case where the company employed non-California residents to work as crewmembers on a vessel that provided maintenance services to offshore oil platforms. When docked at Port Hueneme, California, crewmembers were on duty while the vessel was in port. The vessel returned exclusively to Port Hueneme after visiting each of the oil platforms, which were located outside California's boundaries. On its journey, the ship sailed through the Santa Barbara Channel, which is located in California. Crewmembers also were on duty and working during those voyages. Crewmembers alleged that they were not properly paid minimum wage and overtime or provided meal and rest periods, accurate work records, or complete wage statements as required by California law. The court held that

---

[85] N.Y. Lab. Law § 193(3).
[86] Cal. Lab. Code § 510.
[87] M.G.L. ch. 149, § 150.
[88] Gulf Offshore Logistics, LLC v. Superior Court, 58 Cal. App. 5th 264, 272, 272 Cal. Rptr. 3d 356 (2020), *review denied and ordered not published by, Gulf Offshore Logistics v. Superior Court*, 2021 Cal. LEXIS 2190 (Cal. Mar. 24, 2021).

work performed in California's territorial waters is subject to California employment law even though the waters are also within federal territorial boundaries. Therefore, California law governs the employment relationships at issue here because California served as the base for the crewmembers' work operations, all or most which were performed in California.

§ 3.08. Minimizing Liability by Auditing Payroll Practices.

[1] — Employer "Good Faith" Reliance on Industry Standards Is Insufficient to Avoid Liability Under the Fair Labor Standards Act.

Employers who violate the FLSA are generally liable for the amount of unpaid compensation, plus an additional equal amount as liquidated damages.[89] A district court may, "in its sound discretion," refuse to award liquidated damages if the employer demonstrates good faith and reasonable grounds for believing it was not in violation."[90] The employer "bears the 'substantial burden' of proving the reasonableness of its conduct."[91] An employer cannot show good faith simply by pointing to industry standards (for example, that day-rate compensation for "exempt" employees is common throughout the industry). While industry standards may be relevant, "compliance with industry standards is insufficient to prove good faith."[92] "Courts have held that although evidence of industry standard may not be *sufficient* to establish a good faith defense, it may be *relevant* to such an inquiry."[93]

---

[89] 29 U.S.C. § 216(b).
[90] 29 U.S.C. § 260.
[91] Dacar v. Saybolt, L.P., 914 F.3d 917, 920 (5th Cir. 2018).
[92] Way v. Helix Energy Sols. Grp., Inc., No. H-19-334, 2021 U.S. Dist. LEXIS 82112, at *16 (S.D. Tex. Apr. 29, 2021). *See, e.g.,* Tillis v. S. Floor Covering, Inc., No. 3:16-CV-287-HTW-LRA, 2018 U.S. Dist. LEXIS 162608 (S.D. Miss. Sept. 24, 2018) ("Blind adherence to industry practice is an insufficient basis" for good faith); Reich v. S. New England Telecommunications Corp., 121 F.3d 58 (2d Cir. 1997) ("Nor is good faith demonstrated by ... simple conformity with industry-wide practice.").
[93] Scalia v. Med. Staffing of Am., 2020 U.S. Dist. LEXIS 98604, at *4 (E.D. Va. Mar. 18, 2020); *see* Vega ex rel. Trevino v. Gasper, 36 F.3d 417 (5th Cir. 1994) (noting reliance

[2] — Employers Can Minimize Potential Liability by Auditing Their Payroll Practices.

A wage-hour audit is a systematic way of determining whether the company is complying with federal, state, and local laws regarding the employment relationship and labor relations. Importantly, a wage-hour audit provides a key way to keep up with the increasing regulation of the employment relationship by the legislature and the courts. Thus, wage and hour audits serve several purposes — the most prominent of which is the chance to locate and correct flaws in employee classifications (exempt, non-exempt, independent contractor), payroll, and hours worked. Plaintiffs' attorneys examine every aspect of the payroll process and legal requirements. Every employee who is terminated, demoted, or experiences an unpleasant workplace event is encouraged by Internet and television advertising and Department of Labor outreach to seek the advice of counsel. This challenge has been compounded over the last several years by an increasingly "patchwork" body of wage, wage payment, wage notice, and paid leave laws enacted at the state and city level.

An audit is one means of achieving a level of compliance that greatly reduces the likelihood of litigation. For example, an audit can:

- Identify and proactively address wage-hour issues that could generate employee complaints;
- Respond to changes in the law;
- Prepare for a defense of a lawsuit or agency investigation;
- Show "good faith" efforts to comply with federal and state wage-hour laws (which may help avoid findings of willful violations in a lawsuit or investigation); and
- Help establish and maintain a culture of wage-hour compliance.

---

on industry standard as proof of good faith is relevant, but may not be controlling); *Rosario v. 12425, Inc.*, No. 1:13-cv-23429-UU, 2014 U.S. Dist. LEXIS 193065 (S.D. Fla. 2014) (allowing defendants to present evidence of industry custom as evidence of good faith though noting that such evidence, alone, cannot establish good faith); Morse v. MER Corp., No. 1:08CV1389, 2014 U.S. Dist. LEXIS 17969 (S.D. Ind. Nov. 22, 2010) (denying motion in limine and allowing defendants to introduce evidence of industry standard for the limited purpose of supporting a good faith defense).

To those ends, a proactive internal audit can address matters such as:

- Are your independent contractors appropriately classified?
- Are your exempt employees correctly classified?
- Are your timekeeping records complete and up-to-date, especially for overtime hours and state-mandated breaks?
- Are overtime, bonuses, commissions, and other remuneration properly recorded and paid?
- Are your payroll and HR teams up-to-date on applicable state and local laws?
- Do any company written policies need to be updated?
- Do any managers or supervisors need to be trained or notified of legal updates?

Audits often involve the production of documents that would normally be discoverable in a federal or state Department of Labor investigation or wage-litigation. Consequently, a company should take steps to establish and preserve the attorney-client privilege and work product, to the extent possible, from the outset of the audit.

[3] — Topics to Review When Conducting a Comprehensive Wage-Hour Audit.

Minimum Wage
- Federal (currently $7.25)
- State
- Local

Calculation of Overtime Pay
- Does the company include discretionary bonuses, commissions, and other remuneration in regular rate when calculating OT pay?
- Does the company pay the "blended rate" when employees work at two or more rates of pay in same workweek?
- State OT laws
  - Does the company pay daily OT (1.5 or 2 times) for working over a certain number of hours per day in states that require it?

- Does the company pay OT for working 7 days in the same workweek in states that require it?

Meal and rest breaks
- Comply with federal law, which requires that any break of less than 20 minutes be paid?
- Comply with state laws requiring meal and/or rest breaks for both adults and minors?
- Comply with state meal and rest break laws that apply only to minors?

State Laws Regarding Direct Deposit and Use of Payroll Debit Cards
- Is consent obtained for direct deposit in states requiring such consent?
- Does company use payroll debit cards and, if so, does company comply with state laws regarding such cards?

Deductions from Wages of Non-Exempt Employees
- Do deductions for uniforms or equipment violate federal law by bringing employee's pay below the minimum wage or cutting into overtime pay?
- Do deductions for financial losses, breakage, or lost or damaged items violate federal law by bringing employee's pay below the minimum wage or cutting into overtime pay?
- State law
  - Does state law permit the deduction?
  - Does state law require written authorization from employee for the deduction?
  - Does the company comply with state laws regarding amount/percentage of pay that can be deducted for garnishments/child and spousal support?

Deductions from Salary of Exempt Employees
- Comply with FLSA requirement that only the following deductions may be taken from salary of exempt employee?

- Absence of one or more full days for personal reasons other than sickness or disability;
- Absence of one or more full days for personal reasons other than sickness or disability if employer has a plan for providing compensation for such absences and employee has not yet qualified for plan or has exhausted leave under plan;
- Penalties for violation of safety rules of major significance (must be extremely serious violation);
- Unpaid disciplinary suspensions of one or more full days for violation of written policy;
- First or last week of employment (can pay just for time worked);
- FMLA leave (can pay proportionate amount when employee takes unpaid FMLA leave for part of week); and
- Offset against salary of amount received by employee for jury or witness fees or military pay.

State and Local Laws Regarding Mandatory Paid Sick Leave to Employees

- Does the company comply with state and local mandated paid sick leave requirements?

State Laws Regarding Timing of Payment of Wages to Employees

- Are wages paid to employees at intervals required by state law (*e.g.*, bi-weekly)?
- Are final wages paid by deadline set forth in state law

State Laws Regarding Minimum Allowable Scheduled Shifts/ Reporting Time Pay

- Are non-exempt employees provided with reporting time pay when they work a shift that is less than the minimum allowable scheduled shift permitted under state law?
- Are employees in paid split shift pay when required?

Classification of Employees as Exempt/Non-Exempt
- Are employees paid on salary basis with no improper deductions?
- Does the salary meet the required $684/week threshold?
- If paid a day rate, is there a guaranteed salary of at least $684/week? And, does any additional compensation bear a reasonable relationship to the guaranteed salary amount?
- Do employees' duties satisfy requirements of duties test for an exemption?

State Minor Work Laws
- Comply with state laws regarding maximum number of hours worked per week/day on school and non-school days/weeks for minors?
- Comply with state requirements regarding hours of day when minors are not permitted to work?
- Comply with federal and state requirements regarding types of work minors are not permitted to perform?

Classification of Workers as Independent Contractors Rather than Employees
- Review of 1099 payments for each facility to determine whether any employees are being paid incorrectly as independent contractors

Hours Worked Issues
- Meal and rest breaks.
- Travel time of non-exempt employees.
- Waiting time.
- On-call time.
- Training/meetings.
- Preparatory and concluding activities at beginning and end of work day (*e.g.*, donning and doffing clothes/equipment).
- Practices regarding rounding of time.

FLSA UPDATE § 3.08

Wage Statements
- State law may dictate that certain information be provided on pay stubs.
  - CA has strictest requirements and most severe penalties for employers who do not comply with pay stub requirements.

Vacation
- Federal law does not require employers to provide vacations.
- State laws may affect accrual of vacation and timing of payment for unused accrued vacation upon termination.
  - Does vacation policy comply with state laws, which do not permit "use it or lose it" vacation policies, but allow cap on accrual?

Department of Transportation Regulations
- Does company comply with DOT regulations for employees (*e.g.*, CDL drivers) subject to DOT regulations regarding hours worked, rest periods, logging/recording of time, etc.?

Chapter 4

Protecting Your Brand with Trademarks

Joshua A. Claybourn
Jackson Kelly PLLC
Evansville, Indiana

Synopsis

§ 4.01.	Introduction	68
§ 4.02.	Understanding Trademarks	68
	[1] — Definition of a Trademark	68
	[2] — Types of Trademarks	69
	[3] — Benefits of Registering a Trademark	69
§ 4.03.	Trademark Selection Process	70
	[1] — Developing a Strong and Distinctive Trademark	70
	[2] — Conducting a Thorough Trademark Search	71
	[3] — Importance of Global Trademark Protection	71
§ 4.04.	Trademark Registration Process	72
	[1] — Domestic Trademark Registration	72
	[2] — International Trademark Registration	73
§ 4.05.	Trademark Maintenance and Renewal	74
	[1] — Monitoring the Use of Your Trademark	74
	[2] — Renewal Requirements and Deadlines	74
	[3] — Updating Your Trademark Registrations as Needed	75
§ 4.06.	Trademark Enforcement and Dispute Resolution	75
	[1] — Monitoring and Identifying Potential Infringements	75
	[2] — Cease and Desist Letters and Other Enforcement Actions	75
	[3] — Negotiating Settlements and Coexistence Agreements	76
	[4] — Litigation and Alternative Dispute Resolution Options	76
§ 4.07.	Trademark Protection in Mergers in Acquisitions	77
	[1] — Importance of Strong Trademarks in M&A Activity	77
	[2] — Due Diligence in the Acquisition Process	77
	[3] — Post-Acquisition Integration of Trademarks	78
§ 4.08.	Trademark Best Practices	79
	[1] — Establishing a Trademark Management Strategy	79
	[2] — Regularly Auditing and Updating Your Trademark Portfolio	79
	[3] — Training Employees on Trademark Usage and Enforcement	80
§ 4.09.	Conclusion	80

§ 4.01. Introduction.

The energy and mining industries are highly competitive and heavily regulated sectors that face numerous challenges, including environmental regulations, market fluctuations, social responsibility, and public perception. As a result, companies operating in these industries must place a significant emphasis on protecting their brands to maintain a strong market position and ensure their long-term success. One of the most effective tools for brand protection is the strategic use of trademarks, which serve to safeguard a company's brand identity, reputation, and the value associated with its products or services.

Trademarks play a vital role in brand protection by granting exclusive rights to the use of distinctive signs, such as names, logos, and slogans, in connection with specific goods or services. They help prevent unauthorized use, imitation, or dilution by competitors or third parties, thereby preserving the brand's integrity and minimizing the risk of consumer confusion. Furthermore, strong and protected trademarks are essential during merger and acquisition activities, as they contribute to the overall value of the companies involved and facilitate a smoother integration process.

The goal of this chapter is to provide a comprehensive overview of how to protect your brand within the energy and mining industries through the effective use of trademarks. We will discuss the various aspects of trademark selection, registration, maintenance, enforcement, and integration in mergers and acquisitions, as well as offer best practices for managing your trademark portfolio. Whether you are a new entrant or an established player in these industries, this presentation will equip you with the knowledge and tools necessary to build and maintain a strong brand identity that reflects your company's values, quality, and reputation.

§ 4.02. Understanding Trademarks.
[1] — Definition of a Trademark.

A trademark is a unique sign or symbol that serves to identify and distinguish the goods or services of one business from those of others. It is an essential tool for building brand recognition and value, as well as for preventing consumer confusion in the marketplace. By creating an association between a particular brand and the products or services it offers, a trademark fosters customer trust and loyalty. Trademarks can consist of various elements, such as words, phrases, logos, designs, or a combination of these, and can be registered at national and international levels to secure exclusive rights to their use within specific jurisdictions.

[2] — Types of Trademarks.

Trademarks can be categorized into several types, including:

- *Word marks*: These trademarks consist of text or words, such as brand names, that identify a business's goods or services. For example, "ExxonMobil" is a word mark representing a well-known energy company.
- *Logos*: Logos are distinctive graphic symbols or designs that represent a business and its goods or services. They can be used in conjunction with word marks or independently. For instance, the Chevron Corporation's stylized chevron symbol is a recognizable logo.
- *Slogans*: Slogans are short, catchy phrases or sentences that convey a brand's message or identity. For example, "Beyond Petroleum" is a slogan used by BP, a multinational oil and gas company.
- *Product packaging or trade dress*: Trade dress refers to the visual appearance or packaging of a product, which can be protected as a trademark if it is distinctive and non-functional. For example, the distinctive shape of a Coca-Cola bottle is protected as a trade dress.
- *Sound marks*: These trademarks consist of a specific sound or melody associated with a brand. For instance, the NBC chimes are a famous sound mark that identifies the National Broadcasting Company.
- *Color marks*: In some cases, a specific color or combination of colors can serve as a trademark if it has acquired distinctiveness through exclusive use in association with a particular brand. For example, Tiffany & Co. has trademarked its distinctive shade of blue.

[3] — Benefits of Registering a Trademark.

Registering a trademark provides a range of benefits to businesses, including:

- Public notice of ownership: A registered trademark puts competitors and the public on notice that you claim ownership of the mark and have exclusive rights to its use in connection with the specified goods or services.
- Exclusive rights: Registration grants you the exclusive right to use your trademark in the jurisdiction where it is registered, preventing others from using a confusingly similar mark for similar goods or services.
- Legal presumption of ownership: In the event of a dispute, a registered trademark provides a legal presumption that you are the owner of the mark, shifting the burden of proof to the alleged infringer.
- Ability to enforce rights: Owning a registered trademark enables you to take legal action against infringers, seek damages, and obtain injunctions to stop unauthorized use of your mark.
- Basis for international registration: A domestic trademark registration can serve as the basis for obtaining trademark protection in other countries, simplifying the process of expanding your brand globally.
- Enhanced brand value: A registered trademark can increase the perceived value of your brand, making it more attractive to potential investors, partners, or acquirers during merger and acquisition transactions.

§ 4.03. Trademark Selection Process.
[1] — Developing a Strong and Distinctive Trademark.

- Fanciful, arbitrary, and suggestive marks: The strength of a trademark is determined by its distinctiveness, which influences its ability to prevent consumer confusion and protect the brand's reputation. Fanciful, arbitrary, and suggestive marks are considered strong trademarks due to their inherent distinctiveness. Fanciful marks are invented words with no existing meaning (e.g., "Kodak" for cameras), while arbitrary marks are common words used in an unrelated context (e.g., "Apple" for computers). Suggestive marks, although not as strong as fanciful and arbitrary marks, imply the nature or characteristics of the goods or services without explicitly describing them (e.g., "Microsoft" for computer software).
- Avoiding generic and descriptive marks: Generic and descriptive marks are weaker and more difficult to protect as trademarks. Generic marks

are common terms used to describe a product or service (*e.g.*, "Oil Company"), while descriptive marks merely describe a feature or quality of the goods or services (*e.g.*, "High Performance Drilling"). Since these marks lack distinctiveness, they are generally ineligible for trademark protection. To ensure a strong and protectable trademark, it is essential to avoid generic and descriptive marks in favor of more distinctive options.

[2] — Conducting a Thorough Trademark Search.

Before adopting and registering a trademark, it is crucial to conduct a comprehensive trademark search to determine if the chosen mark is already in use or registered by another party. A thorough search involves reviewing various sources, such as national and international trademark databases, business directories, domain name registries, and social media platforms. By identifying any potential conflicts or similar marks, a trademark search helps minimize the risk of infringement claims and other legal issues that may arise from using a mark that is too similar to an existing one. Engaging the services of a trademark attorney or a professional search firm can be beneficial in ensuring a comprehensive search and analysis of the results.

[3] — Importance of Global Trademark Protection.

In today's interconnected world, it is increasingly important for businesses to consider international trademark protection. This involves registering your trademark in key markets where you operate or plan to expand, preventing unauthorized use, imitation, or dilution by competitors or third parties. International trademark protection not only safeguards your brand's reputation but also contributes to its long-term growth and success in global markets. To achieve this, businesses can either file individual trademark applications in each country of interest or utilize centralized systems like the Madrid System,[1] which simplifies the registration process across multiple jurisdictions. Considering global trademark protection early in the selection

---

[1] *Madrid Protocol for international trademark registration*, U.S. PATENT AND TRADEMARK OFFICE, https://www.uspto.gov/ip-policy/international-protection/madrid-protocol.

§ 4.04

process can help ensure your brand remains strong and competitive in an increasingly globalized marketplace.

§ 4.04. Trademark Registration Process.
[1] — Domestic Trademark Registration.

Registering a trademark domestically typically involves filing an application with the national intellectual property office, such as the United States Patent and Trademark Office (USPTO) in the United States. The process may vary depending on the jurisdiction, but generally includes several steps:

1. *Application preparation*: This stage involves gathering necessary information and materials for the application, such as the chosen trademark, a detailed description of the goods or services associated with the mark, and specimens showing the mark's use in commerce (if applicable). It is important to accurately and completely describe the goods or services to ensure proper coverage and protection.
2. *Formal examination*: After submission, the trademark office will conduct a formal examination to ensure that the application meets all procedural requirements, such as correct classification of goods or services, appropriate specimens, and payment of fees.
3. *Substantive examination*: The trademark office will then conduct a substantive examination to determine if the mark is eligible for registration. This involves assessing the mark's distinctiveness, as well as checking for potential conflicts with existing trademarks.
4. *Publication for opposition*: If the mark passes the substantive examination, it will be published in an official gazette or similar publication, allowing third parties to file oppositions if they believe the mark infringes on their rights. The opposition period varies by jurisdiction but typically lasts for several weeks to a few months.
5. *Registration*: If no oppositions are filed or any oppositions are successfully resolved, the trademark office will issue a registration certificate, granting you exclusive rights to use the mark within the jurisdiction.

[2] — International Trademark Registration.

For businesses seeking to protect their trademarks globally, the Madrid System provides a centralized, cost-effective solution. Administered by the World Intellectual Property Organization (WIPO), the Madrid System allows applicants to file a single application designating multiple countries, streamlining the registration process. The key steps in the international trademark registration process using the Madrid System include:

1. *Base application or registration*: To utilize the Madrid System, you must first have a domestic trademark application or registration (known as the "base" application or registration) in a member country of the Madrid Union.
2. *International application*: You can then file an international application through your national intellectual property office, designating the countries where you seek trademark protection. The application should include information about the base application or registration, the chosen trademark, and the goods or services associated with the mark.
3. *Formal examination by WIPO: WIPO will conduct a formal* examination of the international application to ensure compliance with procedural requirements. If the application meets these requirements, WIPO will record the mark in the International Register and publish it in the WIPO Gazette of International Marks.
4. *Substantive examination by designated countries*: Each designated country will conduct its own substantive examination, assessing the mark's eligibility for registration according to its national laws. If the mark is accepted by a designated country, it will grant protection equivalent to a national registration in that country.
5. *International registration and renewal*: WIPO will issue an international registration certificate and manage renewals for the mark every ten years, simplifying the process of maintaining your global trademark protection.

By understanding and navigating the domestic and international trademark registration processes, businesses can secure valuable protection for their brands, allowing them to compete more effectively in the global marketplace.

§ 4.05. Trademark Maintenance and Renewal.
[1] — Monitoring the Use of Your Trademark.

Once your trademark is registered, it is essential to monitor its use to maintain its strength and prevent it from becoming generic. Proper use of your trademark involves consistently using the mark in connection with the goods or services for which it is registered, as well as ensuring that the mark is not used inappropriately by others. To accomplish this, businesses should establish internal guidelines for the correct use of their trademarks and educate employees on the importance of adhering to these guidelines.

In addition to monitoring your own use of the mark, it is vital to be vigilant in identifying potential infringements or unauthorized use by third parties. This can be achieved by conducting regular searches of online marketplaces, industry publications, and social media platforms, as well as staying informed about new business registrations and domain name registrations. Early detection of potential infringements allows you to take prompt action to protect your brand and maintain the integrity of your trademark.

[2] — Renewal Requirements and Deadlines.

Trademark registrations are not perpetual and must be renewed periodically to maintain your exclusive rights to the mark. While the specific renewal requirements and deadlines vary by jurisdiction, most countries require that trademark owners submit a renewal application, pay the applicable fees, and provide evidence of continued use of the mark.

In the United States, for example, trademark registrations must be renewed between the fifth- and sixth-year following registration, and then every ten years thereafter. During the renewal process, trademark owners must submit a Declaration of Use and/or Excusable Nonuse (Section 8 Declaration), as well as a renewal application (Section 9 Renewal) and the associated fees.[2]

---

[2] *Definitions for maintaining a trademark registration,* U.S. PATENT AND TRADEMARK OFFICE, https://www.uspto.gov/trademarks/maintain/forms-file/definitions-maintaining-trademark.

[3] — Updating Your Trademark Registrations as Needed.

As your business evolves, it is crucial to update your trademark registrations to reflect any changes in the goods or services associated with your mark or any modifications to the mark itself. For example, if your company expands its product offerings or enters new markets, you may need to amend your trademark registration to include additional goods or services or to register your mark in new jurisdictions.

Moreover, if your company undergoes a significant change, such as a merger or acquisition, it is important to update the ownership information associated with your trademark registrations. Failure to do so could result in complications or disputes regarding the ownership and enforceability of your marks.

In conclusion, maintaining and renewing your trademark registrations are essential steps in preserving the value and strength of your brand. By actively monitoring the use of your marks, adhering to renewal requirements and deadlines, and updating your registrations as needed, you can ensure that your trademarks continue to serve as valuable assets in protecting and promoting your business.

§ 4.06. Trademark Enforcement and Dispute Resolution.
[1] — Monitoring and Identifying Potential Infringements.

An essential aspect of protecting your brand and maintaining the strength of your trademarks is actively monitoring and identifying potential infringements. This involves regularly reviewing various sources, such as online marketplaces, industry publications, domain name registries, business directories, and social media platforms, to detect unauthorized use or imitation of your marks by competitors or third parties. By staying vigilant and identifying potential infringements early, you can take prompt action to protect your brand and prevent consumer confusion, dilution, or damage to your brand's reputation.

[2] — Cease and Desist Letters and Other Enforcement Actions.

When a potential infringement is detected, one of the first steps in enforcing your trademark rights is typically to send a cease-and-desist letter to the alleged infringer. This letter serves as a formal notice of your claim to the mark, informs the alleged infringer of the potential legal consequences of their actions, and demands that they cease using the infringing mark immediately. In many cases, a cease-and-desist letter is sufficient to resolve the issue, as the alleged infringer may be unaware of the infringement and may voluntarily comply with your demands.

However, if a cease-and-desist letter is unsuccessful in stopping the infringement, you may need to consider other enforcement actions, such as filing a complaint with the relevant e-commerce platform, requesting a domain name dispute resolution procedure, or seeking injunctive relief from a court to prevent further infringement.

[3] — Negotiating Settlements and Coexistence Agreements.

In some cases, it may be more beneficial to negotiate a settlement or coexistence agreement with the alleged infringer, rather than pursuing more aggressive enforcement actions. Settlement negotiations can lead to mutually agreeable solutions, such as the infringer agreeing to modify their mark or cease using it in exchange for a release of liability.

Coexistence agreements are contracts in which both parties agree to use their respective marks in a manner that minimizes the likelihood of consumer confusion or brand dilution. Such agreements can include provisions specifying the geographic areas in which each party can use their mark, the specific goods or services each mark can be associated with, or other limitations that minimize the potential for conflict.

[4] — Litigation and Alternative Dispute Resolution Options.

If negotiation efforts fail and enforcement actions are not sufficient to stop the infringement, you may need to consider litigation to assert your trademark rights. Trademark litigation typically involves filing a lawsuit in a court with jurisdiction over the matter, seeking remedies such as monetary damages, injunctive relief, and attorney's fees.

However, litigation can be time-consuming, costly, and unpredictable, leading many parties to explore alternative dispute resolution (ADR) options, such as mediation or arbitration. Mediation is a voluntary process in which a neutral third party (the mediator) facilitates negotiations between the parties to help them reach a mutually agreeable resolution. Arbitration, on the other hand, involves a neutral arbitrator or panel of arbitrators hearing the parties' arguments and rendering a binding decision.

Both mediation and arbitration can offer a more efficient, cost-effective, and confidential means of resolving trademark disputes, allowing the parties to preserve their business relationships and focus on their core business objectives.

In conclusion, effective trademark enforcement and dispute resolution are critical to protecting your brand and maintaining the strength of your trademarks. By actively monitoring for potential infringements, pursuing appropriate enforcement actions, engaging in negotiations and settlements, and exploring litigation and ADR options, when necessary, you can safeguard your brand's reputation, value, and competitive advantage in the marketplace.

§ 4.07. Trademark Protection in Mergers in Acquisitions.
[1] — Importance of Strong Trademarks in M&A Activity.

Strong and protected trademarks play a vital role in mergers and acquisitions (M&A) activity, as they significantly contribute to the value of the companies involved. Trademarks represent the goodwill, reputation, and market recognition that a company has built over time. Therefore, in M&A transactions, buyers often view robust trademarks as a key factor in their decision-making process, as they can enhance the value of the merged or acquired company, provide a competitive advantage, and facilitate the integration of products and services under a unified brand identity.

[2] — Due Diligence in the Acquisition Process.

During the M&A process, it is crucial for the acquiring party to conduct thorough due diligence on the target company's trademark portfolio. This includes reviewing the target's trademark registrations, applications, and any pending disputes or challenges, as well as assessing the overall strength and scope of the trademark protection in place. The due diligence process should also involve evaluating any licensing agreements, coexistence agreements, or other contracts related to the target's trademarks, as these may impact the value and transferability of the marks.

§ 4.07

Moreover, due diligence should include an analysis of the target company's trademark usage and enforcement practices, ensuring that the marks have been properly used and maintained to preserve their strength and validity. Failure to conduct a comprehensive due diligence review can result in unforeseen liabilities, disputes, or weakened brand value following the M&A transaction.

[3] — Post-Acquisition Integration of Trademarks.

After the completion of an M&A transaction, it is essential to effectively integrate the acquired trademarks into the buyer's existing portfolio. This process involves several steps, including:

- *Updating ownership records*: To ensure that the acquired trademarks are properly transferred to the buyer, it is necessary to update the ownership records with the relevant trademark offices. This may involve filing assignment documents, paying associated fees, and meeting any additional jurisdiction-specific requirements.
- *Reviewing and harmonizing brand strategies*: The buyer should assess the acquired trademarks in relation to their existing portfolio and consider whether any adjustments to their brand strategy are needed. This may include consolidating overlapping trademarks, retiring or rebranding certain marks, or developing new strategies to maximize the value of the combined portfolio.
- *Ensuring proper use and enforcement*: To maintain the strength of the acquired trademarks, the buyer must ensure that they are used consistently and appropriately in connection with the relevant goods or services. Furthermore, the buyer should continue monitoring for potential infringements and enforce their trademark rights as needed, demonstrating their commitment to protecting the brand's reputation and value.

By recognizing the importance of strong trademarks in M&A activity, conducting thorough due diligence, and effectively integrating acquired trademarks, companies can maximize the value of their combined brand portfolios and ensure a successful transition following an M&A transaction.

§ 4.08. Trademark Best Practices.
[1] — Establishing a Trademark Management Strategy.

Developing a comprehensive trademark management strategy is crucial for businesses looking to protect and strengthen their brands. A well-designed strategy should cover various aspects of trademark protection, including the selection and registration process, monitoring and enforcement, maintenance and renewal, and integration in mergers and acquisitions. Some key elements of an effective trademark management strategy include:

- *Setting clear objectives*: Define your business goals related to brand recognition, market presence, and competitive advantage. This will help you determine the appropriate scope of your trademark protection and guide your decision-making throughout the process.
- *Allocating resources*: Ensure that you have the necessary resources, such as time, budget, and personnel, to effectively manage your trademark portfolio. This may involve hiring dedicated in-house staff or working with external legal counsel or trademark service providers.
- *Establishing policies and procedures*: Develop internal guidelines and procedures for the selection, registration, and use of trademarks, as well as for monitoring and enforcing your trademark rights. This will help ensure consistency and effectiveness in your trademark management efforts.

[2] — Regularly Auditing and Updating Your Trademark Portfolio.

Conducting regular audits of your trademark portfolio is essential for identifying any gaps or weaknesses in your trademark protection and ensuring that your marks remain relevant and valuable. An effective audit should involve:

- *Reviewing your existing trademark registrations*: Assess the scope and strength of your current registrations, considering factors such as geographical coverage, classification of goods or services, and the distinctiveness of your marks.
- *Evaluating your trademark usage*: Ensure that your trademarks are being used consistently and appropriately in connection with the relevant goods or services, as well as in marketing and promotional materials.

■ *Identifying potential updates or expansions*: Based on the findings of your audit, consider whether any updates or expansions to your trademark portfolio are needed, such as registering new marks, renewing or updating existing registrations, or expanding your protection into new markets or product categories.

[3] — Training Employees on Trademark Usage and Enforcement.

Educating employees about the importance of trademarks and their proper usage and enforcement is crucial for maintaining the strength of your brand. A well-informed workforce can help prevent inadvertent misuse or dilution of your marks, as well as more effectively identify and report potential infringements by third parties. Key elements of an effective employee training program include:

■ *Providing information about trademark basics*: Ensure that employees understand the fundamental principles of trademarks, including their purpose, the types of marks, and the registration process.
■ *Sharing internal trademark policies and guidelines*: Familiarize employees with your company's specific trademark policies and guidelines, including the proper use of your marks, the process for reporting potential infringements, and the role of employees in protecting the company's brand.
■ *Offering ongoing training and support*: Provide regular updates and training sessions to keep employees informed about changes in trademark laws or company policies, as well as to reinforce the importance of adhering to best practices in trademark usage and enforcement.

In conlusion, implementing best practices in trademark management, such as establishing a comprehensive strategy, regularly auditing your trademark portfolio, and training employees on trademark usage and enforcement, can help your business protect its brand, maintain a strong market presence, and mitigate the risk of costly disputes or litigation.

§ 4.09. Conclusion.

Trademarks play a critical role in protecting your energy or mining brand by granting exclusive rights to the use of distinctive signs that represent your

TRADEMARKS § 4.09

company's identity, reputation, and the value associated with your products or services. As we have discussed throughout this chapter, effective trademark management involves a proactive approach that encompasses selecting and registering strong marks, maintaining and renewing registrations, monitoring for potential infringements, enforcing your trademark rights, and integrating acquired trademarks in mergers and acquisitions.

The importance of being proactive in trademark management cannot be overstated, as it not only helps protect your brand from unauthorized use, imitation, or dilution, but also contributes to the overall value of your company and its attractiveness in merger and acquisition activities. By implementing the best practices and strategies discussed in this presentation, you can build and maintain a robust brand identity that reflects your company's values, quality, and reputation, and that effectively positions your business for success in the competitive and regulated landscape of the energy and mining industries.

Key takeaways for brand protection in the energy and mining industries include the need for a comprehensive trademark management strategy, the significance of regular audits and employee training, and the value of proactive enforcement and dispute resolution. By keeping these principles in mind and staying informed about evolving trademark laws and practices, you can ensure that your company's brand remains strong, protected, and resilient in the face of the numerous challenges faced by the energy and mining sectors.

Chapter 5

AAPL Joint Operating Agreements: Standards of Operator Conduct, Exculpatory Provisions, and Jury Charges

Michael K. Reer
Harris, Finley & Bogle, P.C.
Fort Worth, Texas

Synopsis

§ 5.01.	Joint Development of Oil and Gas Resources: Unique Problems and Opportunities	84
§ 5.02.	Why Use a Joint Operating Agreement?	84
	[1] — Problem — Cotenancy	84
	[2] — Well Spacing Requirements	87
	[3] — Problem — Well Density Requirements	88
	[4] — Problem — Increasing Capital Expenditures and Economies of Scale	89
	[5] — Solution – The Joint Operating Agreement	89
§ 5.03.	Operator Standards of Conduct	90
	[1] — 1956 Joint Operating Agreement	91
	[2] — 1977 Joint Operating Agreement	92
	[3] — 1982 Joint Operating Agreement	92
	[4] — 1989 Joint Operating Agreement	92
	[5] — 2015 Joint Operating Agreement	96
§ 5.04.	Exculpatory Provisions	96
	[1] — 1956 Joint Operating Agreement	97
	[2] — 1977 Joint Operating Agreement	100
	[3] — 1982 Joint Operating Agreement	103
	[a] — Demonstrating Gross Negligence and Willful Misconduct	107
	[b] — Application of Exculpatory Provision to Affirmative Defenses	109
	[4] — 1989 Joint Operating Agreement	111
	[5] — 2015 Joint Operating Agreement	115
§ 5.05.	Lawsuits: Allocating Cost and Risk	118
	[1] — Costs of Litigation and Settlement	118
	[2] — Getting Answers: The Jury Charge	119
	[3] — Exposure and Liability	120
§ 5.06.	Conclusion	121

§ 5.01. Joint Development of Oil and Gas Resources: Unique Problems and Opportunities.

Joint development of the oil and gas resources within a geographic area by multiple interest owners presents significant efficiencies and cost-savings. Specifically, by combining or pooling their collective interests within a given area, multiple owners avoid unnecessary competition, duplicative infrastructure, and the inefficient utilization of oil and gas reserves. Although parties may choose to jointly develop oil and gas resources through any number of possible arrangements, the rights, duties, and obligations of the parties are most frequently memorialized through form industry agreements published by the American Association of Professional Landmen (AAPL).

AAPL first published a model joint operating agreement in 1956. Since 1956, AAPL published four major revisions of the initial form — in 1977, 1982, 1989, and 2015. This chapter examines the standards of operator conduct, exculpatory clauses, and litigation provisions within the model form — with a particular emphasis on how the rights and duties of the operator have changed through the various iterations of the form agreement.

§ 5.02. Why Use a Joint Operating Agreement?

As oil and gas development progressed from its inception, four primary factors incentivized working interest owners to conduct joint operations: cotenancy; spacing requirements; density requirements; and increasing capital expenditures.[1] The AAPL form joint operating agreements are designed to assist working interest owners in conducting joint operations in response to each of these four issues.

[1] — Problem — Cotenancy.

Cotenancy is a real property concept by which two or more co-owners collectively have unity of possession, commonly by joint tenancy and tenancy

---

[1] *See* Christopher S. Kulander, *Old Faves and New Raves: How Case Law Has Affected Form Joint Operating Agreements — Problems and Solutions (Part One)*, OIL AND GAS, NATURAL RESOURCES, AND ENERGY JOURNAL, Vol. 1. No. 1 (January 2015). (hereinafter cited as *Kulander*)

in common.[2] Cotenancy is a natural result of the "operation of the statute of descent and distribution and commonly followed customs and practices relating to the making of devices of lands."[3] Cotenancy practically results in a divided ownership of the minerals and the working interest.[4] For example, the working interest may be split among multiple lessees to the extent different mineral owners execute leases to different parties.[5]

Divided ownership of the working interest raises significant issues with respect to development. For example, where the mineral interest is divided among multiple cotenants, each owner "has the right to extract minerals from common property without first obtaining the consent of his cotenants."[6] However, the extracting cotenant "must account to [the other cotenants] on the basis of the value of any minerals taken, less the necessary and reasonable costs of production and marketing."[7] On its own, the general rule that any cotenant may develop at its own risk, but must account for and share equally in the profits with other cotenants, disincentivizes development insofar as the developing cotenant is saddled with all the risk and expense of a dry hole but may only share in the reward of successful development to the extent of its ownership interest.

Where the working interest is split between multiple lessors, the cotenancy relationship also carries risk to non-developing lessees with respect to: (a) royalty obligations; and (b) whether the operations of one lessee have the effect of continuing another lessee's lease into the secondary term.[8]

---

[2] *Tenancy*, BLACK'S LAW DICTIONARY (11th Ed. 2019); *see also* Howard Williams & Charles Meyers, *Oil and Gas Law* § 502 (12th ed. 2003, updated and revised by Patrick Martin & Bruce Kramer) [hereinafter cited as *Williams and Meyers*] ("Generically, a cotenancy is formed when two or more persons share 'the unit of exclusive use and possession in property held in common.'").

[3] *See* Todd v. Bruner, 365 S.W.2d 155, 159-60 (Tex. 1963).

[4] Ernest Smith & Jacqueline Lang Weaver, *Texas Law of Oil and Gas* § 17.1.

[5] *Williams and Meyers* § 503.

[6] Byrom v. Pendley, 717 S.W.2d 602, 605 (Tex. 1986).

[7] *Id.*; *See* Cox v. Davison, 397 S.W.2d 200, 201 (Tex. 1965).

[8] *Williams and Meyers* § 503.1.

§ 5.02   ENERGY & MINERAL LAW INSTITUTE

For example, in a 2018 Texas case, the Eastland Court of Appeals considered whether a developing lessee was responsible for making royalty payments to a non-developing lessee's lessor.[9] In holding that the developing lessee and non-developing lessee's lessor were not in a contractual relationship that would require payment, the court found that the obligation to pay royalty to the non-developing lessee's lessor resided with the party that contracted for the liability: the non-developing lessee.[10] This application of contract law principles has the effect of saddling a non-developing lessee with royalty obligations from the date of first production — even though no revenue is owed to the non-developing lessee under real property principles until the "necessary and reasonable costs of production and marketing" are recouped — that is, until a profit is realized.[11]

The obligation to pay royalty on another lessee's well, even prior to payout, is even less ideal to the extent the well does not continue the payor's lease beyond the primary term.[12] For example, in *Earp*, the Oklahoma Supreme Court considered whether a cotenant well held non-developing lessee interests into the secondary term by production absent contractual agreement.[13] In holding that the lease of the non-developing lessee was not held by production through a cotenant well, the Oklahoma Supreme Court noted that "in order to claim the act of drilling as his own, it is obvious that there must be something more than a mere passive acquiescence in the drilling by another lessee under a separate lease."[14] Rather, "when lessees holding under different leases from different lessors enter into an agreement to develop the common property, each agreeing to share in the expense of development and operation, . . . the development and production accomplished by them as a result of such agreement . . . is as much the act of one as it is the act of

---

[9] *See, e.g.*, Devon Energy Prod. Co., L.P. v. Apache Corp., 550 S.W.3d 259 (Tex. App.—Eastland 2018, no pet.).
[10] *Id.*
[11] *See id.*
[12] Earp v. Mid-Continent Petroleum Corp., 27 P.2d 855, 859 (Okla. 1933).
[13] *Id.*
[14] *Id.* at 859.

86

the other and the discovery and production of oil operate as a compliance with the provision of the lease of each of the lessees co-operating in the development."[15]

[2] — Well Spacing Requirements.

Well spacing requirements were adopted for the purpose of limiting the number of wells used in efficiently developing a field.[16] Excessive wells cause economic waste when more wells are drilled than necessary to drain a field efficiently. Further, excessive wells waste natural resources when the reservoir is harmed by a disproportionate rate of withdrawal in areas where wells are clustered.[17] Spacing rules promote economic efficiency by prescribing minimum distances between a proposed well and: (a) any other well drilled in the same area; and (b) property lines.[18] When properly implemented, spacing rules incentivize pooling and unitization of leases as lessees and mineral interest owners combine their respective ownership interests so as to have enough acreage to meet spacing requirements for a well.[19]

Although the most well-known well spacing requirement is Texas Railroad Commission Rule 37, well spacing has long been a part of oil and gas regulations in other jurisdictions.[20] For example, Pennsylvania's Oil and Gas Conservation Law, passed in 1961, has detailed provisions for the regulation of well spacing in formations below the Onondaga — including

---

[15] *Id.* Commentators have cautioned that *Earp*, like many lease interpretation cases, has limitations based on the specific language of the lease at issue. For example, the lease at issue in *Earp* provided that only production "by the lessee" would hold the lease into the secondary term — a fact that may distinguish *Earp* from disputes concerning other lease forms. *See Williams and Meyers* § 503.1.

[16] Browning Oil Co., Inc. v. Luecke, 38 S.W.3d 625, 633 (Tex. App.—Austin 2000, pet. denied).

[17] Ernest Smith & Jacqueline Lang Weaver, *Texas Law of Oil and Gas* § 9.3. Professors Smith and Weaver note "it has been estimated that more than 100 million dollars a year was spent in drilling and operating unnecessary wells in Texas from 1947 to 1952 . . . ."

[18] *See, e.g.,* 16 Tex. Admin. Code § 3.37.

[19] *See Kulander*, at 4-5.

[20] *See, e.g.,* 58 P.S. § 401.

§ 5.02   ENERGY & MINERAL LAW INSTITUTE

the Utica shale.[21] Likewise, the Ohio Administrative Code provides lease-line spacing requirements depending on the depth of the well.[22]

[3] — Problem – Well Density Requirements.

Well density requirements are conceptually "closely tied" to well spacing requirements, "and the two rules together prevent clustering of wells."[23] Well density rules generally require the assignment of acreage to a well based on either the default state rule (*e.g.*, 40 acres per well in Texas) or on field rules adopted by the applicable state regulatory authority.[24] Field rules are designed to establish the acreage that wells in a specific field can drain effectively, considering the effect of current completion techniques.[25]

As with well spacing requirements, the Pennsylvania Oil and Gas Conservation Law contains provisions for the regulation of well density.[26] The Ohio Administrative Code requires anywhere from one to ten acres for drilling units depending on the depth of the well.[27]

---

[21] *See* 48 P.S. § 407.

[22] Ohio Admin. Code § 1501:9-1 (requiring "not less than one hundred feet from any boundary" for wells less than 1,000 feet in depth, "not less than two hundred thirty feet from any boundary" for wells between 1,000 and 2,000 feet in depth, and "not less than three hundred feet from any boundary" for wells in excess of 2,000 feet); *see also* W. Va. Code St. R. § 39-1-4 (providing spacing requirements for vertical and horizontal deep wells, such as, 500 feet of spacing between a well and unit boundary measured perpendicularly where the units are operated by different operators).

[23] Ernest Smith & Jacqueline Lang Weaver, *Texas Law of Oil and Gas* § 9.3[B].

[24] *Id.*

[25] *Id.*

[26] 58 PS § 407 ("The commission shall, within forty-five days after the application for spacing is filed, either enter an order establishing spacing units and specifying the size and shape of the units, which shall be such as will, in the opinion of the commission, result in the efficient and economic development of the pool as a whole or shall enter an order dismissing the application.")

[27] Ohio Admin. Code § 1501:9-1 (requiring one acre drilling unit for wells less than 1,000 feet in depth, five acre drilling units for wells between 1,000 and 2,000 feet in depth, and 10 acre drilling units for wells exceeding 2,000 feet in depth).

[4] — Problem — Increasing Capital Expenditures and Economies of Scale.

As the oil and gas industry matured, the trend in development was to drill deeper, and thus more expensive, wells.[28] For example, in 2016 the U.S. Energy Information Agency estimated the average cost of a horizontal well exceeded $6,000,000 in nearly every shale basin in the country.[29]

As with the cost of drilling and development, midstream costs and expenses have increased. Operators commonly negotiate with gathering companies for the construction and operation of midstream infrastructure—such as gathering lines and processing facilities—based in part on the contractual dedication of future oil and gas production from a given geographical area to these facilities.[30] At least theoretically, the operator may capitalize on economies of scale by dedicating production from as large of a geographic area as possible.

[5] — Solution — The Joint Operating Agreement.

An agreement by which lessees pool resources and jointly develop acreage (*i.e.*, the joint operating agreement) was the obvious solution to each of these problems. At first, operators each developed a preferred form joint operating agreement, which led to extended negotiations and "form wars" over specific provisions.[31] The inefficiency involved with a multitude of forms and in negotiating a new form for each proposed development detracted from the overall goal joint operations sought to achieve — operational efficiency.

The history of the AAPL form joint operating agreements dates back to 1952, when landmen from Tulsa and Oklahoma City decided there was likely enough similarity between company-specific joint operating agreements to attempt an industry standard form.[32] The landmen invited 28 larger oil

---

[28] *Kulander*, at 4-5.
[29] *Trends in U.S. Oil and Gas Upstream Costs*, U.S. ENERGY INFORMATION ADMINISTRATION (March 2016) (available at https://www.eia.gov/analysis/studies/drilling/pdf/upstream.pdf).
[30] *See, e.g.*, Sabine Oil & Gas Corp. v. HPIP Gonzalez Holdings, LLC, 550 B.R. 59 (Bankr. S.D.N.Y. 2016).
[31] *Kulander*, at 5.
[32] J.O. Young, *Oil and Gas Operating Agreements: Producers 88 Operating Agreements, Selected Problems and Suggested Solutions*, 20 ROCKY MTN. MIN. L. INST. 197, 100-01 (1975).

and gas companies to participate in the effort to draft a standard form, and after four years of drafting the form was presented to the Annual Meeting of AAPL in Denver, Colorado.[33]

The first AAPL form joint operating agreement was published in 1956.[34] Subsequently, revised forms were published in 1977, 1982, 1989, and 2015. The last two versions—1989 and 2015—were made in response to specific industry concerns. The 1989 version was published in response to the mid-1980s banking crises and general plummeting of oil and gas prices.[35] The 2015 version was published in response to advances in oil and gas completion technologies, and specifically horizontal development.[36]

In general, the model form joint operating agreement solves many of the problems discussed above. For example, the model form allows the parties to: (a) designate a single operator; (b) hold all leases within the contract area through a single development scheme; (c) propose operations; (d) elect to participate or not participate in proposed operations; and (e) allocate risk and reward for proposed operations based on whether parties elected to participate.[37] Significantly, the drafters of the model form attempted to strike a balance between protecting the rights of non-operators and incentivizing parties to accept the duties and responsibilities of operatorship. This balance is reflected in many provisions within the model form, but particularly in the standards of conduct owed by the operator to the non-operator and the exculpatory provision, which excuses the operator from certain liabilities not attributable to gross negligence or willful misconduct.

§ 5.03. Operator Standards of Conduct.

Through every version of the joint operating agreement, Article Five (titled either "Operator of Unit" or "Operator") has contained the contractual

---

[33] *Id.*
[34] 1956 AAPL Joint Operating Agreement. The AAPL form operating agreement is also known as the "610 Model Form."
[35] *Kulander*, at 6.
[36] *See*, Jeff Weems, Changes Incorporated Into the AAPL 2015 610 Model Form, Inst. for Energy Law 68th Annual Oil & Gas Law Conference (2016). (hereinafter cited as *Weems*)
[37] *See, e.g.*, 1956 AAPL Joint Operating Agreement, Article 5.

standard of conduct the operator owes non-operators in conducting operations or activities within the contract area.[38] The sentence in the joint operating agreement specifying the standard of conduct also includes an exculpatory provision. For the purposes of this chapter, the exculpatory provision is considered separately below.[39]

In general, the form joint operating agreement has applied a higher standard of conduct to operators as versions progressed, even as the scope of the exculpatory provision also expanded. The increasingly higher standards of conduct appear designed to encourage activity and operations within the contract area, and the timely completion of development activities.

[1] — 1956 Joint Operating Agreement.

The 1956 Joint Operating Agreement gives the operator authority to "conduct and direct and have full control of all operations on the Unit Area, as permitted and required by, and within the limits of, this agreement."[40] In exchange for giving the operator full control over operations within the contract area, the joint operating agreement requires that the operator "conduct all operations in a good and workmanlike manner . . . ."[41]

Surprisingly few courts have considered the specifics of what it means to conduct operations in a "good and workmanlike manner," particularly given that the standard has been included in every AAPL onshore joint operating agreement to date. However, a "good and workmanlike manner" generally means "that quality of work performed by one who has the knowledge, training, or experience necessary for the successful practice of a trade or occupation and performed in a manner generally considered proficient by those capable of judging such work."[42] More simply stated: "Good and workmanlike manner means in such a way that a workman of average skill

---

[38] *See, e.g., id.*
[39] *See*, 1956 AAPL Joint Operating Agreement, Article 5, Section 1.04 "Exculpatory Provisions."
[40] 1956 AAPL Joint Operating Agreement, Article 5.
[41] *Id.*
[42] Parkway Co. v. Woodruff, 901 S.W.2d 434, 446 (Tex. 1995).

and intelligence, the conscientious workman, would do the job. It is good, average work."[43]

[2] — 1977 Joint Operating Agreement.

The 1977 Joint Operating Agreement revised and reformatted the original model form into the format most practitioners are used to seeing today. Although the 1977 version altered some verbiage (*e.g.*, substituting the defined term "contract area" for the previously used "unit area"), the version did not change either the basic scope of the operator's authority (over "all operations on the Contract area as permitted and required by, and within the limits of, this agreement") or the original requirement that the operator "conduct all such operations in a good and workmanlike manner . . . ."[44]

[3] — 1982 Joint Operating Agreement.

The changes to the model joint operating agreement reflected in the 1982 version generally address non-operational issues, such as commonly shared burdens, subsequently created interests, minimum commencement time, and issues related to regulatory agencies.[45] Therefore, the revisions left the scope and standard of conduct related to operator operations unchanged.[46]

[4] — 1989 Joint Operating Agreement.

The 1989 Joint Operating Agreement was drafted, in part, in reaction to the general downturn in oil and gas prices during the 1980s.[47] Professor Kulander has written that the significant changes between the 1982 and 1989 forms reflect the changing economic conditions occurring in the mid-1980s:

---

[43] Fairbanks, Morse & Co. v. Miller, 195 P. 1083, 1090 (Okla. 1921).
[44] 1977 AAPL Joint Operating Agreement, Article 5.
[45] James C.T. Hardwick, *The 1982 Model Form Operating Agreement: Changes and Continuing Concerns*, 8-1, 8-2 to 8-4, ROCKY MT. MIN. L. FDN. (1983).
[46] 1982 AAPL Joint Operating Agreement, Article V.A.
[47] Thomas Schroedter & Lewis Masburg, *An Introduction to the AAPL Model Form Operating Agreement*, 1-1, 1-8. ROCKY MT. MIN. L. FDN. (1990) (noting that the AAPL appointed a revision committee in March 1986 to draft a new version of the model form primarily in those areas which dealt with the impact of the collapse of oil and gas prices in 1982). (hereinafter cited as *Schroedter*).

The 1989 Form was revised during the bleakness of the mid and late 1980s, when oil prices sank, banks failed, and bankruptcies in the oil and gas business washed over upstream operations, resulting in parties defaulting on their financial and operational obligations. These events highlighted shortcomings with the first three form JOAs — namely deadbeat operators and non-operators.[48]

In particular, industry concern existed that the terms of the 1982 Joint Operating Agreement were being misinterpreted and misused by parties that were not in a financial position to participate in an operation. Rather than elect "non-consent" to a proposed operation (and face the risk penalty in Article VII), these parties commonly sought to delay operations until participation was more realistic from a financial standpoint.[49]

The 1989 Joint Operating Agreement, perhaps in response to concerns over "deadbeat operators," significantly expanded the standard of care applied to activities undertaken pursuant to the operating agreement.[50] Specifically, the 1989 Joint Operating Agreement requires the operator to "conduct its activities under this agreement as a reasonable prudent operator, in a good and workmanlike manner, with due diligence and dispatch, in accordance with good oilfield practice, and in compliance with applicable law and regulation."[51]

The addition of the requirements that the operator act as a reasonably prudent operator, with due diligence and dispatch, in accordance with good oilfield practice, and in compliance with applicable law and regulations are best understood in view of the committee's concerns over inactive operators.

A "reasonably prudent operator" means "an operator of ordinary prudence, that is having neither the highest nor the lowest prudence, but on the contrary, an operator of average prudence and intelligence, acting

---

[48] *Kulander*, at 6.
[49] *Schroedter*, at 1-20.
[50] 1989 AAPL Joint Operating Agreement, Article V.A; *see also Schroedter*, at 1-8 ("Articles V and VII of the 1989 version expand and clarify the Operator's responsibilities, both operationally and financially.").
[51] *Id.*

§ 5.03   ENERGY & MINERAL LAW INSTITUTE

with ordinary diligence under the same or similar circumstances."[52] The addition of the "reasonable prudent operator" standard seems, at first glance, duplicative of the preexisting requirement that the operator conduct operations in a "good and workmanlike manner."[53] One possible explanation for the addition of the reasonably prudent operator standard is a concern from the committee that "deadbeat" and inactive operators would expose the non-operators to liability with respect to lessor implied covenant claims.[54] For example, many of the leading cases on implied covenant law measure compliance through the reasonably prudent operator standard:

> The standard of care in testing the performance of implied covenants by lessees is that of a reasonably prudent operator under the same or similar facts and circumstances. The reasonably prudent operator concept is an essential part of every implied covenant. Every claim of improper operation by a lessor against a lessee should be tested against the general duty of the lessee to conduct operations as a reasonably prudent operator in order to carry out the purposes of the oil and gas lease.[55]

Due diligence "means that measure of care, prudence and application of effort and skill exercised by an individual in his particular specialty."[56] Likewise, Black's Law Dictionary defines "dispatch" as a "prompt completion of something."[57] The 1989 Joint Operating Agreement requires the operator to apply reasonable effort and skill to achieve the prompt completion of

---

[52] *See* Good v. TXO Production Corp., 763 S.W.2d 59, 60 (Tex. App.—Amarillo 1988, writ denied.).

[53] *Id.* ("reasonably prudent operator" standard satisfied with "average prudence" and "ordinary diligence") *with Fairbanks*, 195 P. at 1090 (defining "good and workmanlike" as "good, average work.").

[54] *See* Amoco Prod. Co. v. Alexander, 622 S.W.2d 563, 567-68 (Tex. 1981).

[55] *Id.* (internal citations omitted).

[56] Thompson v. Henderson, 45 S.W.3d 283, 288 (Tex. App.—Dallas 2001, pet. denied); *see also* Cook v. Duncan, 301 S.E.2d 837, 841 (W. Va. 1983) (due diligence means the exercise of a reasonable effort).

[57] BLACK'S LAW DICTIONARY (11th Ed. 2019).

activities for which the operator has responsibility.[58] Again, this addition reflects the concern of the committee over the proliferation of inactive operators seeking to delay operations until their financial outlook improved rather than going non-consent and paying the risk penalty articulated in the joint operating agreement.

"Good oilfield practice" means "that operations are carried out in a proper and workmanlike manner."[59] The Williams and Meyers treatise notes that the term "has been used in the same way as the phrase 'everything is A.P.I.,' which refers to the American Petroleum Institute's set of standards covering aspects of petroleum operations."[60]

The requirement that operators conduct activities in accordance with "applicable law and regulation" is likely in response to "deadbeat" operators falling behind on regulatory reporting and well maintenance standards required by state regulatory authorities. In many states, inability or refusal to comply with well maintenance and reporting standards can trigger a notice of noncompliance, loss of authority to operate the well, or even a regulatory order to plug and abandon the well.[61] To the extent the operator fails to comply with applicable law or regulation, Article V.B of the 1989 Joint Operating Agreement allows the non-operators to remove the existing operator and select a new one.[62]

In general, the changes made in the 1989 Joint Operating Agreement were not well received. A contemporary commentary of the 1989 model form notes that "[d]espite the extensive experience of the committee members, as reflected by the high quality of both the Working Draft and the First Draft, there was a reaction (and an overreaction) on the part of many of the majors that the drafts, and particularly the Working Draft, were not sufficiently

---

[58] 1989 AAPL Joint Operating Agreement, Article V.A.
[59] Howard Williams & Charles Meyers, *Manual of Oil and Gas Terms*, 372, (12th ed. 2003, updated and revised by Patrick Martin & Bruce Kramer).
[60] *Id.*
[61] *See, e.g., Oil and Gas Monitoring and Enforcement Plan: Fiscal Year 2023*, RAILROAD COMMISSION OF TEXAS.
[62] 1989 AAPL Joint Operating Agreement, Article V.B.

oriented to a major oil company point of view."[63] However, despite the initial cold reception of the 1989 Joint Operating Agreement, it remained AAPL's standard form-610 for over 25 years.

[5] — 2015 Joint Operating Agreement.

After the publication of the 1989 Joint Operating Agreement, the oil and gas industry underwent significant change. "Throughout the 1990s and 2000s, the use of horizontal drilling grew steadily and in May 2009 reached the point at which the percentage of wells drilled horizontally exceeded that of vertical wells."[64] In response, the AAPL created a modified version of the 1989 Joint Operating Agreement in 2013 specifically designed for use in the horizontal context.[65] The "horizontal form" was created as an interim step, "meant to expeditiously get a Model Form into circulation that addressed many of the common issues involving horizontal development" but without reflecting "all of the changes the committee [was] considering."[66]

In 2015, the committee submitted an amended joint operating agreement, which received approval.[67] Although the committee generally rewrote Article V to improve the overall readability of the article, it did not substantively change the standard of conduct required by the 1989 Joint Operating Agreement.[68]

§ 5.04 Exculpatory Provisions.

All versions of the AAPL Joint Operating Agreement contain an exculpatory provision that provides some degree of protection to the operator. An exculpatory clause is a "clause in a contract designed to relieve one party of liability to the other for specified injury or loss incurred in performance

---

[63] *Schroedter*, at 1-18.
[64] Worth Carlin & Jeff Weems, *Changes Within the AAPL 610 – 1989 Model Form Operating Agreement: Horizontal Modifications and Other Development Issues in Major Shale Plays*, 5-1, 5-4 Rocky Mt. Min. L. Fdn. (2014).
[65] *Id.* at 5-7.
[66] *Id.*
[67] *Weems.*
[68] 2015 AAPL Joint Operating Agreement, Article V.A.

of the contract."[69] In general, the law in oil and gas producing states favors the strict construction of exculpatory provisions against parties seeking to enforce them.[70]

Like with the provisions applicable to operator standards of conduct, the AAPL drafting committees have made several significant changes to the scope of the exculpatory provision over time.

[1] — 1956 Joint Operating Agreement.

The exculpatory provision began with the 1956 Joint Operating Agreement, which provided that the operator "shall have no liability as Operator to the other parties for losses sustained, or liabilities incurred, except as may result from gross negligence or from breach of the provisions of this agreement."[71] The scope of the 1956 exculpatory provision is markedly narrow compared to subsequent versions, and only excuses liability related to certain off-the-contract claims, such as ordinary negligence.[72] As a result, operators remained liable for breach of the joint operating agreement—including breach of the duty to conduct operations in a "good and workmanlike" manner.[73]

The "gross negligence" carveout to the exculpatory provision is a mainstay in every version of the model form. However, the standard of conduct necessary to overcome the exculpatory provision is typically a matter defined by the jurisdiction in which the contract area is located.[74] Oil and

---

[69] Howard Williams & Charles Meyers, *Manual of Oil and Gas Terms*, 372, 373 (12th ed. 2003, updated and revised by Patrick Martin & Bruce Kramer).

[70] *See, e.g.*, Bryan v. City of Cotter, 344 S.W.3d 654, 658 (Ark. 2009) ("Contracts that exempt a party from liability for negligence are not favored by law. Thus, exculpatory clauses are strictly construed against the party relying on them, and the contract must clearly set out what negligent liability is to be avoided."); Zimmer v. Mitchell and Ness, 385 A.2d 437, 439 (Pa. Super. Ct. 1978); Reed v. University of North Dakota, 589 N.W.2d 880 (N.D. 1999); Chadwick v. Colt Ross Outfitters, Inc., 100 P.3d 465 (Colo. 2004); Geczi v. Lifetime Fitness, 973 N.E.2d 801, 804 (10th Dist. Ohio 2012); Jewett v. Capital Nat. Bank of Austin, 618 S.W.2d 109, 112 (Tex. App.—Waco 1981, writ ref'd n.r.e.).

[71] 1956 AAPL Joint Operating Agreement, Article 5.

[72] *Id.*

[73] *Id.*

[74] *Id.*

§ 5.04   ENERGY & MINERAL LAW INSTITUTE

gas producing jurisdictions generally agree with the gist of the term "gross negligence," but there are undoubtedly differences in the proof required from jurisdiction to jurisdiction:

> ***Arkansas***: Arkansas defines "gross negligence" as "the failure to use even slight care."[75]
>
> ***Colorado***: Colorado defines "gross negligence" as "willful and wanton conduct, that is, action committed recklessly, with conscious disregard for the safety of others."[76]
>
> ***New Mexico***: New Mexico defines "gross negligence" as "an act or omission done without the exercise of even slight care under the circumstances."[77] New Mexico formally abolished the distinction between ordinary and gross negligence when it adopted the doctrine of comparative negligence.[78]
>
> ***North Dakota***: North Dakota defines "gross negligence" as "to all intents and purposes, no care at all. It is the omission of such care which even the most inattentive and thoughtless persons seldom fail to take of their own affairs, and it is such conduct as evidences a reckless temperament. It is such a lack of care that it is practically willful in its nature."[79]
>
> ***Ohio***: Ohio defines "gross negligence" as "the failure to exercise any or very slight care" or "a failure to exercise even that care which a careless person would use."[80]

---

[75] Spence v. Vaught, 367 S.W.2d 238, 512 (Ark. 1963).
[76] Jones v. Dressel, 623 P.2d 370, 373 (Colo. 1981).
[77] Paiz v. State Farm Fire and Cas. Co., 880 P.2d 300, 302 n.1 (N.M. 1994).
[78] Scott v. Rizzo, 634 P.2d 1234, 1239 (N.M. 1981) *but see* Govich v. North American Systems, Inc., 814 P.2d 94, 101 (N.M. 1991 ("New Mexico courts never have recognized degrees of negligence. Rather, the standard in all cases has been 'ordinary care under the circumstances.'").
[79] Sheets v. Pendergrast, 106 N.W.2d 1, 5 (N.D. 1960).
[80] Winkle v. Zettler Funeral Homes, Inc., 912 N.E.2d 151, 209 (Ohio App. 3d 2009).

Oklahoma: Oklahoma statutorily defines "gross negligence" as "the want of slight care and diligence."[81]

Pennsylvania: Pennsylvania defines "gross negligence" as a "form of negligence where the facts support substantially more than ordinary carelessness, inadvertence, laxity, or indifference."[82] "The behavior of the defendant must be flagrant, grossly deviating from the ordinary standard of care."[83]

Texas: Texas defines "gross negligence" as "an act or omission which, when viewed objectively from the standpoint of the defendant at the time of the occurrence, involved an extreme degree of risk considering the probability and magnitude of the potential harm to others and of which the defendant had actual, subjective awareness of the risk involved but nevertheless proceeded with conscious indifference to the rights, safety, or welfare of others."[84]

West Virginia: West Virginia does not appear to have a well-established common law definition of "gross negligence," but at least one statute defines "gross negligence" as "voluntary and conscious conduct, including a failure to act, by a person who, at the time of the conduct, knew that the conduct was likely to be harmful to . . . another person."[85] In some cases, the courts have established "gross negligence" as "an utter disregard of prudence amounting to complete neglect . . . ."[86]

Wyoming: Wyoming defines "gross negligence" as "great or extreme negligence."[87] It "includes an element of carelessness so great or

---

[81] 25 Okl. St. Ann. § 6 ("Slight negligence consists in the want of great care and diligence; ordinary negligence in the want of ordinary care and diligence; and gross negligence in the want of slight care and diligence.").
[82] Albright v. Abington Mem'l Hosp., 696 A.2d 1159, 1164 (Pa. 1997).
[83] Id.
[84] IP Petroleum Co., Inc. v. Wevanco Energy, L.L.C., 116 S.W.3d 888, 897 (Tex. App.—Houston [1st Dist.] 2003, pet. denied).
[85] W. Va. Code § 55-7D-2.
[86] Dodrill v. Young, 102 S.E.2d 724, 730 (W. Va. 1958).
[87] Moore v. Kondziela, 405 P.2d 788, 789 (Wyo. 1965).

§ 5.04   ENERGY & MINERAL LAW INSTITUTE

extreme that the jury can say that there was a degree of negligence substantially greater than would constitute ordinary negligence."[88]

[2] — 1977 Joint Operating Agreement.

The 1977 Joint Operating Agreement significantly expanded the scope of the exculpatory provision: "[The operator] shall conduct all such operations in a good and workmanlike manner, but it shall have no liability as Operator to the other parties for losses sustained or liabilities incurred, except such as may result from gross negligence or willful misconduct."[89] The 1977 form thereby includes an important revision to the exculpatory provision, adding "willful misconduct" to the list of activities not included within the exculpatory clause, but removing reference to "breach" of the operating agreement.[90]

"Willful misconduct" joins "gross negligence" on every subsequent model form. As with "gross negligence," significant differences exist in the standards for "willful misconduct" from jurisdiction to jurisdiction:

> *Arkansas*: Arkansas defines "willful misconduct" as the failure to use even slight care and "the actor knows, or the situation is so extremely dangerous that he should know, that his act or failure to act will probably cause harm."[91]
>
> *Colorado*: Colorado defines "willful misconduct" as "conduct purposefully committed under circumstances where the actor realizes that the conduct is dangerous but nonetheless engages in the conduct without regard to the safety of others."[92]

---

[88] *Id.*
[89] 1977 AAPL Joint Operating Agreement, Article V.A.
[90] *Compare id. with* 1956 AAPL Joint Operating Agreement, Article 5.
[91] Spence v. Vaught, 367 S.W.2d 238, 512 (Ark. 1963). To the extent that willful misconduct encompasses all gross negligence under Arkansas law, the Joint Operating Agreement's reference to willful misconduct is at least arguably surplusage as applied to Arkansas.
[92] Jones v. Dressel, 623 P.2d 370, 373 (Colo. 1981).

New Mexico: New Mexico defines "willful misconduct" as "the intentioned doing of a harmful act without just cause or excuse or an intentional act done in utter disregard for the consequences."[93]

Ohio: Ohio defines "willful misconduct" as "something more than negligence. Willful misconduct implies an intentional deviation from a clear duty or from a definite rule of conduct, a deliberate purpose not to discharge some duty necessary to safety, or purposely doing wrongful acts with knowledge or appreciation of the likelihood of resulting injury."[94]

Oklahoma: Under Oklahoma law, willful misconduct "depends upon the facts of a particular case, and necessarily involves deliberate, intentional, or wanton conduct in doing or omitting to perform acts, with knowledge or appreciation of the fact, on the part of the culpable person, that danger is likely to result therefrom."[95]

Pennsylvania: Pennsylvania defines "willful misconduct" as conduct whereby "the actor desired to bring about the result that followed, or at least that he was aware that it was substantially certain to ensue."[96]

Texas: Texas defines "willful misconduct" as "a specific intent" by the defendant "to cause substantial injury to" the plaintiff.[97]

West Virginia: Under West Virginia law, "willful misconduct means more than negligence and carries the idea of deliberation and intentional wrongdoing. Willful misconduct includes all conscious or intentional violations of definite law or rules of conduct, as distinguished from inadvertent, unconscious, or involuntary violations."[98]

---

[93] Delgado v. Phelps Dodge Chino, Inc., 34 P.3d 1148, 1156 (N.M. 2001).
[94] Tighe v. Diamond, 80 N.E.2d 122, 127 (Ohio 1948).
[95] Sixkiller v. Summers, 680 P.2d 360 n.2 (Okla. 1984).
[96] Evans v. Philadelphia Trans. Co., 212 A.2d 440, 443 (Pa. 1965).
[97] IP Petroleum Co., Inc. v. Wevanco Energy, L.L.C., 116 S.W.3d 888, 897 (Tex. App.—Houston [1st Dist.] 2003, pet. denied), at 897.
[98] Thompson v. State Compensation Com'r, 54 S.E.2d 13, 18 (W. Va. 1949).

§ 5.04   ENERGY & MINERAL LAW INSTITUTE

Wyoming: Wyoming distinguishes between ordinary negligence and willful misconduct based on the "actor's state of mind."[99] "In order to prove that an actor has engaged in willful misconduct, one must demonstrate that he acted with a state of mind that approaches intent to do harm . . . [C]ourts allow a party to establish that willful misconduct has occurred by demonstrating that an actor has intentionally committed an act of unreasonable character in disregard of a known or obvious risk that is so great as to make it highly probable that harm will follow."[100]

The 1977 Joint Operating Agreement states it is subject to the law of the state in which the contract area occurs.[101] In the event the contract area is in two or more states, the law of the state where most of the land in the contract area is located governs.[102]

Virtually no case law exists interpreting the scope and application of the 1956 and 1977 exculpatory provisions.[103] Some commentators expressed concern regarding whether the exculpatory provision was broad enough to cover indemnity.[104] For example, in a case discussing facts that occurred offshore Louisiana, a drilling contractor negligently lowered a barge onto a

---

[99] Bryant v. Hornbuckle, 728 P.2d 1132, 1136 (Wyo. 1986).

[100] *Id.*

[101] 1977 AAPL Joint Operating Agreement, Article XIV. The 1982 Joint Operating Agreement contains a similar provision, providing that the law of the state in which the contract area is located will govern the agreement and all matters pertaining thereto, including, but not limited to, non-performance, breach, remedies, procedures, rights, duties, and interpretation or construction. The 1956 Joint Operating Agreement does not contain a choice of law provision.

[102] 1977 AAPL Joint Operating Agreement, Article XIV. In contrast, the 1982 Joint Operating Agreement provides an empty space for the parties to write in their selected jurisdiction to the extent the contract area occurs in two or more states.

[103] James C.T. Hardwick, *The 1982 Model Form Operating Agreement: Changes and Continuing Concerns*, 8-1, 8-2 to 8-4, Rocky Mt. Min. L. Fdn. (1983) at 8-22; *see* MDU Barnett Ltd. Partnership v. Chesapeake Exploration Ltd. Partnership, Civ. Act. No. H-12-2528, 2014 WL 585740, at *7 (S.D. Tex. Feb. 14, 2014) (noting that the exculpatory provision in the 1977 Joint Operating Agreement should be interpreted consistent with the exculpatory provision in the 1982 Joint Operating Agreement).

[104] *See* James C.T. Hardwick, *The 1982 Model Form Operating Agreement: Changes and Continuing Concerns*, 8-1, 8-2 to 8-4, Rocky Mt. Min. L. Fdn. (1983), at 8-22.

third-party pipeline.[105] The pipeline company brought a claim against the operator, but the court did not reach the issue of whether the operator could seek indemnity from non-operating interest owners for the claim.[106] At least one commentator thought the most likely result was that the operator should charge the joint account for the liability and then rely on the exculpatory provision to the extent the non-operators challenged the charge.[107]

[3] — 1982 Joint Operating Agreement.

Consistent with the 1982 Joint Operating Agreement's focus on clarifying issues pertaining to title (such as preexisting burdens), the model form did not make any change to the exculpatory provision.[108] As with the 1977 Joint Operating Agreement, the 1982 model form provides the operator "shall have no liability as Operator to the other parties for losses sustained or liabilities incurred, except as may result from gross negligence or willful misconduct."[109]

The 1982 Joint Operating Agreement exculpatory provision is the first with significant case law interpretation. Courts interpreting the exculpatory clause have uniformly applied the clause to "operations" conducted in furtherance of the joint operating agreement.[110] For example, in *Palace*

---

[105] Transcontinental Gas Pipe Line Corp. v. Mr. Charlie, 294 F.Supp. 1025 (E.D. La. 1968) *affirmed in part, reversed in part*, Transcontinental Gas Pipe Line Corp. v. Mobile Drill. Barge, 424 F.2d 684 (5th Cir. 1970).

[106] *Id.*

[107] James C.T. Hardwick, *The 1982 Model Form Operating Agreement: Changes and Continuing Concerns*, 8-1, 8-2 to 8-4, Rocky Mt. Min. L. Fdn. (1983), at 8-24. At least arguably, the operator would also be able to discharge lawsuit liability through Article X, which allows the operator settle any damage claim or suit up to a specified amount without prior permission from the non-operators. Article X expressly provides that the expense of "discharging such claim or suit shall be at the joint expenses of the parties participating in the operation from which the claim or suit arises." 1977 AAPL Joint Operating Agreement, Article X. The 1956 Joint Operating Agreement contains a similar provision. 1956 AAPL Joint Operating Agreement, Article 28.

[108] *Compare* 1977 AAPL Joint Operating Agreement, Article V.A *with* 1982 AAPL Joint Operating Agreement, Article V.A.

[109] 1982 AAPL Joint Operating Agreement, Article V.A.

[110] *See, e.g.*, Palace Exploration Co. v. Petroleum Development Co., 374 F.3d 951, 954 (10th Cir. 2004).

§ 5.04

Exploration Co. v. Petroleum Development Co, the U.S. Court of Appeals for the Tenth Circuit applied the exculpatory provision to a claim that the operator drilled a well at the wrong location.[111]

In contrast, courts have traditionally construed the exculpatory provision in the 1982 Joint Operating Agreement narrowly with respect to non-operational activities, consistent with the general principle that exculpatory provisions should be narrowly construed.[112] For example, in *Palace Exploration Co. v. Petroleum Development Co,* the El Paso Court of Appeals declined to apply the exculpatory provision to a claim that the operator breached the 1982 Joint Operating Agreement by first sending an authorization for expenditure letter and by then failing to perform all or substantially all of the work proposed under the letter. The court concluded "that the exculpatory clause is limited to claims based upon an allegation that [the operator] failed to act as a reasonably prudent operator and does not apply to a claim that it breached the JOA."[113] Likewise, the U.S. District Court for the Southern District of Texas refused to apply the exculpatory clause to a claim for breaches of the joint operating agreement's accounting provisions, which "do not concern [the operator's] conduct as the well operator in the Barnett Shale Prospect Area."[114]

Other Texas appellate courts have consistently reached similar results, and in 2013 the Texas Supreme Court summarized case law on the scope of the 1982 exculpatory provision by noting that "the clause extends only to claims that the operator failed to act as a reasonably prudent operator for operations under the contract, and not for other breaches of the JOA."[115]

---

[111] *Id.*
[112] *See, e.g.,* Reeder v. Wood County Energy, LLC, 395 S.W.3d 789, 793 (Tex. 2012); *c* 20 S.W.3d 741 (Tex. App.—El Paso 200, no pet.).
[113] *Id.,* at 759; *see also* MDU Barnett, 2014 WL 585740, at *7 ("The Texas intermediate appellate courts have uniformly found that the phrase 'all such operations' referred back to 'operations on the Contract Area,' and held that the exculpatory clause was limited to the operator's activities at the wellsite and did not extend to other breaches of the agreement.").
[114] MDU Barnett, 2014 WL 585740, at *8.
[115] Reeder v. Wood County Energy, LLC, 395 S.W.3d 789, 793 (Tex. 2012); *c* 20 S.W.3d 741 (Tex. App.—El Paso 200, no pet.).

The Texas limitations on the scope of the 1982 exculpatory provision are also found in other jurisdictions.[116] For example, the Tenth Circuit has found that two categories of activities are not within the scope of the exculpatory clause. First, applying Colorado law, the Tenth Circuit found that the 1982 exculpatory clause did not apply to "nonperformance of duties imposed by the contract," such as failing to obtain working interest owner consent to a substantial change in the basic method of operation.[117] Second, applying Wyoming law, the Tenth Circuit found "the exculpatory clause has no application to claims that an operator has failed to abide by specific and express contractual duties assigned in the JOA."[118] Rather, the Tenth Circuit reiterated the exculpatory clause clearly applies to "tortious actions and . . . implied duties that come with the covenant of good and workmanlike performance."[119]

However, it is important to note that a minority of courts have rejected the view that the 1982 exculpatory provision should be constricted to off-the-contract claims and allegations that would violate the reasonably prudent

---

[116] *See, e.g.*, Shell Rocky Mountain Prod., LLC v. Ultra Resources, Inc., 415 F.3d 1158 (10th Cir. 2005); Amoco Rocmount Co. v. Anshutz Corp., 7 F.3d 909 (10th Cir. 1993).

[117] Amoco Rocmount Co. v. Anshutz Corp., 7 F.3d 909, 923 (10th Cir. 1993).

[118] Shell Rocky Mountain Prod., LLC v. Ultra Resources, Inc., 415 F.3d 1158 (10th Cir. 2005); *see also* Castle Tex. Prod. Ltd. P'ship v. Long Trusts, 134 S.W.3d 267, 283 n.4 (Tex. App.—Tyler 2003 pet. denied) (declining to apply exculpatory provision to claim that operator did not properly account for non-operating interest owner's proportionate share of gas and condensate); IP Petroleum Co., Inc. v. Wevanco Energy, LLC, 116 S.W.3d 888 (Tex. App.—Houston [1st Dist.] 2003, no pet.) (applying exculpatory provision where non-operator alleged that operator improperly conducted drilling operations on the lease); Cone v. Fagadau Energy Corp., 68 S.W.3d 147 (Tex. App.—Eastland 2001, pet. denied) (declining to apply exculpatory provision where claim by non-operator concerned accounting issues).

[119] Shell Rocky Mountain Prod., LLC v. Ultra Resources, Inc., 415 F.3d 1158 (10th Cir. 2005). The Tenth Circuit's limitation of the 1982 exculpatory clause to negligence in field operations was adopted in the form of an "Erie guess" by the U.S. District Court for the Eastern District of Louisiana in 2017. *See* Shell Offshore Inc. v. Eni Petroleum US LLC, No. 16-15537, 2017 WL 4226154, at *6 (E.D. La. Sept. 21, 2017) ("Applying the exculpatory clause to the operator's administrative duties and the rights of the non-operators, particularly as set forth in Exhibit C, would undermine the force of these provisions. As noted by one authority on oil and gas operating agreements, 'it is difficult to perceive why the parties would include explicit and detailed directions on administrative matters that are supplemental to 'operations' if they did not intend the operator to be liable for breach of those matters.'").

§ 5.04   ENERGY & MINERAL LAW INSTITUTE

operator standard.[120] For example, in *Stine v. Marathon Oil Co*, the U.S. Court of Appeals for the Fifth Circuit commented that the "tenor of the wording of the exculpatory clause is that [the operator] is not liable for good faith performance of duties under this agreement, but is liable for acts outside the scope of [its] powers under the agreement.[121] Further, the court found:

> It is clear to us that the protection of the exculpatory clause extends not only to 'acts unique to the operator,' as the district court expressed it, but also to any acts done under the authority of the JOA 'as operator.' This protection clearly extends to breaches of the JOA.[122]

Given the trend in case law that the 1982 Joint Operating Agreement exculpatory provision only protects against liability related to "operations," some parties have attempted to "plead around" the exculpatory provision by casting their claims in terms of breach of the agreement's notice provisions.[123] For example, in *Matrix*, the non-operator alleged the operator drilled the well in the wrong location.[124] However, rather than plead the claim as negligent operations—which would clearly run afoul of the exculpatory clause—the non-operator pleaded the claim as breach of the joint operating agreement

---

[120] *See, e.g.*, Stine v. Marathon Oil Co., 976 F.2d 254, 261 (5th Cir. 1992).

[121] *Id.*, at 261. *See also* Caddo Oil Co. v. O'Brien, 908 F.2d 13, 17 (5th Cir. 1990) (operator excused from accounting to nonoperator for charges for operations and was not held to a fiduciary standard because operating agreement made operator liable only for willful misconduct); Grace-Cajun Oil Co. No. Two v. Damson Oil Corp., 897 F.2d 1364, 1366 (5th Cir. 1990).

[122] *Id.*; *see also* PYR Energy Cop. v. Samson Res. Co., 470 F.Supp.2d 709, 725 (E.D. Tex. 2007) (finding *Stine* survived pre-2013 Texas intermediate appellate court decisions). Of course, the 1990 reasoning of the Fifth Circuit, which was based on Texas law, is unlikely to have survived the Texas Supreme Court's 2013 decision in *Reeder*, which more narrowly interprets the exculpatory provision. *See* Erie Railroad Co. v. Tompkins, 304 U.S. 64, 78 (1938); MDU Barnett, 2014 WL 585740, at *7 ("The court concludes that *Reeder* clearly abrogates *Stine*, and the court defers to the Texas Supreme Court's construction of state law.").

[123] *See, e.g.*, Matrix Prod. Co. v. Ricks Exploration Inc., 102 P.3d 1285, 1286 (Ct. App. N.M. 2004).

[124] *Id.*

notice provision.[125] The New Mexico Court of Appeals rejected this effort, holding that notice of the well was properly given, "and that any error in this case was not in the notice provided but in performing the drilling operation."[126]

[a] — Demonstrating Gross Negligence and Willful Misconduct.

Few non-operators have succeeded in overcoming the post-1982 exculpatory provision once applied.[127] *Apache Corp. v. Castex Offshore, Inc* represents a notable exception.[128] In *Castex*, there was no dispute that the claims brought by the non-operator were within the scope of the exculpatory clause.[129] The non-operator alleged the operator committed gross negligence and misconduct during operations at two separate projects: Belle Isle and Potomac.[130]

The crux of the non-operator's claims regarding the Belle Isle project was that the operator was grossly negligent in overspending the project.[131] Specifically, the operator sent an initial request for expenditure for the project in the amount of $16.9 million but spent a total of $102 million completing the project.[132] During trial, the non-operator presented evidence that the cost overruns were the result of a myriad of factors caused by the operator, including purchasing construction equipment and materials prior to

---

[125] *Id.* Article VI.B to the 1982 Joint Operating Agreement requires "[s]hould any party hereto desire to drill any well on the Contract Area other than the well provided for in Article VI.A., or to rework, deepen or plug back a dry hole drilled at the joint expense of all parties or a well jointly owned by all the parties and not then producing in paying quantities, the party desiring to drill, rework, or deepen or plug back such a well shall give the other parties written notice of the proposed operation, specifying the work to be performed, the location, proposed depth, objective formation and the estimated cost of the operation."

[126] Matrix Prod. Co. v. Ricks Exploration Inc., 102 P.3d 1285, 1286 (Ct. App. N.M. 2004).

[127] *But see* Apache Corp. v. Castex Offshore, Inc., 626 S.W.3d 371, 384 (Tex. App.—Houston [14th Dist.] 2021, pet. denied).

[128] *See id.*

[129] *Id.*

[130] *Id.* at 377, 385.

[131] *Id.* at 377.

[132] *Id.*

§ 5.04 ENERGY & MINERAL LAW INSTITUTE

completion of engineering (which caused wasted equipment and materials) and changing project specifications (which caused multiple redesigns).[133] The non-operator also presented evidence that employees of the operator knew the cost overruns were far more egregious than those actually reported to their superiors and the non-operators.[134]

Based on the evidence presented, the Houston Court of Appeals found sufficient evidence for the jury's finding of gross negligence, writing that there was "a substantial basis for making an implied finding that [the operator's employees] knew, but did not care, about [their] overspending."[135]

The Potomac project was situated in the shallow waters of a bay.[136] Problems with the drilling necessitated five sidetracks, and only "after the drilling of a fifth sidetrack was the well able to produce any gas, and that production did not last for very long."[137] The non-operator sued the operator, "claiming that [the operator] had mismanaged the drilling of the well by failing to set certain liners, which would have protected the gas reserves from the influx of water" that hampered production.[138] The non-operator also "sought damages for its share of the cost overruns in drilling the well, and for its share of gas reserves that were lost because of [the operator's] mismanagement."[139] The non-operator presented evidence to the jury that the operator "deliberately left three open pathways for cross-flow," which ultimately damaged or ruined the well.[140] Based on the evidence presented, the jury found willful misconduct but not gross negligence.[141] The finding of willful misconduct did not survive the evidence sufficiency challenge at the Houston Court of Appeals because even if the evidence established the operator intended to leave the sidetracks open (allowing for the possibility

---

[133] *Id.* at 379.
[134] *Id.*
[135] *Id.* at 384.
[136] *Id.* at 386.
[137] *Id.* at 385.
[138] *Id.*
[139] *Id.*
[140] *Id.* at 389.
[141] *Id.*

of crossflow), there was no evidence the operator intended for the harm to occur.[142] Rather, the Houston Court of Appeals wrote the non-operator "could have overcome that exculpatory clause with legally sufficient evidence that [the operator] knew, but did not care, that it was mismanaging the drilling operation."[143]

Although the Houston Court of Appeals found insufficient evidence to support a finding of willful misconduct, the conclusion that the non-operator could have succeeded by demonstrating that the operator "knew, but did not care, that it was mismanaging the drilling operation" appears at odds with Texas and Louisiana law requiring the jury to find the defendant had "a specific intent . . . to cause substantial injury to" the plaintiff.[144]

[b] — Application of Exculpatory Provision to Affirmative Defenses.

The exculpatory provision of the 1982 Joint Operating Agreement shields operators from both claims and affirmative defenses within the scope of the clause.[145] For example, in *Chesapeake Operating, Inc. v. Sanchez Oil & Gas Corp* (a case in the U.S. District Court for the Western District of Texas in which the court applied Louisiana law), the working interest owner refused to pay its proportionate share of operating expenses as required by the terms of the joint operating agreement.[146] When the operator brought suit to collect payment for the operating expenses, the working interest owner pleaded the affirmative defense of prior material breach, alleging the operator failed to conduct operations in a good and workmanlike manner.[147] The working interest owner argued the prior material breach of the joint

---

[142] *Id.* at 393.
[143] *Id.*
[144] *Compare id. with* IP Petroleum Co., Inc. v. Wevanco Energy, L.L.C., 116 S.W.3d 888, 897 (Tex. App.—Houston [1st Dist.] 2003, pet. denied), at 897.
[145] *See, e.g.,* Chesapeake Operating, Inc. v. Sanchez Oil & Gas Corp., No. H-11-1890, 2012 WL 2133554, at *3 (S.D. Tex. June 12, 2012).
[146] *Id.*
[147] *Id.*

§ 5.04

operating agreement excused any additional performance by the working interest owner—including payment for the disputed operations.[148]

The operator moved to dismiss the affirmative defenses on the basis that the exculpatory clause barred the affirmative defense of prior material breach.[149] The working interest owner argued that the joint operating agreement's exculpatory clause did not apply because it was not seeking to establish "liability."[150] This reasoning was squarely rejected by the court:

> While the Court agrees that this clause is usually applied when a party asserts a claim or counterclaim against the Operator, here even though Sanchez has not asserted an affirmative *claim*, it essentially seeks to hold [the operator] liable because [the operator] will be left responsible for Sanchez's share of the operating expenses if the affirmative defenses were to be upheld. The court thus HOLDS that Sanchez cannot escape the exculpatory clause by filing affirmative defenses rather than a counterclaim.[151]

The reasoning in *Sanchez* has been accepted by the only Texas appellate court to examine the issue of whether the Joint Operating Agreement exculpatory clause bars both affirmative claims and defenses.[152] In *Crimson Exploration Operating, Inc. v. BPX Operating Co.*, the non-operator refused to pay its proportionate share of costs associated with a well blowout, and then pleaded the affirmative defense of prior material breach when sued by the operator.[153] Although the appellate court acknowledged that "[i]t is a fundamental principle of contract law that when one party to a contract commits a material breach of that contract, the other party is discharged

---

[148] *Id.*
[149] *Id.*
[150] *Id.*
[151] *Id.*
[152] Crimson Exploration Operating, Inc. v. BPX Operating Co., No. 14-20-00070-CV, 2021 WL 786541 (Tex. App.—Houston [1st Dist.] Mar. 2, 2021, pet. denied) (mem. op.). In *Crimson*, the Houston appellate court applied the 1989 Joint Operating Agreement exculpatory provision to affirmative defenses.
[153] *Id.* at *1.

or excused from performance," the court concluded that the non-operator "cannot escape the exculpatory clause by filing an affirmative defense to [the operator's] action rather than a counterclaim asserting [the operator's] prior material breach."[154]

The reasoning in *Sanchez* was also recently accepted by the U.S. District Court for the Western District of Louisiana, which held that the joint operating agreement's exculpatory provision precluded the affirmative defense of prior material breach as a means to avoid paying operating expenses in the absence of gross negligence or willful misconduct.[155]

[4] — 1989 Joint Operating Agreement.

In contrast to the 1982 model form, the 1989 Joint Operating Agreement contains an exculpatory clause providing that with respect to "its ***activities under this agreement*** . . . in no event shall [operator] have any liability as Operator to the other parties for losses sustained or liabilities incurred except such as may result from gross negligence or willful misconduct."[156] Courts and legal commentators have noted the 1989 version exculpates liability for all "activities under this agreement" instead of "all such operations," arguably providing for "more expansive exoneration of the operator."[157]

Indeed, several courts have summarized the effect of the exculpatory clause in the 1989 Joint Operating Agreement as setting "the standard to adjudicate the breach of contract claims."[158] For example, in *Bradford Energy Capital, LLC v. SWEPI LP*, the U.S. District Court for the Western District of Pennsylvania applied the exculpatory clause in granting summary judgment

---

[154] *Id.* at *4, 5.
[155] Key Operating and Prod. Co., LLC v. White Capital Group, LLC, No. 6:21-CV-03555, 2023 WL 349837, at *7 (W.D. La. Jan. 1, 2013).
[156] 1989 AAPL Joint Operating Agreement, Article V.A (emphasis added).
[157] Reeder v. Wood County Energy, LLC, 395 S.W.3d 789, 794 (Tex. 2012); Robert C. Bledsoe, *The Operating Agreement: Matters Not Covered or Inadequately Covered*, 47 Rocky Mtn. Min. L. Inst. § 15.03[1] (2001).
[158] Crimson Exploration Operating, Inc. v. BPX Operating Co., No. 14-20-00070-CV, 2021 WL 786541 (Tex. App.—Houston [1st Dist.] Mar. 2, 2021, pet. denied) (mem. op.) at *4; Bradford Energy Capital, LLC v. SWEPI LP, No. 17-1231, 2020 WL 5747841 (W.D. Pa. Sept. 25, 2020).

§ 5.04   ENERGY & MINERAL LAW INSTITUTE

against a non-operator's claim for breach related to the operator's refusal to complete and turn a well to sales.[159] The court found that the summary judgment evidence demonstrated that whether to complete and put the well into production was a matter of "business judgment"—not a matter of gross negligence or willful misconduct.[160]

The Texas Supreme Court reached a similarly broad result when considering "whether the exculpatory clause in the JOA sets the standard to adjudicate . . . breach of contract claims . . . ."[161] In applying the 1989 exculpatory provision to a breach of contract claim, the court found a meaningful difference between the 1982 and 1989 exculpatory provisions:

> Reading the clause as written, we conclude that the model form transformation is significant, as the change in language broadens the clause's protection of operators. The model forms from 1977 and 1982 both contained clauses that protected operators from "all such operations," while the 1989 model form protects "its activities." The modifier "such" references operations under the JOA, while the deletion of that word and the use of the term "its activities" includes actions under the JOA that are not limited to operations. The modification implicates a broader scope of conduct following the language of the contract."[162]

As with the 1982 Joint Operating Agreement, the exculpatory clause in the 1989 version bars the affirmative defense of prior material breach absent a showing of gross negligence or willful misconduct.[163]

---

[159] Bradford Energy Capital, LLC v. SWEPI LP, No. 17-1231, 2020 WL 5747841 (W.D. Pa. Sept. 25, 2020).
[160] *Id.*
[161] Reeder v. Wood County Energy, LLC, 395 S.W.3d 789, 792 (Tex. 2012).
[162] *Id.* at 795.
[163] Crimson Exploration Operating, Inc. v. BPX Operating Co., No. 14-20-00070-CV, 2021 WL 786541 (Tex. App.—Houston [1st Dist.] Mar. 2, 2021, pet. denied) (mem. op.) at *5.

The exculpatory provision within the 1989 Joint Operating Agreement arguably provides the broadest possible protection to operators, insulating operators from liability in tort and contract incurred without gross negligence or willful misconduct. Indeed, any effort to extend the exculpatory provision further (*e.g.*, to excuse gross negligence or willful misconduct) would likely make the exculpatory provision void as a matter of public policy.[164]

Despite the broad language used by the exculpatory provision in the 1989 Joint Operating Agreement, and the expansive reading given to the clause by many courts, some limits still exist.[165] For example, in *Bachtell Enterprises, LLC v. Ankor E&P Holdings Corporation*, the Houston Court of Appeals found that the exculpatory clause did not excuse a failure by the operator to obtain non-operator consent for charges in excess of $50,000.[166] In finding that the exculpatory clause did not apply, the ourt wrote:

> The question squarely before us, as an apparent matter of first impression, is whether 'activities' is so broad as to protect an operator from any breach of contract so that the operator can have no liability for breach of any contractual provision, absent willfulness. We decline to extend the reach of *Reeder* that far. As the *Reeder* court noted, exculpatory clauses are 'designed to relieve one party of liability to the other for specified injury or loss incurred in the performance of the contract. In other words, it is a defense designed to protect one party against risks and losses, but it is not meant

---

[164] *See* Zachry Const. Corp. v. Port of Houston Auth. of Harris Cty., 449 S.W.3d 98, 116 (Tex. 2014) (holding contractual provisions exempting a party from tort liability for harm caused intentionally or recklessly are unenforceable on grounds of public policy); Jones v. Dressel, 623 P.2d 370, 373 (Colo. 1981) (exculpatory agreements do not bar civil liability for gross negligence); Feleccia v. Lackawanna College, 215 A.3d 3, 21 (Pa. 2019) (waiver regarding gross negligence not enforceable) *but see* Martin v. A.C.G., Inc., 965 P.2d 955, 997 (Okla. Civ. App. 1998) (gross negligence waiver not contrary to "clear mandate of public policy as articulated by constitutional, statutory or decisional law which shows this to be a threat to the public policy.").

[165] Bachtell Enterprises, LLC v. Ankor E&P Holdings Corporation, 651 S.W.3d 514, 522 (Tex. App.—Houston [14th Dist.] 2022, no pet.).

[166] *Id.* The operator in *Bachtell* brought suit against the non-operator seeking payment and the non-operator pleaded the affirmative defense of prior material breach.

§ 5.04   ENERGY & MINERAL LAW INSTITUTE

for offensive use to impose liabilities knowingly incurred without consent.[167]

Although the *Bachtell* court correctly notes that *Reeder* does not expressly require application of the exculpatory provision to every breach of contract claim related to the 1989 Joint Operating Agreement, *Reeder* analyzes the application of the exculpatory provision to breach of contract claims generally without reference to the specific breaches alleged at the trial court.[168] This would seem to suggest that the Texas Supreme Court intended for its analysis in *Reeder* to be more far-reaching than the facts immediately before the court.[169] Rather, it seems more likely that *Bachtell* is ultimately limited to its facts given the equities involved.[170] Asking the court to force the non-operator to pay for an expenditure that was never authorized on the basis of the exculpatory clause (even though the terms of the joint operating agreement expressly required such authorization) may have simply been a step too far for the Houston Court of Appeals.[171]

However, if gross negligence and willful misconduct are the standard by which liability for tort and breach of the joint operating agreement are judged, non-operating working interest owners might wonder why the joint operating agreement includes any reference to other standards, such as "reasonably prudent operator," "good and workmanlike manner," "with due diligence and dispatch," "in accordance with good oilfield practice," and " in compliance with applicable law and regulation."[172] These non-operating working interest owners might complain the exculpatory provision has completely swallowed all other standards of care in the joint operating agreement and rendered them surplusage.[173]

---

[167] *Id.*
[168] *Compare id. with* Reeder v. Wood County Energy, LLC, 395 S.W.3d 789, 792 (Tex. 2012).
[169] Reeder v. Wood County Energy, LLC, 395 S.W.3d 789, 792-95 (Tex. 2012).
[170] *See generally*, Bachtell Enterprises, LLC v. Ankor E&P Holdings Corporation, 651 S.W.3d 514, 522 (Tex. App.—Houston [14th Dist.] 2022, no pet.).
[171] *See generally, id.*
[172] 1989 AAPL Joint Operating Agreement, Article V.A.
[173] *See, e.g.*, Certain Underwriters at Lloyd's of London Subscribing to Policy v. Cardtronics, Inc., 438 S.W.3d 770, 776 (Tex. App.—Houston [1st Dist.] 2014, no pet.).

Although the heightened standards of operation in 1989 Joint Operating Agreement are unlikely to create new avenues for operator liability given the scope of the exculpatory provision, the standards nonetheless retain meaning in the context of the drafting committee's overall goal of removing "deadbeat operators." The 1989 Joint Operating Agreement includes a more robust operator removal provision that incorporates the heightened standards of operation:

Operator may be removed for good cause by the affirmative vote of Non-Operators owning a majority interest based on ownership . . . For purposes hereof, "good cause" shall mean not only gross negligence or willful misconduct but also the material breach of or inability to meet the standards of operation contained in Article V.A or material failure or inability to perform its obligations under this agreement.[174]

In contrast, the 1982 Joint Operating Agreement only provides that the operator "may be removed if it fails or refuses to carry out its duties hereunder, or becomes insolvent, bankrupt, or is placed in receivership . . . ."[175] The 1989 Joint Operating Agreement expressly incorporates the heightened standards of operation included within Article V.A, and removes any applicability of the exculpatory provision to the operator removal clause.[176]

In sum, the 1989 Joint Operating Agreement provides heightened standards for operations—which may be used by the non-operators to remove operators that fall short of the standards. The heightened standards are balanced with a more robust exculpatory provision, which effectively leaves operator removal as the sole remedy for breach of the agreement absent gross negligence or willful misconduct.

[5] — 2015 Joint Operating Agreement.

The 2015 Joint Operating Agreement contains an exculpatory clause providing that "in no event shall [operator] have any liability as Operator to the other parties for losses sustained or liabilities incurred *in connection*

---

[174] 1989 AAPL Joint Operating Agreement, Article V.B.
[175] 1982 AAPL Joint Operating Agreement, Article V.B.
[176] 1989 AAPL Joint Operating Agreement, Article V.B.

§ 5.04   ENERGY & MINERAL LAW INSTITUTE

with authorized or approved operations under this agreement except such as may result from gross negligence or willful misconduct.[177]

The 2015 version reinstates the 1982 Joint Operating Agreement reference to "operations" and deletes the 1989 reference to "activities," ostensibly paring back the exculpatory clause.[178] Indeed, members of the drafting committee confirmed the revisions evidence an intent to return the construction of the exculpatory clause to its pre-*Reeder* status quo.[179]

Although there are no widely reported decisions concerning the scope of the 2015 version, the language in the 2015 Joint Operating Agreement is potentially problematic for operators and non-operators alike. At least two commentators have suggested the exculpatory clause extends beyond the limits of the 1982 Joint Operating Agreement, despite what the drafting committee intended:

> Unfortunately, the 2015 AAPL Form 610 is not a perfect model of clarity. The 2015 version does *not* expressly state that its exculpatory clause applies only to the operator's operational decisions. To the contrary, the works "in connection with" are broad and arguably enable an operator to contend that the exculpatory clause in the 2015 version limits its liability for any actions that are in any way *connected to or related to* its approved operations.[180]

Conversely, the limitation on the exculpatory clause to "authorized or approved" operations may introduce unfortunate ambiguity for the operator

---

[177] 2015 AAPL Joint Operating Agreement, Article V.A (emphasis added).

[178] *Compare id. with* 1982 AAPL Joint Operating Agreement, Article V.A and 1989 AAPL Joint Operating Agreement, Article V.A.

[179] *See* Frederick M. MacDonald, *The A.A.P.L. Form 610-2015 Model Form Joint Operating Agreement—Commentary of the Form 610 Revision Task Force, Joint Operations and the New AAPL Form 610-2015 Model Form Operating Agreement* 1-1, 1-9 to 1-10, Rocky Mt. Min. L. Fdn. (2017) ("Under the revised language, it is clear that the limitation of the Operator's liability to its gross negligence or willful misconduct only applies to authorized or approve operations, as distinguished from breach of the Operating Agreement itself.").

[180] Byron Keeling & Anna Fredrickson, *Exculpatory Clauses for Operators: When Do They Apply and What Do They Mean?* 10-1, 10-9 Rocky Mt. Min. L. Fdn. (2021).

to the extent the clause invites disagreement concerning whether operations were properly "authorized or approved."[181] For example, the 2015 Joint Operating Agreement requires operators to give a written proposal for operations subsequent to the initial well.[182] For horizontal wells, the written proposal must include: "(1) that the proposed operation is a Horizontal Well operation; (2) drilling and Completion plans specifying the proposed: (i) Total Measured Depth(s), (ii) surface hole location(s), (iii) Terminus/Termini, (iv) Displacement(s), (v) utilization and scheduling of rig(s) (Spudder Rig, drilling, and Completion), and (vi) stimulation operations, staging and sizing; and (3) estimated drilling and Completion costs as set forth in an AFE."[183] The joint operating agreement further provides that "[i]f Operator, in its reasonable judgment, deviates from an approved proposal based upon information derived from facts and circumstances determined subsequent to the commencement of the operations relating to such proposal (including, without limitation, revision of the originally proposed Completion staging and design), such deviations in and of themselves will not result in liability of the Operator to the Parties."[184]

To the extent a well deviates from the detailed written proposal, the non-operator may argue the exculpatory provision does not apply because the operation was not properly authorized or approved. Whether the deviation was the result of "information derived from facts and circumstances determined subsequent to the commencement of the operations relating to such proposal" is likely a fact intensive inquiry.

Until more case law is generated concerning the scope and applicability of the 2015 exculpatory clause, some risk exists for operators and non-operators alike. Although the drafting committee expressed an intent to return to the pre-1989 status quo, the 2015 exculpatory clause does not replicate the language in the 1982 Joint Operating Agreement. Rather, by using language that is arguably less precise than that used by the 1982 agreement, the 2015

---

[181] *See* 2015 AAPL Joint Operating Agreement, Article V.A.
[182] *Id.* at Article VI.B.
[183] *Id.*
[184] *Id.* at Article VI.E.

Joint Operating Agreement has introduced a level of uncertainty that will likely remain until case law establishes the exact scope of the exculpatory clause.

§ 5.05 Lawsuits: Allocating Cost and Risk.

Each version of the model form joint operating agreement contains additional protection for the operator in the event of litigation. In general, the joint operating agreements allow the operator to: (1) charge reasonable defense costs to the joint account; (2) settle claims with some or no involvement from the non-operators; and (3) charge back certain liabilities to the joint account.

[1] — Costs of Litigation and Settlement.

The 1956 Joint Operating Agreement allows the operator to settle pre-lawsuit claims in amounts less than $1,000.[185] The operator is permitted to charge the settlement amount to the joint account.[186] In contrast, the hiring of outside counsel to defend against a lawsuit and the settlement of claims brought in a lawsuit requires consent from all parties.[187]

The 1977 Joint Operating Agreement removes the distinction between pre-suit claims and claims brought in a lawsuit.[188] The limit of the operator's discretion to settle claims charged to the joint account is determined by the parties prior to execution of the joint operating agreement through a fill-in-the-blank. Further, "[a]ll costs and expense of handling, settling, or otherwise discharging such claim or suit shall be at the joint expense of the parties."[189] Non-operators against which claims are made "on account of any matter arising from operations" are entitled to the same protection.[190] The changes made in 1977 were continued into the 1982 and 1989 forms.[191]

---

[185] 1956 AAPL Joint Operating Agreement, Article 28.
[186] *Id.*
[187] *Id.*
[188] 1977 AAPL Joint Operating Agreement, Article X.
[189] *Id.*
[190] *Id.*
[191] 1982 AAPL Joint Operating Agreement, Article X; 1989 AAPL Joint Operating Agreement, Article X.

The committee to the 2015 Joint Operating Agreement made a significant change to how lawsuits above the threshold amount were handled. Previous versions of the form provided that if a lawsuit demand exceeded the operator settlement authority "the parties hereto shall assume and take over the further handling of the claim or suit, unless such authority is delegated to Operator."[192] In contrast, the 2015 form provides that "Operator shall promptly give notice to Non-Operators and Operator shall assume and handle the claim or suit on behalf of all parties unless, within 14 days after receipt of such notice, a party gives notice to Operator and the other parties of its affirmative election to assume and handle the claim or suit on its own behalf, which assumption and handling shall be done at said party's own expense and over and above the party's proportionate share chargeable to the joint account as hereinafter provided."[193] The 2015 model form approach appears more pragmatic than having all parties collectively participate in litigation decision making.

[2] — Getting Answers: The Jury Charge

In 2018, the Committee on Pattern Jury Charges for the State Bar of Texas published the most recent edition of *Texas Pattern Jury Charges for Oil & Gas*, which includes questions directly pertaining to breach of joint operating agreements. The *Texas Pattern Jury Charge for Oil & Gas* includes separate jury questions for breach of a standard of conduct and the exculpatory clause.[194]

With respect to breach, the Pattern Jury Charge instructs the jury the answer "yes" or "no" to the following question:

Did *Don Davis* fail to comply with the joint operating agreement?
[set forth provisions or conduct at issue, if appropriate]

[You are instructed that the joint operating agreement requires the operator to conduct operations [insert appropriate standard of care as set forth in the JOA].][195]

---

[192] *See, e.g.*, 1982 AAPL Joint Operating Agreement, Article X.
[193] 2015 AAPL Joint Operating Agreement, Article X.
[194] Texas Pattern Jury Charge for Oil and Gas 305.27, 305.28 (2018).
[195] *Id.* at 305.27.

The Pattern Jury Charge includes two "yes" or "no" follow-up questions contingent on a "Yes" to the standard of conduct question:

Did *Don Davis's* failure to comply result from willful misconduct?

Did *Don Davis's* failure to comply result from gross negligence?[196]

The Pattern Jury Charge suggests inserting the appropriate definition of "gross negligence."[197]

The structure of the pattern jury charge requires the trial court to determine whether the exculpatory provision applies to the wrongful conduct alleged. This is consistent with the principle that the rights, duties, and obligations of the parties under an unambiguous contract are determined as a matter of law.[198]

[3] — Exposure and Liability.

Under Article X of the 1956 Joint Operating Agreement, liability for adjudicated claims is apportioned to all parties to the extent the liability constitutes a "joint loss."[199] The 1956 model does not give a precise definition of "joint loss," which is only used with respect to certain title failures within the contract area.[200] The 1977 Joint Operating Agreement immediately clarified that all costs of discharging claims or suits is "at the joint expense of the parties."[201] The 1982 Joint Operating Agreement again changed Article X, this time to clarify that only "parties participating in the operation from

---

[196] *Id.* at 305.28.

[197] *Id.*

[198] ACS Investors, Inc. v. McLaughlin, 943 S.W.2d 426, 430 (Tex. 1997) ("We may determine the parties' rights and obligations under an unambiguous contract as a matter of law."); Seringetti Constr. Co. v. Cincinnati, 553 N.E.2d 1371 (Ohio 1988).

[199] 1956 AAPL Joint Operating Agreement, Article 28.

[200] *See, id.* at Article 2.C.

[201] 1956 AAPL Joint Operating Agreement, Article X.

which the claim or suit arises" retain liability.[202] The 1982 change was retained by both the 1989 and 2015 model forms.[203]

§ 5.06 Conclusion.

The model form Joint Operating Agreements are just that — model forms and templates. The model forms are national templates that do not lend themselves to a one-size-fits-all mentality.[204] Rather, the forms themselves include space for the parties to modify the form language and draft any new terms to meet their specific needs.[205] To the extent the parties to a joint operating agreement have strong preferences concerning standards of conduct or the scope of the exculpatory provision, the parties may negotiate and memorialize these preferences in the agreement no matter what model form is utilized as the base.

---

[202] 1982 AAPL Joint Operating Agreement, Article X.
[203] 1989 AAPL Joint Operating Agreement, Article X; 2015 AAPL Joint Operating Agreement, Article X.
[204] *See* Frederick M. MacDonald, *The A.A.P.L. Form 610-2015 Model Form Joint Operating Agreement—Commentary of the Form 610 Revision Task Force, Joint Operations and the New AAPL Form 610-2015 Model Form Operating Agreement* 1-1, 1-9 to 1-10, Rocky Mt. Min. L. Fdn. (2017) at 1-4.
[205] *See, e.g.,* 1989 AAPL Joint Operating Agreement, Article XVI.

Chapter 6

PHMSA/LDAR Rulemaking: What's Proposed and What's Next

Keith J. Coyle
Abigail M. Reecer
Babst Calland
District of Columbia

Synopsis

§ 6.01.	Introduction 123
§ 6.02.	Background on PHMSA Rulemaking.................................. 124
	[1] — Risk Assessment 125
	[2] — Gas Pipeline Advisory Committee 126
	[3] — Post-GPAC Process 126
	[4] — Administrative and Judicial Review 127
§ 6.03.	2020 PIPES Act Congressional Mandate 128
§ 6.04.	May 2023 Proposed Rule on LDAR.................................... 128
	[1] — Scope 129
	[a] — Increase Leakage Surveys and Patrols 130
	[b] — Development of Advanced Leak Detection Programs 131
	[c] — Leak Grade and Repair Requirements 131
	[d] — Exceptions for Compressor Stations.................. 132
	[e] — Reporting.. 133
	[f] — Mitigating Emissions from Venting.................... 133
	[g] — Design, Configuration, and Maintenance of Pressure Relief Devices 133
	[h] — Qualifications 134
	[i] — LNG Facilities 134
	[j] — Underground Natural Gas Storage Facilities 135
	[2] — Comments on the May 2023 Proposed Rule on LDAR.. 135
	[3] — Next Steps 135

§ 6.01. Introduction.

The Pipeline and Hazardous Material Safety Administration (PHMSA) is in the process of developing new leak detection and repair (LDAR) regulations that could have a lasting impact on the operation and maintenance of the nation's gas pipeline facilities. Prompted by a congressional mandate in the Protecting Our Infrastructure of Pipelines and Enhancing Safety (PIPES) Act of 2020[1], this paper examines the LDAR regulations that PHMSA proposed in May 2023 and provides insight into the process for finalizing and seeking judicial review of those regulations.

§ 6.02. Background on PHMSA Rulemaking.

PHMSA administers a national pipeline safety program pursuant to the pipeline safety laws. The pipeline safety laws generally provide PHMSA with authority to regulate gas pipeline facilities and persons engaged in the transportation of gas, subject to certain exceptions.[2] PHMSA has used that authority to prescribe comprehensive minimum federal safety standards for gas pipeline facilities. These safety standards are codified by regulation at 49 C.F.R. Part 192. PHMSA has also prescribed certain registration and reporting requirements for gas pipeline facilities that are codified by regulation at 49 C.F.R. Parts 190 and 191.

PHMSA's general authority to prescribe safety standards for gas pipeline facilities is set forth in 49 U.S.C. § 60102. Section 60102 creates a hybrid rulemaking process that exceeds the basic notice-and-comment requirements in the Administrative Procedure Act (APA).[3] The additional procedures that PHMSA is required to follow include preparing a risk assessment for each proposed safety standard and presenting that risk assessment and the proposed safety standard to a federal advisory committee for review.

After the advisory committee completes its review, the subsequent phases of the PHMSA rulemaking process are similar to those that apply throughout the federal government. PHMSA then issues a final rule that can be subject to further administrative or judicial review. Each of these steps in the rulemaking process is briefly discussed below.

---

[1] Protecting Our Infrastructure of Pipelines and Enhancing Safety Act of 2020, Pub. L. 116-260, div. R, title II (2020). (hereinafter cited as *PIPES Act of 2020*)

[2] 49 U.S.C. §§ 60101-60102 (as amended by *PIPES Act of 2020*, §§ 203, 204, 206); 49 C.F.R. § 192.1.

[3] GPA Midstream Ass'n v. United States Dep't of Transportation, 67 F.4th 1188, 1196-97 (D.C. Cir. 2023). *See* Administrative Procedure Act (APA), 5 U.S.C. §§ 551 – 559, 701 – 706.

[1] — Risk Assessment.

Section 60102(b)(2) contains a list of factors that PHMSA must consider "[w]hen prescribing any standards" under certain statutory provisions.[4] Those factors include "the reasonably identifiable or estimated benefits [and costs] expected to result from implementation or compliance with the standard."[5] PHMSA must conduct a "risk assessment" to obtain that cost-benefit information, and in doing so must:

> (A) identify the regulatory and nonregulatory options that the Secretary considered in prescribing a proposed standard; (B) identify the costs and benefits associated with the proposed standard; (C) include—(i) an explanation of the reasons for the selection of the proposed standard in lieu of the other options identified; and (ii) with respect to each of those other options, a brief explanation of the reasons that the Secretary did not select the option; and (D) identify technical data or other information upon which the risk assessment information and proposed standard is based.[6]

The D.C. Circuit recently granted petition for judicial review of a final rule where PHMSA failed to comply with the risk assessment requirements in *GPA Midstream Association and American Petroleum Institute v. United States Department of Transportation and Pipeline and Hazardous Safety Administration*.[7] The D.C. Circuit vacated the portions of a final rule that required the use of rupture-mitigation valves for gathering lines, holding that PHMSA acted arbitrarily and capriciously in failing to comply with the risk assessment requirements in the pipeline safety laws at the proposed rule stage and to explain, let alone consider, why the rulemaking's safety standard would be practicable and make sense for gathering lines until issuing the final rule, when there could be no peer review or public comment.

---

[4] 49 U.S.C. § 60102(b)(2).
[5] 49 U.S.C. § 60102(b)(2)(D)-(E).
[6] 49 U.S.C. § 60102(b)(3).
[7] GPA Midstream Ass'n v. United States Dep't of Transportation, 67 F.4th at 1199.

§ 6.02 ENERGY & MINERAL LAW INSTITUTE

[2] — Gas Pipeline Advisory Committee.

PHMSA is required to provide "the risk assessment information and other analyses supporting each proposed standard" to the Gas Pipeline Advisory Committee ("GPAC"), a federal advisory committee comprised of representatives from the government, industry, and general public, that is responsible for reviewing and providing non-binding recommendations on pipeline safety rulemaking proposals.[8]

Once the GPAC is provided the information by PHMSA, it is required to "prepare and submit [to PHMSA] a report on the technical feasibility, reasonableness, cost-effectiveness, and practicability of the proposed standard and include in the report recommended actions" within 90 days of receiving the proposed standard and supporting analyses.[9] PHMSA must, within 90 days of receiving the GPAC report, "provide a written response" to the GPAC "concerning all significant peer review comments and recommended alternatives contained in the report." PHMSA must "publish the reasons" for rejecting any conclusions of the GPAC in a rulemaking proceeding.[10]

[3] — Post-GPAC Process.

After the GPAC process is complete, the agency reviews the comments received and analyzes them to decide whether to proceed with the proposed rulemaking, issue a new or modified proposal, or withdraw the proposal.[11] If PHMSA decides to proceed, it develops a final rule for submission to the Secretary of Transportation. The final rule must include a preamble with a response to the significant issues raised in public comments and a statement providing the basis and purpose of the rule. The Office of the Secretary (OST) then reviews the final rule to ensure consistency with the administration's

---

[8] 49 U.S.C. § 60115(c)(1)(A). Congress added the requirement for peer review of proposed standards by the GPAC "to bring more rationality to federal pipeline safety standard setting and broaden participation by requiring [Office of Pipeline Safety] to consider more carefully comments received from these bodies." Report of the Committee on Commerce, Science, and Transportation on S. 1505, S. Rept. 104-334, at 3-4 (July 26, 1996).

[9] 49 U.S.C. § 60115(c)(2).

[10] 49 U.S.C. § 60115(c).

[11] Exec. Order No.12866: Regulatory Planning and Review (1993).

objectives and departmental rules, policies, and procedures.[12] All major rulemakings, with some exceptions, must be reviewed and cleared by OST.

The final rule is then sent to the Office of Management & Budget (OMB) for review pursuant to the terms of executive orders for cost-benefit and other purposes.[13] The OMB review helps to promote adequate interagency review of draft proposed and final regulatory actions, so that such actions are coordinated with other agencies to avoid inconsistent, incompatible, or duplicative policies. OMB review helps to ensure that agencies carefully consider the consequences of rules (including both benefits and costs) before they proceed. During the course of OMB's review of a draft rule, it may decide to return the rule to the agency for reconsideration. This might occur if the quality of the agency's analysis is inadequate, if the rule is not justified by the analysis, if the rule is not consistent with the regulatory principles stated in Executive Order 12866 or with the President's policies and priorities, or if the rule unnecessarily conflicts with other Executive Branch agency rules or efforts.[14] Once OMB's review is complete, the final rule can be returned to PHMSA for publication in the *Federal Register*.[15]

[4] — Administrative and Judicial Review.

Final rules can be subject to further administrative or judicial review. In the case of the former, any interested person may petition the Associate Administrator for reconsideration of a final rule. Interested parties can seek administrative review by filing a petition for reconsideration within 30 days of the final rule's publication in the *Federal Register*.[16] The filing of a petition does not stay the effectiveness of the final rule.[17] Any interested person

---

[12] *See* Rulemaking and Guidance Procedures, DOT Order 2100.6A (June 7, 2021).
[13] *See e.g.*, Exec. Order No. 12866: Regulatory Planning and Review (1993); Exec. Order No. 13563: Improving Regulation and Regulatory Review (2011).
[14] *See* OMB Circular No. A-4, Regulatory Analysis (2003) (providing guidance on the development of regulatory analyses).
[15] A final legislative rule cannot be made effective in less than 30 days after publication. 5 U.S.C. § 553(d). The Administrative Procedure Act provisions at 5 U.S.C. 553 require proposed rules to be published in the Federal Register. *See also* 49 CFR § 190.329.
[16] 49 CFR § 190.335.
[17] 49 CFR § 190.338(c).

may appeal the denial of a petition for reconsideration to the Administrator within 20 days.[18] The filing of an appeal also does not stay the effectiveness of the final rule.

A person adversely affected by a regulation may also file a petition for judicial review in the United States Court of Appeals for the District of Columbia Circuit or in the court of appeals of the United States for the circuit in which the person resides or has its principal place of business.[19] The petition must be filed no later than 89 days after the regulation is issued or, in the case where further administrative review is sought, the order denying the petition for reconsideration or appeal is issued.[20] In the case of a regulation, the date used is the date the regulation is available for public inspection at Office of Federal Register or publication in the *Federal Register*.[21] Pursuant to Rule 15 of the Federal Rules of Appellate Procedures, the petition for review must contain the name of each party seeking review, name of the agency, and the order to be reviewed.[22]

§ 6.03. 2020 PIPES Act Congressional Mandate.

Intent on establishing minimum performance standards reflecting capabilities of commercially available advanced technologies, the 2020 PIPES Act was signed into law by the U.S. Congress on December 27, 2020.[23] In addition to reauthorizing the federal pipeline safety program through September 30, 2023, the 2020 PIPES Act amended certain provisions in the Pipeline Safety Act.[24] Section 113 of the PIPES Act directed PHMSA to promulgate final regulations by December 27, 2021, requiring operators of gas transmission, distribution pipelines, and certain gathering lines to conduct LDAR programs. Congress explicitly limited the application of the required LDAR programs to operators of regulated gathering lines in a Class 2, 3,

---

[18] 49 CFR § 190.338(b).
[19] 49 U.S.C. § 60119(a).
[20] 49 CFR § 190.337(b).
[21] 49 CFR § 190.335.
[22] Fed. Rule App. Procedure 15.
[23] *PIPES Act of 2020*, Pub. L. 116-260, div. R, title II.
[24] 49 U.S.C. § 60101 *et seq.*

or 4 location, new and existing gas transmission pipeline facilities, and new and existing gas distribution facilities.[25] This requirement did not extend to onshore gas gathering lines in Class 1 locations, which only recently became subject to the Agency's jurisdiction under the Pipeline Safety Act after being exempt for more than five decades.[26]

§ 6.04. May 2023 Proposed Rule on LDAR.

On May 18, 2023, PHMSA published a proposed rule in the *Federal Register* in Docket No. PHMSA-2021-0039 (NPRM).[27] The NPRM includes significant changes to the reporting requirements in 49 C.F.R. Part 191 and safety standards in 49 C.F.R. Part 192 for gas pipeline facilities. PHMSA proposes these changes primarily to address certain provisions in the 2020 PIPES Act.[28]

[1] — Scope.

PHMSA proposed to amend the safety standards and reporting requirements for gas pipeline facilities to, among other things: increase the frequency of leakage survey and patrolling requirements; introduce leakage survey and repair requirements for liquefied natural gas (LNG) facilities; require grading and repairs of leaks; reduce the use of blowdowns and intentional venting; impose design, configuration, and maintenance requirements for relief devices to reduce emissions; expand reporting requirements; and require regulated onshore and offshore gathering lines submit geospatial pipeline location data to the National Pipeline Mapping System (NPMS). PHMSA proposes a six-month effective date for this rulemaking.[29]

---

[25] 49 U.S.C. § 60102(q).
[26] Pipeline Safety: Safety of Gas Gathering Pipelines: Extension of Reporting Requirements, Regulation of Large, High-Pressure Lines, and Other Related Amendments, 86 Fed. Reg. 63, 266 (Nov. 15, 2021).
[27] Pipeline Safety: Gas Pipeline Leak Detection and Repair, 88 Fed. Reg. 31,890 (May 18, 2023) (hereinafter cited as *2023 NPRM*).
[28] *PIPES Act of 2020,* Division R, 134 Stat. 1181, 2210.
[29] *2023 NPRM.*

§ 6.04   ENERGY & MINERAL LAW INSTITUTE

Among other notable features of the proposal, the scope of this NPRM extends beyond the section 113 congressional mandate by including Type C gathering lines, underground natural gas storage facilities, and LNG facilities.[30] The statutory mandate was limited to regulated gathering lines in a Class 2, 3, or 4 location, and new and existing gas transmission and distribution pipelines.[31] The NPRM also includes provisions intended to avoid overlap with existing Environmental Protection Agency (EPA) leak detection and repair (LDAR) regulations at 40 CFR Part 60, Subpart OOOOa, and EPA's proposed regulations that would be codified at 40 CFR Part 60, Subparts OOOOb and OOOOc.[32] The scope of these anti-overlap provisions is unclear, and the provisions could prove difficult to implement from a practical perspective.[33]

[a] — Increase Leakage Surveys and Patrols.

With the exception of distribution pipelines located within business districts, PHMSA proposes to increase the frequency of leakage surveys and right-of-way patrols for pipeline facilities and introduces these requirements for Type B and C gathering pipelines.[34] PHMSA proposes that transmission operators conduct right-of-way patrols every 45 days with a minimum of 12 patrols each calendar year.[35] The proposal reflects a significant expansion of the current obligations.

PHMSA proposes to expand the leakage survey obligation to all valves, flanges, meters, regulators, tie-ins, and launcher and receiver facilities.[36] Further, the NPRM would restrict leakage surveys that exclusively use human senses to offshore pipelines below the waterline, or, with the prior approval of PHMSA, onshore transmission and gathering lines located outside of high

---

[30] *Id.*
[31] *PIPES Act of 2020*, § 113.
[32] *2023 NPRM*, at 31938-39.
[33] *Id.*
[34] *Id* at 31972.
[35] *Id.* at 31974.
[36] *Id.* at 31975.

consequence areas or in Class 1 or 2 locations.[37] For all other leakage surveys, an operator must deploy leak detection technologies that meet PHMSA's proposed detection sensitivity requirements.[38] The proposed frequencies for the leakage surveys vary based on the type and location of the pipeline, valve, flange, tie-in or launcher and receiver facility.

[b] — Development of Advanced Leak Detection Programs.

PHMSA proposes to require that operators develop a written Advanced Leak Detection Program (ALDP).[39] Operators would need to develop procedures that specify how they intend to perform leakage surveys, as well as pinpoint and investigate leaks. Among other requirements, operators would need to identify the leak detection technology they intend to use in their programs after considering several prescribed factors, and an operator's ALDP must select a leak detection device that is capable of detecting and pinpointing all leaks that have a sufficient release rate to produce a reading of five parts per million when measured from a distance of 5 feet or less from the pipeline or within a wall-to-wall paved area.[40] It is not clear whether this leak detection device sensitivity threshold is practicable or consistent with existing EPA LDAR regulations.

[c] — Leak Grade and Repair Requirements.

PHMSA proposes stringent leak grade and repair regulations that would require operators to classify and repair all detected leaks on their pipeline systems. Operators would need to determine whether detected leaks qualify as grade 1 (most severe), grade 2, or grade 3 (least severe) based on pre-defined narrative criteria or specified percentages of the lower explosive limit (LEL).[41] A grade 2 leak would need to be repaired within 6 months of detection, but an operator must also re-evaluate the leak every 30 days until

---

[37] *Id.* at 31974, 31977.
[38] *Id.* at 31963.
[39] *Id.* at 31978.
[40] *Id.*
[41] *Id.*

§ 6.04   ENERGY & MINERAL LAW INSTITUTE

the repair is complete.[42] In addition, an operator would be required to develop procedures to prioritize grade 2 leak repairs, and a grade 2 leak located on a transmission line or Type A gathering line in a High Consequence Area (HCA), or a Class 3 or 4 location would require repair within 30 days.[43] A grade 3 leak would need to be repaired within 24 months of detection, and re-evaluated every 6 months until the repair is complete, unless the operator replaces the pipeline segment containing the leak within 5 years of detection.[44] The proposal would establish post-repair inspection and leak repair verification requirements, provide for the downgrading and upgrading of leak classifications, and allow an operator to request that PHMSA extend the regulatory deadlines for completing for repairs.[45] PHMSA's proposed leak grading scheme is not an approach adopted by EPA in its LDAR regulations, which generally include a concentration-based leak definition above which a repair is required.

[d] — Exceptions for Compressor Stations.

PHMSA would not apply the proposed leakage survey, patrolling, ALDP, leak grade and repair, and personnel qualification requirements to compressor stations on gas transmission or gathering lines if the compressor station is already subject to the EPA's LDAR standards.[46] More specifically, compressor stations would be exempt from these proposed PHMSA requirements if they are subject to EPA's methane detection monitoring and repair requirements under 40 CFR Part 60, Subparts OOOOa or OOOOb, or relevant standards in an EPA-approved State Plan or Federal Plan that is at least as stringent as EPA's proposed requirements at 40 CFR Part 60, Subpart OOOOc.[47] The EPA "requirements" PHMSA references as being in place under 40 CFR Part 60, Subparts OOOOb and OOOOc are the subject of a proposed rulemaking by EPA, and they have not been promulgated in final

---

[42] *Id.*
[43] *Id.*
[44] *Id.*
[45] *Id.* at 31977.
[46] *Id.* at 31939.
[47] *Id.*

form.[48] Furthermore, EPA's proposed greenhouse gas emission guidelines under 40 CFR Part 60, Subpart OOOOc, if finalized, would generally apply to compressor stations constructed prior to November 15, 2021, but these emission guidelines would be implemented directly by states after what could be a lengthy EPA review and approval process.

[e] — Reporting.

PHMSA is proposing to amend Part 191 to require operators to report estimated emissions attributed to leaks, other estimated emissions from stationary sources, and the number and grade of leaks an operator detects and repairs. PHMSA is also introducing a new large-volume gas release report that would require an operator to report within 30 days an unintentional or intentional release of one million cubic feet or more from a gas pipeline facility.[49] The NPRM would also require operators to submit data about offshore gas gathering lines, and Type A, Type B, and Type C gas gathering lines to the NPMS.[50] This provision exceeds the existing statutory mandate for NPMS.

[f] — Mitigating Emissions from Venting.

To limit methane emissions caused by venting events such as blowdowns and tank boil-off, the NPRM would require operators of gas transmission, Type A gathering, regulated offshore pipelines, and LNG facilities to choose from a list of emission reduction methodologies, such as routing gas to a flare stack or reducing the operating pressure of a line prior to venting.[51] Operators would be required to document the methodologies they choose and describe how the chosen methodologies reduce emissions.

[g] — Design, Configuration, and Maintenance of Pressure Relief Devices.

The NPRM would require a documented engineering analysis to demonstrate that new, replaced, relocated, or otherwise changed pressure

---

[48] *Id.*
[49] *Id.* at 31955, 31967, 31972.
[50] *Id.*
[51] *Id.* at 31979.

§ 6.04

relief and limiting devices on Part 192-regulated pipelines have been designed and configured to minimize unnecessary releases of gas.[52] Operators must also develop operations and maintenance procedures to assess pressure relief devices as well as procedures to provide for the repair or replacement of the devices, if necessary.

[h] — Qualifications.

The NPRM would require personnel that conduct leakage surveys, leak grading, and leak investigations on certain facilities to be operator qualified under Part 192, subpart N.[53]

[i] — LNG Facilities.

PHMSA proposes to require operators to conduct quarterly leakage surveys of equipment or components at LNG facilities that contain methane or LNG.[54] The surveys would require use of leak detection equipment capable of detecting a methane leak that produces a reading of at least 5 parts per million when located within 5 feet of the equipment being surveyed.[55] PHMSA would require LNG facility operators to develop procedures to eliminate leaks and minimize releases of gas, conduct leak surveys and address any methane leaks according to their maintenance procedures or abnormal operating procedures.[56] PHMSA also proposes that LNG operators adopt blowdown and boiloff emission reduction methodologies from a PHMSA-proposed list. PHMSA's list includes use of a flare or isolation of smaller piping segments, but also would allow operators to propose their own "alternative method," if the operator can demonstrate it would reduce emissions by 50 percent as compared to taking no emission mitigation measures.[57]

---

[52] *Id.*
[53] *Id.* at 31978.
[54] *Id.* at 31932, 31979.
[55] *Id.* at 31979.
[56] *Id.*
[57] *Id.*

[j] — Underground Natural Gas Storage Facilities.

The NPRM proposes to amend Sec. 192.12(c) to require operator procedural manuals to include procedures for eliminating leaks and minimizing releases of gas from storage facilities.[58]

[2] — Comments on the May 2023 Proposed Rule on LDAR

All NPRMs are required to be open for public comment.[59] The public can comment on anything in an NPRM, including any analyses the agency has prepared for the proposal (i.e., risk assessment and economic analysis.)[60] Comments on the May 2023 NPRM were originally due by July 17, 2023. PHMSA received requests to extend the comment period and thus extended the deadline to August 16, 2023. Since the release of the NPRM, almost 35,000 comments have been submitted.

[3] — Next Steps.

Now that the deadline for public comment has passed, GPAC will meet to review the comments received and analyze them to decide whether to proceed with the proposed rulemaking, issue a new or modified proposal, or withdraw the proposal. GPAC will hold a public meeting the from November 27, 2023, to December 1, 2023, to discuss the NPRM. Thereafter, public comments on the proceedings of the GPAC meeting must be submitted by January 5, 2024. Following the GPAC meeting, PHMSA will evaluate the GPAC's recommendations and, if appropriate, develop a final rule for review by the Secretary of Transportation and OMB. After that review is complete, PHMSA can publish a final rule that addresses the comments received and relevant information from the GPAC meeting report. That final rule, which is expected to be issued sometime in 2024, could then be subject to further administrative or judicial review.

---

[58] *Id.* at 31973.
[59] 49 C.F.R. § 190.317-323.
[60] The U.S. Department of Transportation provides guidance on how the public can provide effective comments. *See* https://www.transportation.gov/regulations/guidance.

Chapter 7

Who Owns the Pore Space? A State-by-State Overview of Pore Space Ownership for Geological Carbon Capture, Utilization, and Storage

Ryan Haddad
Lucas Liben
Simone Senior
Reed Smith, LLP
Pittsburgh, Pennsylvania[1]

Synopsis

§ 7.01.	Introduction	137
§ 7.02.	The "American Rule"	138
§ 7.03.	The "English Rule"	141
§ 7.04.	Undecided Jurisdictions...	141
§ 7.05.	Conclusion	146

§ 7.01. Introduction.

Geological carbon capture, utilization, and storage (CCUS) is the process of capturing and removing carbon-dioxide (CO_2) from emission sources or the Earth's atmosphere and storing it in subsurface geological formations.[2] When such geological formations are depleted of their natural gas and other fossil fuels, "pore space" remains.[3] Pore space is the microscopic space between sand, rock, and other sediment into which captured CO_2 can be injected and stored for permanent sequestration or future use and

---

[1] Ryan Haddad, Lucas Liben, and Simone Senior are energy and natural resources attorneys at Reed Smith LLP.
[2] *What's the Difference between Geological and Biologic Carbon Sequestration?* UNITED STATES GEOLOGICAL SURVEY, U.S. DEP'T OF THE INTERIOR, https://www.usgs.gov/faqs/whats-difference-between-geologic-and-biologic-carbon-sequestration.
[3] *Pore Space*, SCIENCEDIRECT, https://www.sciencedirect.com/topics/earth-and-planetary-sciences/pore-space.

distribution.[4] CCUS presents stakeholders with a fundamental question: who owns the rights to the pore space?

This chapter provides an overview of each state's position on pore space ownership according to applicable case law and legislation. As summarized below in Part II and Part III, certain states follow the majority, "American Rule", holding that the surface owner owns the rights to the pore space, while other states follow the minority, "English Rule", under which the mineral owner possesses the right to the pore space. Part IV discusses the states that have conflicting case law on pore space ownership, states that have proposed legislation on pore space ownership which was subsequently defeated, and states that have not yet directly addressed pore space ownership in case law or legislation.

§ 7.02. The "American Rule."

The American Rule — providing that pore space is owned by the surface owner — is currently the majority rule within the United States. The following ten states have codified the American Rule by enacting legislation establishing, or creating a presumption, that pore space is owned by the surface owner: California,[5] Indiana,[6] Kentucky,[7] Montana,[8] Nebraska,[9]

---

[4] *Id.*

[5] CAL. PUB. RES. CODE § 71462(a) (Deering 2022) ("Title to any geologic storage reservoir is vested in the owner of the overlying surface estate unless it has been severed and separately conveyed.").

[6] IND. CODE 14-39-2-3(b) ("After June 30, 2022, the ownership of pore space is vested in the surface estate of real property that is divided into a surface estate and a mineral estate unless such rights are explicitly acquired by conveyance document").

[7] KY. REV. STAT. ANN. § 353.800(8) (LexisNexis 2011) (Defining "pore space owner" as "the surface owner unless the pore space has been severed from the surface estate, in which case the pore space owner shall include all persons reasonably known to own an interest in the pore space").

[8] MONT. CODE ANN. 82-11-180(3) ("If the ownership of the geologic storage reservoir cannot be determined from the deeds or severance documents related to the property by reviewing statutory or common law, it is presumed that the surface owner owns the geologic storage reservoir.").

[9] NEB. REV. STAT. § 57-1604(1) ("Title to any reservoir estate underlying the surface of lands and waters is vested in the owner of the overlying surface estate unless it has been severed and separately conveyed.").

North Dakota,[10] Oklahoma,[11] Utah,[12] West Virginia,[13] and Wyoming.[14] Two states, Illinois[15] and New York,[16] have proposed, but not yet passed, legislation adopting the American Rule. Illinois courts have not directly addressed the ownership of pore space, however, certain case law described below in Louisiana, Michigan, New Mexico,[17] New York, and South Dakota suggest that courts in these states generally follow the American Rule.

The United States District Court for the Western District of Louisiana has held that a surface owner owns the pore space, stating that "[w]hether a state is governed by an 'ownership' or 'nonownership' theory of mineral rights, the mineral owner cannot be considered to have ownership of the subsurface estate containing the spaces where the minerals are found."[18]

---

[10] N.D. Cent. Code § 47-31-02 ("Title to pore space in all strata underlying the surface of lands and waters is vested in the owner of the overlying surface estate.")

[11] Okla. Stat. tit. 60 § 6 (2023) ("[P]ore space is real property and, until title to the pore space or rights, interests or estates in the pore space are separately transferred, pore space is property of the person or persons holding title to the land surface above it.")

[12] Utah Code Ann. § 40-6-20.5 (LexisNexis 2022) ("Title to pore space underlying the surface estate is vested in the owner of the surface estate.")

[13] W. Va. Code § 22-11B-18(a), (d) (2022) ("Title to pore space in all strata underlying the surface of lands and waters is vested in the owner of the overlying surface estate" and "there shall be a rebuttable presumption that for all transactions prior to the effective date of this article, that the pore space remains vested with the surface owner unless there was a clear and unambiguous reservation, conveyance, and/or severance of the pore space from the surface upon the face of the instruments.")

[14] Wyo. Stat. Ann. § 34-1-152 (2023), effective July 1, 2023 ("The ownership of all pore space in all strata below the surface lands and waters of this state is declared to be vested in the several owners of the surface above the strata.")

[15] H.B. 3119, 103 Gen. Assemb., Reg. Sess. (Ill. 2023) ("Title to pore space is vested in the surface owner of the overlying surface estate.")

[16] S.B. 10971, 2010 Leg. (N.Y. 2010) ("The ownership of all pore space in all strata below the surface lands and waters . . . is declared to be vested in the several owners of the surface above the strata."). According to the New York State Senate archives, this bill has not had any activity since being referred to the Environmental Conservation in May 2010, available at https://www.nysenate.gov/legislation/bills/2009/a10971/amendment/original.

[17] In 2010, New Mexico proposed, but did not pass, legislation that would have followed the American Rule. S.B. 145, 49th Leg. 2nd Sess. (N.M. 2010) ("The ownership of all pore space of this state is vested in the several owners of the overlying surface, unless ownership of the pore space has been previously severed.")

[18] United States v. 43.42 Acres of Land, 520 F. Supp. 1042, 1046 (W.D. La. 1981).

Similarly, the Louisiana Court of Appeals has established that "[s]urface ownership . . . includes the right to the use of the reservoir underlying the [land] for storage purposes."[19]

The Michigan Court of Appeals has held that "the storage space, once it has been evacuated of minerals and gas, belongs to the surface owner."[20]

The Supreme Court of New Mexico has held that the mineral estate is limited to the rights to "explore for, discover, develop, and remove oil and gas" and does not include the rights to the "solids of the earth":

> [while] the right . . . to explore for, discover, develop, and remove oil and gas[] conveys an interest in real estate, it does not convey a greater interest in the soil, except the oil and gas, than to enable the owner of the lease to use the soil in carrying out and availing the leases of the above-named rights. . . . The lessee is not the owner of the solids of the earth . . . He, at most, is the owner of the oil and gas, in place, and merely has the right to use the solid portion so far as necessary to bore for, discover, and bring to the surface the oil and gas.[21]

The Appellate Division of the Supreme Court of New York held that a surface owner's grant of the right to extract minerals "cannot be construed to include the right to store gas piped in from foreign fields," as storage rights should remain with the grantor, surface owner when not explicitly conveyed.[22] Further, the United States Court of Appeals for the Second Circuit found that a mineral owner, the grantee of a conveyance of salt mines, held title only to the salt and not the excavation cavity.[23] The court, however, stated that

---

[19] S. Nat.Gas Co. v. Sutton, 406 So. 2d 669, 671 (2d Cir.1981).
[20] Dep't of Transp. v. Goike, 560 N.W.2d 365, 365 (Mich. Ct. App. 1996).
[21] Jones-Noland Drilling Co. v. Bixby, 282 P. 382, 383 (N.M. 1929); *see also A Blueprint for the Regulation of Geologic Sequestration of Carbon Dioxide in New Mexico*, Mark E. Fesmire et. al., N.M. Energy, Mins., Nat. Res. Dep't, Oil Cons. Div., 6 (Dec. 1, 2007) ("Pore space . . . likely belongs not to the mineral interest but to the surface owner, who would have the sole power to grant storage rights for the purpose of sequestering carbon dioxide").
[22] Miles v. Home Gas Co., 35 A.D.2d 1042, 1043 (N.Y. App. Div. 1970); 358 N.Y.S.2d 846 (Sup. Ct. 1974); 364 N.Y.S.2d 213 (App. Div. 1975).
[23] Int'l Salt Co. v. Geostow, 878 F.2d 570, 574-75, 577 (2d Cir. 1989).

the mineral owner "has the exclusive right to the use and enjoyment of an excavated cavity so long as the mine has not been exhausted or abandoned."[24]

The United States District Court for the District of South Dakota also held in favor of the American Rule in a case involving surface owner plaintiffs: "[t]he pore space beneath [the plaintiffs'] property belongs to [the plaintiffs'] surface estate in the same manner that all the non-mineral material beneath the physical boundaries of [the plaintiffs'] property belongs to [the plaintiffs'] surface estate."[25] The court reasoned that because the plaintiffs "did not specifically reserve ownership of the pore space or other non-mineral interests" and "only reserved the minerals themselves as well as the right to explore for and develop those minerals" in the warranty deed at issue, they retained ownership of the pore space as the surface owners.[26]

§ 7.03. The "English Rule."

The English Rule — providing that pore space is owned by the mineral owner — is currently the minority rule within the United States. The rule is derived from the British Commonwealth and is commonly used in the United Kingdom, Canada, and Australia, where the respective governments own most mineral rights.[27] The Supreme Court of Alaska has taken a position in favor of the English Rule with respect to state-owned land. That court rejected the American Rule in holding that rights to the pore space at issue "belong to . . . [the] owners of the minerals rather than the city as owner of the surface estate."[28] The court reasoned that (a) the rights at issue were governed by the Alaska Land Act, (b) the Act reserves to Alaska the right to natural resources found in and on the land, and (c) the Act is interpreted

---

[24] *Id.* (emphasis added)
[25] Brown v. Cont'l Res., Inc., 2021 U.S. Dist. LEXIS 252396, *17.
[26] *Id.*
[27] Elizabeth Lokey Aldrich et al., Energy Policy Inst., *Analysis of Existing and Possible Regimes for Carbon Capture and Sequestration: A Review for Policymakers* 17-20 (Apr. 2011), available at https://www.ourenergypolicy.org/wp-content/uploads/2015/06/epi-ccs-pore-space-regimes.pdf.
[28] City of Kenai v. Cook Inlet Nat. Gas Storage Alaska, LLC, 373 P.3d 473, 484 (Alaska 2016).

to apply to pore space storage rights.[29] Other state courts have conflicting rulings for both the American Rule and the English Rule, as described further in Part IV below.

§ 7.04. Undecided Jurisdictions.

The law with respect to pore space ownership is presently undecided in Ohio, Pennsylvania, and Texas, as described below. In addition, the following states have proposed, but subsequently defeated, legislation on pore space ownership and do not currently have case law resolving the issue: Arkansas,[30] Colorado,[31] and Kansas.[32] The remaining twenty-seven states, in addition to the District of Columbia, have not directly addressed pore space ownership in legislation or case law: Alabama, Arizona, Connecticut, Delaware, Florida, Georgia, Hawaii, Idaho, Iowa, Maine, Maryland, Massachusetts, Minnesota, Mississippi, Missouri, Nevada, New Hampshire, New Jersey, North Carolina, Oregon, Rhode Island, South Carolina, Tennessee, Vermont, Virginia, Washington, and Wisconsin.

Columbia Gas Transmission Corp. v. Smail[33] appears to be the most recent Ohio case addressing pore space ownership, decided in 1986. In this case, the District Court for the Northern District of Ohio, while

---

[29] Id. at 480–81, 484; ALASKA STAT. § 38.05.125(a).

[30] In 2011, Arkansas proposed, but did not pass, legislation that would have followed the American Rule, establishing that "a conveyance of the surface ownership of real property may be deemed to be a conveyance of the reservoir and pore space" except in delineated circumstances, such as when the pore space has been previously severed or reserved from the surface ownership. H.B. 1450, 88 Gen. Assemb., Reg. Sess. (Ark. 2011), 15-72-1106(a)(1), available at https://legiscan.com/AR/text/HB1450/2011.

[31] In January 2023, by the direction of Governor Jared Polis, the Colorado Oil & Gas Conservation Commission, Department of Natural Resources, published a legislative proposal, recommending that Colorado legislation "state that the surface owner is the owner of the underlying pore space unless it has been expressly conveyed," available at https://cogcc.state.co.us/documents/library/special_projects/CCUS_Framework_Legislative_Proposal.pdf.

[32] In 2012, Kansas proposed, but did not pass, legislation that would have followed the American Rule, stating that "the ownership of all pore space . . . is declared to be vested in the several owners of the surface above the strata." S.B. 271, (Kan. 2012).

[33] Columbia Gas Transmission Corp. v. Smail, 1986 U.S. Dist. LEXIS 22580, *13 (N.D. Ohio July 18, 1986).

acknowledging that Ohio courts have not explicitly ruled on pore space ownership, "[found] persuasive the rationale ... that one who injects natural gas into storage facilities in the ground does not lose title to the gas when he stores it,"[34] thus suggesting that it favors the American Rule. The case was preceded by a similar Ohio ruling in 1911, holding that a plaintiff who acquired the "right to drill for oil and gas" did not also acquire the "right of storage."[35] Conversely, the Supreme Court of Ohio ruled in 1907 more closely to the English Rule, holding that a "mine owner has the right to use as he may choose, but without injury to the owner of the soil, the space left by excavation of the mineral ... [and] [i]t results from the absolute proprietorship over the mineral in place, that the owner thereof has a like interest in the containing chamber until the termination of the estate."[36] Accordingly, it is unsettled whether Ohio has or will adopt the majority or minority rule with respect to pore space ownership.

Similar to Ohio, Pennsylvania case law does not provide a clear position on pore space ownership. In *U.S. Steel Corp. v. Hoge*,[37] surface owners sold portions of the coal seam underlying their property to United States Steel Corporation (U.S. Steel), while reserving the right to drill and operate through the coal seam to access oil and gas.[38] The surface owners thereafter conveyed this reserved right to Mary Cunningham.[39] After Cunningham began drilling wells to recover coalbed gas from the coal seam, U.S. Steel initiated an action to terminate the drilling and determine the ownership of, and right to develop,

---

[34] Columbia Gas Transmission Corp. v. Smail, 1986 U.S. Dist. LEXIS 22580, *13 (N.D. Ohio July 18, 1986).
[35] Chartiers Oil v. Curtiss, 1911 Ohio Misc. LEXIS 241, at *9-10 (Ohio Misc. 1911) ("It follows that the plaintiff has the right to drill for oil and gas upon the lands of the defendants described in the petition, together with such right of ingress and egress upon the surface of said lands as may be necessary for that purpose ... [i]t ought not, however, have a right of storage upon this tract, other than as may be incidental to the immediate production and marketing of oil, as it has other adjacent lands on which such right of storage exists.").
[36] Moore v. Indian Camp Coal Co., 80 N.E. 6, 8 (Ohio 1907).
[37] U.S. Steel Corp. v. Hoge, 468 A.2d 1380 (Pa. 1983).
[38] U.S. Steel Corp. v. Hoge, 468 A.2d 1380, 1381-82 (Pa. 1983).
[39] *Id.* at 1382.

the coalbed gas.[40] The Supreme Court of Pennsylvania ultimately found that even though the language of the conveyance to Cunningham generally included the right to drill through the coal seam for oil and gas, the court found it "inconceivable that the parties intended a reservation of all types of gas" because, at that time, coalbed gas was "only a waste product with well-known dangerous propensities."[41] Further, the court stated that "as a general rule, subterranean gas is owned by whoever has title to the property in which the gas is resting."[42] The *Hoge* ruling appears to mirror the principles of the English Rule, however, it is unclear how Pennsylvania courts would apply *Hoge* to the issue of pore space ownership.

The American Rule is reflected in a 1990 decision by the Superior Court of Pennsylvania. In *Pomposini v. T.W. Phillips Gas & Oil Co.*,[43] the court held that the surface estate retains the right to natural gas storage unless the oil and gas lease explicitly conveys such right to another party.[44] The court reasoned that "the right to extract gas did not include the right to use the cavernous spaces owned by the lessor for the storage of gas in the absence of an express agreement therefor."[45] A nineteenth century decision by the Supreme Court of Pennsylvania also supports the American Rule, indicating that there is a general principle in Pennsylvania that "[t]he ownership of the surface carries with it, if there is no obstacle to the application of the general rule, title downwards to the center of the earth and upwards indefinitely."[46]

In November 2022, Pennsylvania Senator Gene Yaw proposed the enactment of the "Carbon Dioxide Geologic Sequestration Primacy Act," intending to create Pennsylvania-specific legislation around the legal and regulatory ramifications of CCUS.[47] Senator Yaw stated that the proposed

---

[40] *Id.*
[41] *Id.* at 1384-85.
[42] *Id.* at 1383.
[43] Pomposini v. T.W. Phillips Gas & Oil Co., 580 A.2d 776 (Pa. Super. Ct. 1990).
[44] *See* Pomposini v. T.W. Phillips Gas & Oil Co., 580 A.2d 776, 778-79 (Pa. Super. Ct. 1990).
[45] *Id.*
[46] Delaware & H. Canal Co. v. Hughes, 183 Pa. 66, 68.
[47] S.B. 1361, 2022 Gen. Assemb., Reg. Sess. (Pa. 2022).

legislation would "designate property rights around storage sites in deep geologic formations."[48] The legislation has not yet been enacted, however it illustrates potential movement towards solidifying Pennsylvania's position on pore space ownership.

The most recent litigation in Texas on the issue, *Myers-Woodward, LLC v. Underground Services Markham, LLC*,[49] decided in June 2022, held in favor of the American Rule—that pore space belongs to the surface estate owner.[50] The matter was subsequently appealed to the Supreme Court of Texas and is currently pending before the court. Prior Texas cases have similarly supported the American Rule while others have leaned toward the English Rule.

For example, in 1969, the United States Court of Claims in *Emeny v. United States*[51] held in favor of the American Rule, finding that the surface owner retained rights to the pore space.[52] Applying Texas law, the court held that "the property of the respective landowners . . . included the geological structures beneath the surface, including any such structure that might be suitable for the underground storage of 'foreign' or 'extraneous' gas produced elsewhere."[53] In 1974, the Supreme Court of Texas pointed to *Emeny* as a supporting citation when holding that the defendant, surface owner "owns the lands in fee simple, and this includes not only the surface and mineral estates, but also the matrix of the underlying earth, i.e., the reservoir storage space, subject only to the reserved right of the [plaintiffs] to the payment

---

[48] Memorandum, from Senator Gene Yaw, dated March 30, 2022, regarding Pennsylvania Geologic Storage of Carbon Dioxide Act, available at https://www.legis.state.pa.us/cfdocs/Legis/CSM/showMemoPublic.cfm?chamber=S&SPick=20210&cosponId=37118.
[49] Myers-Woodward, LLC v. Underground Servs. Markham, LLC, 2022 Tex. App. LEXIS 4082, *28.
[50] Myers-Woodward, LLC v. Underground Servs. Markham, LLC, 2022 Tex. App. LEXIS 4082, *28-29 (stating that, "we decline to follow *Mapco* in this case. . . . we conclude that as a matter of law, as the surface owner, Myers owns the subsurface of the property, including the caverns at issue here.").
[51] Emeny v. United States, 412 F.2d 1319 (Ct. Cl. 1969).
[52] Emeny v. United States, 412 F.2d 1319, 1323 (Ct. Cl. 1969).
[53] *Id.* at 1323.

§ 7.05   ENERGY & MINERAL LAW INSTITUTE

of royalties on minerals that are produced and saved."[54] Other cases have positively cited Emeny, such as a 2013 Texas Court of Appeals case, holding that "ownership of the hydrocarbons [residing within the pore space] does not give the mineral owner ownership of the earth surrounding those substances."[55] On the other hand, a 1991 Texas Court of Appeals holding appears to be in favor of the English Rule. In *Mapco, Inc. v. Carter*,[56] the court confirmed that Texas "follow[s] the rule of law that mineral owners retain and still possess and own an ownership interest after the underground storage facility has been constructed and completed or the stratum depleted. These mineral owners are vested with ownership and title rights, including compensation for the use of the cavern."[57]

§ 7.05.   Conclusion.

Pore space ownership proves to be a developing area of law with varying positions on the subject. In summary, ten states have codified the American Rule (California, Indiana, Kentucky, Montana, Nebraska, North Dakota, Oklahoma, Utah, West Virginia, and Wyoming); Illinois and New York have proposed, but not yet passed, legislation adopting the American Rule; and courts in Louisiana, Michigan, New Mexico, and New York generally follow the American Rule. The Supreme Court of Alaska has ruled in favor of the English Rule, while Ohio, Pennsylvania, South Dakota, and Texas have not taken a clear position on pore space ownership. Arkansas, Colorado, and Kansas have proposed, but subsequently defeated, legislation on pore space ownership and do not currently have case law resolving the issue. Lastly,

---

[54]   Humble Oil & Ref. Co. v. West, 508 S.W.2d 812, 815 (Tex. 1974).
[55]   Springer Ranch, Ltd. v. Jones, 421 S.W.3d 273, 283 (Tex. App. 2013) (*citing Emeny*, 412 F.2d at 1319). *See also* FPL Farming, Ltd. v. Tex. Natural Res. Conservation Comm'n, No. 03-02-00477-CV, 2003 Tex. App. LEXIS 1074, at *10 (Tex. App. Feb. 6, 2003) (noting that the court was "assuming without deciding" that the surface owner owned the subsurface space at issue).
[56]   Mapco, Inc. v. Carter, 808 S.W.2d 262, 277 (Tex. App.), *rev'd on other grounds*, 817 S.W.2d 686 (Tex. 1991).
[57]   Mapco, Inc. v. Carter, 808 S.W.2d 262, 277 (Tex. App.), *rev'd on other grounds*, 817 S.W.2d 686 (Tex. 1991).

the remaining twenty-seven states, in addition to the District of Columbia, have not directly addressed pore space ownership in legislation or case law: Alabama, Arizona, Connecticut, Delaware, Florida, Georgia, Hawaii, Idaho, Iowa, Maine, Maryland, Massachusetts, Minnesota, Mississippi, Missouri, Nevada, New Hampshire, New Jersey, North Carolina, Oregon, Rhode Island, South Carolina, Tennessee, Vermont, Virginia, Washington, and Wisconsin.

Chapter 8

MSHA and OSHA Safety Enforcement in the Biden Administration: What's Changing and Where Are We Headed in Enforcement?

Mark E. Heath
Spilman, Thomas & Battle PLLC
Charleston, West Virginia

Chris Petersen
Fisher & Phillips LLP
Denver, Colorado

Synopsis

§ 8.01.	Introduction 151
§ 8.02.	What to Expect from MSHA in 2023: An Employer's Guide to Developments in Workplace Safety 151
	[1] — Increased Penalties 151
	[2] — Special Assessments Return with Significant Use 151
	[3] — Special Investigations Are Rising to Levels Under Previous Democratic Administrations 152
	[4] — Pattern of Violations Are Back 154
	[a] — Why Increased Use of Pattern of Violation Is a Serious Concern 154
	[5] — Impact Inspections Returned in January 2023 155
	[a] — One Potential Issue with Impact Inspections 156
	[6] — New Regulations 156
	[7] — Global Settlements Return? 156
	[8] — Issues at the Federal Mine Safety Health and Review Commission 157
	[a] — Settlement Approvals.. 157
	[b] — How the Mine Act Addresses Settlements 157
	[i] — Past Practice 157
	[c] — Current Appeals 158
	[d] — Where Are We Headed? 160
	[e] — Future Impacts? 160
	[f] — What Can Companies Do Now? 161
	[9] — OSHA vs. MSHA Jurisdiction: Still an Issue 161
	[a] — MSHA Jurisdiction 161
	[b] — OSHA and OSH Act Overview 161

	[i] — Key Enforcement Differences	162
	[c] — Memorandum of Understanding of 1979 Between MSHA and OSHA	162
	[d] — *Maxxim Rebuild Co. v. FMSHRC*	162
	[e] — *KC Transport, Inc. v. WEVA*	163
	[f] — What Should Employers Do to Address the Issue?	164
	[10] — Status of Commission and Vote Swings	264
§ 8.03.	**What to Expect from OSHA in 2023: An Employer's Guide to Developments in Workplace Safety**	**165**
	[1] — What to Expect from OSHA in 2023	165
	[2] — OSHA's Offcial 2023 Agenda	165
	[a] — Prevention of Workplace Violence in Health Care and Social Assistance	165
	[b] — Heat Illness in Prevention in Outdoor and Indoor Work Settings	165
	[c] — Infectious Disease	166
	[d] — Occupational Exposure to COVID-19 in Healthcare Settings	166
	[e] — Improve Tracking of Workplace Injuries and Illnesses	166
	[f] — Worker Walkaround Representative Designation Process	166
	[g] — Lock Out/Tag Out Update	167
	[3] — New Head of the Department of Labor	167
	[4] — OIRA Now Pro-Regulation	167
	[5] — A New Urgency- Resorting to Regulatory Mode	168
	[6] — OSHA and Clouds in the Economic Horizon	168
	[a] — The Heat Standard	169
	[b] — OSHA Updates HazCom Standard	169
	[c] — OSHA Updates to the PSM Standard	170
	[d] — Healthcare COVID-19 Rule	170
	[i] — Increasing Infections	170
	[ii] — Coverage Concerns	171
	[iii] — Potentially Illegal	172
	[e] — A New Infectious Disease Standard	172
	[7] — Expect to Be Inspected	173
	[a] — Instance-by-Instance Citations	174
	[i] — Grouping Will Be Discouraged to Inspection Procedures	176
	[b] — The Fairfax Memo — Changes to Inspection	176
	[i] — Revisiting 'Fairfax Memo'	177

[ii] — Who Gets Say 177
[iii] — Defending the Policy 178
[c] — Beware Agency Sharing 178

§ 8.01. Introduction.

As we are now several years into the Biden Administration, it is apparent there has been a consistent tightening of enforcement by both Occupational Safety and Health Administration (OSHA) and the Mine Safety and Health Administration (MSHA), with incremental changes taking place across the enforcement tools of both agencies. Some increased enforcement activity has been the statutory adjustment of penalties, the increased use of Section 110(c) individual penalties and application of some standards not focused on during the Trump Administration. This chapter looks at some the changes that have occurred, their impact on companies and employees and where we are likely headed.

§ 8.02. What to Expect from MSHA in 2023: An Employer's Guide to Developments in Workplace Safety.

[1] — Increased Penalties.

As an operation of statute, MSHA penalties have increased. The maximum for citations and orders is now $85,580. Flagrant orders are now $313,790. Failure to correct orders have risen to $9,271. Possession of smoking materials underground is $391. Orders are now a minimum of $2,853 and 104(b) orders are $5,703 minimum.[1]

[2] — Special Assessments Return with Significant Use.

Common from 2008-2016, MSHA is returning to the use of Special Assessments for serious paper, particularly those related to fatalities. By using a special assessment, penalties can go to the maximum limits when not justified under the points table. For instance, a citation issued under Section

---

[1] Federal Civil Penalties Inflation Adjustment Act Annual Adjustments for 2023 (final rule), 88 Fed. Reg. 2210 (published January 13, 2023).

104(d)1 of the Federal Mine Safety and Health Act of 1977 could be $30,000 in a regular assessment based on points only. The special assessment process allows the agency to use the facts of the accident to increase penalties, often to the statutory maximum of $85,580 per citation or order.

Recently, in a fatality from the last two years – one order on points totaled the max of $85,580 and the second order was then specially assessment at $85,580. The two orders from the fatal then totaled $171,160. The operators only choice to challenge these penalties is to appeal the assessment to get a hearing before a Federal Mine Safety and Health Review Commission (FMSHRC or Commission) administrative law judge.

[3] — Special Investigations Are Rising to Levels Under Previous Democratic Administrations.

Special Investigations are trending up along with individual penalties against agents of the operator – typically superintendents, foremen, electricians and other examiners. Special Investigations generally follow agency increases in issuing serious paper. In the last two years, the number of special investigations have increased. They had declined in the Trump Administration.

Further, when the agency does seek penalties against individuals under Section 110(c) of the Federal Mine Safety and Health Act of 1977, the amount of the penalties have increased. In one recent case involving a superintendent, 110(c) penalties totaled $9,200 for two orders.

A recent MSHA press release shows how all these enforcement trends work together:

US Department of Labor finds Illinois mine operator tried to conceal underground fire, endangered miners, misled probe; proposes nearly $1.2M in civil penalties[2]

---

[2] Press Release, U.S. Dep't of Labor, US Department of Labor finds Illinois mine operator tried to conceal underground fire, endangered miners, misled probe; proposes nearly $1.2M in civil penalties (June 17, 2022) (available at https://www.dol.gov/newsroom/releases/msha/msha20220617#:~:text=MSHA%20cited%20the%20operator%20for,on%20the%20morning%20of%20Aug).

MSHA finds M-Class Mining didn't tell miners of a dangerous fire hazard, continued operations MSHA News Release Posted: [June 17, 2022]

WASHINGTON – The U.S. Department of Labor's Mine Safety and Health Administration has proposed nearly $1.2 million in civil penalties to M-Class Mining LLC, a Macedonia, Illinois, coal mine operator. MSHA cited the operator for continuing to operate the mine without evacuating miners with a fire underground and failing to notify MSHA of the fire. The fire broke out on a longwall section on Aug. 13, 2021.

Late on the morning of Aug. 14, 2021, after learning of the unextinguished fire through an anonymous complaint, MSHA issued an order to withdraw all miners from the mine and began an accident investigation. The investigation found that the operator allowed continued coal production and did not take immediate actions to protect the safety and health of miners.

Specifically, MSHA inspectors determined M-Class Mining LLC failed to follow the approved Mine Emergency Evacuation and Firefighting Program and evacuate the miners; did not notify MSHA within 15 minutes of the fire's start as the law requires; and failed to fully comply with federal orders to withdraw miners from the mine.

M-Class Mining LLC deliberately jeopardized the lives of the very miners it was responsible for protecting, and violated numerous important safety and health standards in the process," said Assistant Secretary for Mine Safety and Health Chris Williamson. "The fact that this operator continued business as usual while miners underground had no idea there was an ongoing fire hazard more than justifies the civil penalties that we propose." MSHA issued 14 citations to the M-Class mine, including 10 related to the operator's reckless disregard for the

§ 8.02   ENERGY & MINERAL LAW INSTITUTE

miners' safety and health. Two of the 10 proposed citations are flagrant: for the operator not evacuating the mine when the fire was located, and for allowing miners to work underground without being tracked by the mine tracking system. A flagrant violation may be assessed the highest penalty allowed by law.

MSHA has assessed $1,165,396 in proposed penalties for the violations.

[4] — Pattern of Violations Are Back.

Under 30 CFR 104, MSHA can identify mine operators alleged to have a recurring pattern of Significant and Substantial (S&S) violations.[3] Pattern of Violations was in the original Mine Act but was not used by MSHA until the early 2000s. Use of this tool dropped off under the Trump Administration. During those four years, no new mines were placed on pattern status.

Based on a formula that keys on S&S violations, a pattern order requires the shut down of production in areas covered by the Pattern Order until the citation or order is abated and MSHA releases the site.

There are now two mines under Pattern orders.[4]

[a] — Why Increased Use of Pattern of Violation Is a Serious Concern.

If a mine receives notice of a Pattern of Violations (POV) and subsequently receives additional S&S violations, federal law allows MSHA to withdraw miners from the affected area except those necessary to correct the violation. An operator can be removed from Section 104(e) sanctions if no S&S violations are found within 90 days of the POV notice's issuance.

---

[3] *Pattern of Violation*, MINE SAFETY AND HEALTH ADMINISTRATION, https://www.msha.gov/compliance-and-enforcement/pattern-violations-pov.

[4] Press Release, U.S. Dep't of Labor, US Department of Labor issues Pattern of Violations notice to Morton Salt Inc., Weeks Island Mine and Mill in Louisiana, citing safety concerns (December 2, 2022) (available at https://www.dol.gov/newsroom/releases/msha/msha20221202).

Following that, a POV designation can be terminated after a full inspection of the entire mine results in no S&S violations.

MSHA offers two online calculators to help mine operators monitor compliance, including the Pattern of Violations Calculator,[5] which allows mine operators to monitor performance under the POV screening criteria and alerts mine operators that corrective actions are needed, and the Significant and Substantial Calculator,[6] which enables mine operators to monitor their S&S violations. It is the responsibility of mine operators to track their violation and injury histories to determine whether they need to take action to avoid triggering a POV notice.

[5] — Impact Inspections Returned in January 2023.

MSHA initiated impact inspections in April 2010 after the explosion at the Upper Big Branch Mine in West Virginia claimed the lives of 29 miners.[7] From March 2020 through December 2022, MSHA stated it conducted targeted inspections at mines that warranted additional enforcement activity.

MSHA resumed conducting regular monthly impact inspections in January 2023 and is publishing the results on its website.[8] The agency also issues press releases which are then picked up by the media.[9]

---

[5] *POV Calculator*, MINE SAFETY AND HEALTH ADMINISTRATION, https://www.msha.gov/data-and-reports/data-sources-and-calculators/pov-calculator

[6] *S&S Calculator*, MINE SAFETY AND HEALTH ADMINISTRATION https://www.msha.gov/data-and-reports/data-sources-and-calculators/ss-calculator.

[7] Impact inspections are separate from the mandatory regular inspection program, and focus on mines that meet several factors such as a pattern of violations or a history of Significant and Substantial violations at inspection. *See Sam Creasey, Why We Use Impact Inspections to Protect Miners* https://blog.dol.gov/2023/10/04/why-we-use-impact-inspections-to-protect-miners, U.S. DEPARTMENT OF LABOR BLOG, October 4, 2023, https://blog.dol.gov/2023/10/04/why-we-use-impact-inspections-to-protect-miners.

[8] https://www.msha.gov/monthly-impact-inspection-results.

[9] *See, e.g.*, Press Release, U.S. Dep't of Labor, US Department of Labor announces findings of impact inspections at US mines with histories of repeated health or safety violations (March 28, 2023) (available at https://www.dol.gov/newsroom/releases/msha/msha20230328).

[a] — One Potential Issue with Impact Inspections.

In the past, when a district did not have a mine that qualified for an impact inspection, the district was required to pick one mine for a visit. This meant when the results were released publicly, it appeared a mine that did not require an impact inspection had compliance issues. It remains to see how this will work in the new system of impact inspections.

[6] — New Regulations.

MSHA is considering a number of new regulations.

A silica regulation is on its way. The current MSHA silica standard is 100. OSHA standard is fifty. We are likely to see a MSHA standard for silica of fifty. The regulatory process started in 2019 and finished with the Notice of Proposed Rule Making in September 2023.[10]

Powered Haulage updates were issued in the fall of 2023.[11] Study of respirable coal mine dust rule; testing, evaluation and approval of electric motor driven mine equipment and accessories (Part 18); and exposures to diesel exhaust remain under consideration.[12]

[7] — Global Settlements Return?

Global settlements were common in 2010s and have gotten little attention since. A new settlement recently raised the issue, but it is not known if this is a one-time event.[13]

---

[10] Press Release, U.S. Dep't of Labor, Federal judge orders Blackhawk Mining, subsidiaries to pay $349K in penalties to resolve more than 530 violations (February 15, 2023)(available at https://www.dol.gov/newsroom/releases/sol/sol20230215#:~:text=WASHINGTON%20%E2%80%93%20A%20federal%20administrative%20law,inspectors%20identified%20at%2014%20mines).

[11] Safety Program for Surface Mobile Equipment (Final Rule), 88 Fed. Reg. 87904 (issued December 20, 2023).

[12] *See* MSHA.gov website for all regulatory changes under consideration.

[13] Press Release, U.S. Dep't of Labor, Federal judge orders Blackhawk Mining, subsidiaries to pay $349K in penalties to resolve more than 530 violations (February 15, 2023)(available at https://www.dol.gov/newsroom/releases/sol/sol20230215#:~:text=WASHINGTON%20%E2%80%93%20A%20federal%20administrative%20law,inspectors%20identified%20at%2014%20mines).

[8] — Issues at the Federal Mine Safety Health and Review Commission.

There are several key issues under review at FMSHRC, although a 2-2 tie in Commission members is likely slowing down the process.

[a] — Settlement Approvals.

Issues continue to arise on who controls settlements – the Commission administrative law judges (ALJs) or the parties – MSHA and the mining operator or individual respondent.

In most cases, ALJs have traditionally approved the settlement between the parties. That is changing with multiple ALJs requiring the parties to submit multiple motions, each with additional information, trying to convince the ALJ that the settlement should be approved. In eight plus cases, the ALJs have refused and the cases are before the commission. None have been argued to date. Decisions are likely in next 18 months. Decisional meetings on the first two were held on May 14, 2024.

[b] — How the Mine Act Addresses Settlements.

Section 110(k) of the Federal Mine Safety and Health Act of 1977 provides that "[n]o proposed *penalty* which has been contested before the Commission. . . shall be compromised, mitigated, or settled except with the approval of the Commission."[14] This has been a fairly stable area of the law, with only occasional disputes in significant cases on whether the ALJ had to approve settlement between the parties that modified citations and orders. Generally, some ALJs would request additional information to justify settlements, but most were approved with little questioning.

[i] — Past Practice.

Occasionally, significant cases would result in ALJ questions, but in the end they were approved.

For example, former Chief ALJ at the Commission, Judge Robert Lesnick, now retired, questioned a global settlement of citations from

---

[14] 30 U.S.C. § 820(k) (emphasis added).

§ 8.02   ENERGY & MINERAL LAW INSTITUTE

Aracoma after a 2006 mine fire. He required argument by company counsel and the Solicitor, but the ALJ ultimately approved the monetary reductions that were part of a civil settlement and was also part of a settlement of criminal charges against the company. The ALJ questioned whether MSHA fine was enough and quoted the Chief Executive Officer's salary to questions the reductions. The settlement covered 102 dockets and 1,302 citations. A total of $2.8 million in MSHA fines reduced to $1.7 million.[15]

[c]— Current Appeals.

There are now at least eight appeals before the Commission on settlement authority, who makes the decision, who decides what is significant and substantial and other issues.

Three of the appeals, *Knight Hawk*,[16] *Bluestone*[17] and *Greenbrier Minerals*[18] all look at the ability to remove a significant and substantial designation without ALJ review or approval. Under previous decisions, the Secretary's decisions to designate, or not to designate, a violation as S&S are unreviewable enforcement decisions. Such decisions are not penalties subject to Commission approval under Section 110(k) left entirely to the Secretary's discretion.[19]

Some current ALJs challenge this interpretation of the holding.

In *Knight Hawk Coal*,[20] there are three citations at issue. The Operator agreed to pay a S&S citations on a trailing cable damage. Secretary removed S&S on a zip tie used on connection instead of a bolt and failure to follow roof control plan. Parties submitted motion three times to ALJ and all were denied. The Secretary argued S&S is a special finding not subject to Commission review. Monetary reduction of $2,007 to $137.

---

[15] *See* Aracoma Coal Company, WEVA 2006-654 (Dec. 23, 2008) (Judge Lesnick).
[16] Knight Hawk Coal, LAKE 2021-0160.
[17] Bluestone Oil, WEVA 2022-0176.
[18] Greenbrier Minerals, LLC., WEVA 2022-0294.
[19] Mechanicsvillle, 18 FMSHRC 879-80.
[20] Knight Hawk Coal, LAKE 2021-0160.

SAFETY ENFORCEMENT § 8.02

In *Rulon Harper Coal*,[21] WEST 2022-0249 and 0250, the ALJ denies Secretary's argument it can remove S&S at any time. Parties file amended settlement agreement, denied again. Two settlements denied: $22,134 to $7,227 and $22,944 to $3,936.

In *Greenbrier Minerals, LLC.*, WEVA 2022-0294,[22] there are six citations at issue: two vacated, four settled. Operator agreed to settle four with reduction from 1,960 to $1,213.

In *Bluestone Oil*, WEVA 2022-0176,[23] the ALJ disagreed on withdrawal of S&S and Commission certified review with Knight Hawk.

Showing that work arounds don't always work is *Genesis Alkali*.[24] Judge Miller denies settlement. In middle of different motions to settle, company withdrew appeal of seven citations and the Secretary vacated 18 citations. It did not work. The ALJ treats these developments at as another submission of settlement and denies it. Commission agrees to review.

In *County Line Stone Co.*,[25] *Consol of Pennsylvania Company LLC*[26] and *Ramaco Resources LLC.*,[27] the Secretary sought to vacate citations and asserts its right to do so at any time. The ALJ requires certification from the parties that the dismissals are independent and not related to settlement of other citations in the case.

In *Perry County Resources*,[28] the ALJ rejects settlement of one of five citations reduced to low negligence, $530 to $264. Rest paid as issued.

ALJ demands right to review 104b orders associated with settlement motions before approval. The same issue arose in *Appalachian Resources West Virginia*[29] and is now before the commission.

---

[21] Rulon Harper Coal, WEST 2022-0249 and 0250.
[22] Greenbrier Minerals, LLC., WEVA 2022-0294.
[23] Bluestone Oil, WEVA 2022-0176.
[24] Genesis Alkali, WEST 2022-0189 ALJ.
[25] County Line Stone Co. YORK 2022-0003.
[26] Consol of Pennsylvania Company LLC PENN 2021-0108.
[27] Ramaco Resources LLC, WEVA 2022-0260.
[28] Perry County Resources, KENT 2022-0024.
[29] Appalachian Resources West Virginia WEVA 2022-0301 and WEVA 2022-428.

§ 8.02   ENERGY & MINERAL LAW INSTITUTE

Questions unresolved?
- Where is the line on requests to justify settlements?
- What records requests and review of records can an ALJ make?
- Will ALJs want to review inspector notes?
- In serious cases, would it include state accident reports and citations?
- Special investigation records and statements?
- Company investigations?
- Part 50 records?
- Dust sampling?
- Workers compensation records?

The list is long and complicated.

If relied on by the ALJ, does an appeal of a denial of settlement mean these records are examined by the Commission in the appeal process?

[d] — Where Are We Headed?

Obviously, with the number of decisions on appeal, a number of opinions are about to issue that could radically rewrite the settlement approval process and increase the role and power of ALJs. Ultimately, this could remove power from the operator and Secretary to resolve enforcement at the mine site and give it to the ALJ.

The Secretary can at times reduce violations to change enforcement at a mine or get an agreement of operator to not challenge other citations.

[e] — Future Impacts?

These inquiries for records not normally reviewed are occurring at a time when FMSHRC caseloads, particularly in coal mining, have declined. If the Commission decides the ALJ has broad power to request records for review and has strong powers under Section 110(k) to determine what is an appropriate settlement, how would such a broad and time-consuming process function under heavy caseloads? In 2010-2012, the Commission had caseloads of over 20,000 contests. Settlements were used as a way to quickly clear out smaller cases or those that both sides – company and Solicitor – agreed should be quickly settled. A cumbersome settlement approval process would negate an important tool to control Commission caseloads.

[f] — What Can Companies Do Now?

Document reasons for settlement and paper changes. Go into as much detail as you can. Be prepared to give more information to the ALJ to get approval. That can include explaining the company view on why the incident happened and mitigating circumstances. If can't convince ALJ, could be lengthy process at Commission to get relief. Prepare for real possibility the parties will not control settlements in the future.

Perhaps MSHA could strengthen the 10-day conference process to address concerns when issues are between the agency and operator only. That could include penalty agreements at 10-day conferences.

[9] — OSHA vs. MSHA Jurisdiction: Still an Issue.

MSHA: employers who are engaged in underground and surface mining, related operations, and preparation and milling of the minerals extracted.

OSHA: all employers who engage in business affecting commerce except those employers covered by another federal agency.

[a] — MSHA Jurisdiction,

MSHA covers all mining activity in United States for coal and all other minerals. In coal mining, MSHA jurisdiction begins after initial timbering. Normally commercial timbering well in advance of mining is not covered by MSHA. Development of the mine is MSHA. Reclamation of disturbed area is MSHA. Routine water treatment and monitoring of site after reclamation is completed is likely OSHA. Key issue is: where is that line?

[b] — OSHA and OSH Act Overview.

The Occupational Safety and Health Administration (OSHA) has the authority to create and enforce workplace health and safety standards.[30] OSH Review Commission provides appellate review.

The Act applies to all employers "engaged in a business affecting commerce who has employees, but does not include the United States or

---

[30] 29 U.S.C. § 651 (OSH Act).

§ 8.02   ENERGY & MINERAL LAW INSTITUTE

any state."[31] Act does not apply to employers whose business practices are under the jurisdiction of other Federal agencies

[i] — Key Enforcement Differences.

Inspection scope and frequencies:

MSHA: surface mines no less than two times per year and MSHA: underground mines no less than four times per year.[32]

Many small OSHA operators are never inspected unless a fatal, call-in complaint or serious incident.

[c] — Memorandum of Understanding of 1979 Between MSHA and OSHA.

The 1979 Memorandum of Understanding (MOU) between MSHA and OSHA serves as guidance for determining the jurisdiction of the two agencies. General principle: Unsafe and unhealthful working conditions on mine sites and milling operations, apply Mine Act. When MSHA declines coverage, the issue goes to OSHA.

[d] — *Maxxim Rebuild Co. v. FMSHRC*.[33]

Rebuild Shops refers to a number of repair shops, truck shops off mine sites. Maxxim Rebuild, a subsidiary of Alpha Natural Resources (Alpha), had a rebuild shop adjacent to an Alpha mine in West Virginia and it moved the shop to an abandoned mine site in Kentucky. The shop had not been inspected when it was located in West Virginia. MSHA asserted jurisdiction over the Kentucky shop. Both the ALJ and the Commission upheld jurisdiction.

The Sixth Circuit Court of Appeals reverses, finding the fact the mine needed a repair shop "does not transform the Sidney Shop into a mine anymore than it could have transformed the Jeffrey Company Plant into a mine in the past or a Caterpillar Plant into a mine in the future." This decision

---

[31] 29 C.F.R § 1975.3(d).
[32] 30 U.S.C. 22 § 813.
[33] Maxxim Rebuild Co. v. Fed. Mine Safety & Health Review Comm'n, 848 F.3d 737 (6th Cir. 2017).

162

is only binding in the Sixth Circuit (Ohio, Kentucky, Tennessee, Indiana), but other Circuits can follow it if they want to.

[e] — *KC Transport, Inc. v. WEVA.*[34]

This FMSHRC Decision shows this issue may be coming back into play. In a two to one decision, the Commission, reversing the ALJ, determined a truck yard off mine property and not bonded was not under MSHA jurisdiction and also found no jurisdiction over the trucks.

The inspector was looking to abate violations on a trucking contractor he wrote while trucks were on MSHA covered permits. The inspector goes to a truck yard off permitted property to check the trucks for abatement. He then sees additional alleged violations of MSHA standards in the truck yard off permit. He cites them.

The ALJ states MSHA did not have jurisdiction over the trucks as mobile mine sites, but ruled there was MSHA jurisdiction over the off-permit truck yard.

The Commission disagreed and found no jurisdiction over trucks or worksite. The Secretary appealed the Commission Decision to the DC Circuit Court of Appeals.

In August of 2023, the DC Circuit Court of Appeals in a two to one decision:

1) reversed the Commission opinion finding no jurisdiction; and
2) returned the case to the Commission for examination of whether MSHA jurisdiction could exist on whether a truck or truck shop that is as an operator.[35]

An appeal to the United States Supreme Court is ongoing. With the potential changes in Commission make-up, this issue is likely to return to the Commission.

---

[34] KC Transport v. Secretary of Labor, MSHA, 77 F.4th 1022 (Aug. 1, 2023), rehearing denied, 2023 W.L. 6466441 (Oct. 3, 2023).
[35] KC Transport v. Secretary of Labor, MSHA, 77 F.4th 1022 (Aug. 1, 2023), rehearing denied, 2023 W.L. 6466441 (Oct. 3, 2023).

[f] — What Should Employers Do to Address the Issue?

Conduct a full inventory of all property you own. When were they last inspected by MSHA. If its been several years, is there any active mining or reclamation to be done? If only environmental compliance, its likely OSHA.

Review OSHA requirements for the non- MSHA work sites you own or operate.

[10] — Status of Commission and Vote Swings.

The Commission remains at four members: two from the union/employee perspective and two from the industry perspective. That leaves many cases with a potential tie, in which ALJ decision stands.

The White House makes the nominations. A Commission Clerk did not clear Committee in December 2022, but was re-nominated in 2023. The Senate has not voted on the nomination.

Whoever control White House appoints majority under an unwritten practice. So Democrats typically appoint union background members and Republicans appoint industry attorneys. Commissioners do not have to be a lawyer. Terms run for six years, so majority does not automatically change with new President. From 2017 to August of 2021, it was three to two in favor of the employer, then two to one in favor of the employer until August 31, 2022 when former Chair Art Traynor was not reappointed by the White House and his term expired. Currently it is a two to two tie. Commission will be three to two employer when or if last member is confirmed.

By statute, two Commissioners can grant review, but it takes three members to decide a case. Appeals of Commission decisions go to Court of Appeals for DC Circuit or to Court of Appeals where mine is located. When there is only one member, the Commission cannot act and appeals go directly to Court of Appeals.

§ 8.03. What to Expect from OSHA in 2023: An Employer's Guide to Developments in Workplace Safety.

[1] — What to Expect from OSHA in 2023.

While some employers may be ready to relegate workplace safety to the back burner where it was before the pandemic, you know that's not a smart move. Most employees understand OSHA is going to flex its newly carved muscles in 2023, soon to be unleashing an army of newly hired investigators onto an unsuspecting public. But while employers know they should not just be crossing your fingers and hoping to be spared, you are not sure what to do now to prepare. This chapter will reveal the 10 most critical trends you can expect in the new year and provide practical guidance to help employers on their way. This chapter will discuss the state of workplace safety as COVID-19 seems to be in retreat, what OSHA initiatives and rulemaking you can expect in the coming months, and how workplace inspections will be different going forward.

[2] — OSHA's Official 2023 Agenda.

[a] — Prevention of Workplace Violence in Health Care and Social Assistance.

This is at the pre-rule stage. OSHA published a Request for Information (RFI) in December 2016, soliciting information primarily from health care employers, workers, and other subject matter experts on impacts of violence, prevention strategies, and other information useful to the agency. A broad coalition of labor unions and the National Nurses United each petitioned OSHA for a standard preventing workplace violence in health care. In January 2017, OSHA granted the petitions. To develop a workplace standard, OSHA is preparing a Small Business Regulatory Enforcement Fairness Act (SBREFA) panel.

[b] — Heat Illness in Prevention in Outdoor and Indoor Work Settings.

This is at the pre-rule stage. OSHA previously published an advance notice of proposed rulemaking (ANPRM) on October 27, 2021, to explore rulemaking on a heat stress standard. Given the broad scope of regulatory efforts and technical considerations, the agency is continuing its dialogue and engagement with stakeholders to explore a rulemaking.

[c] — Infectious Disease.

A Notice of Proposed Rulemaking (A) is slated for September 2023. OSHA continues to examine regulatory alternatives for control measures to protect employees from infectious disease exposure to pathogens that can cause significant disease. The agency cites workplaces where such control measures might be necessary including health care, emergency response, prisons, homeless shelters, drug treatment programs, and other occupational settings where employees can be at increased risk of exposure to potentially infected people.

[d] — Occupational Exposure to COVID-19 in Healthcare Settings.

A final rule was slated for December 2022; OSHA is continuing to work towards a final standard. This rulemaking derives from OSHA's emergency temporary standard on the healthcare industry. The agency believes the danger faced by healthcare workers continues to be of the highest concern and measures to prevent the spread of COVID-19 are still needed to protect them.

[e] — Improve Tracking of Workplace Injuries and Illnesses.

A final rule is slated for March 2023. In March 2022, OSHA issued a proposed rule that would amend its occupational injury and illness recordkeeping regulation to require certain employers, those with 100 or more employees in certain designated industries, to electronically submit 300, 301 and 300a each year. The comment period closed June 30, 2022.

[f] — Worker Walkaround Representative Designation Process.

A Notice of Proposed Rulemaking was slated for May 2023. This rulemaking will clarify the right of workers and certified bargaining units to specify a worker or union representative to accompany an OSHA inspector during the inspection process/facility walkaround, regardless of whether the representative is an employee of the employer, if in the judgment of the Compliance Safety and Health Officer such person is reasonably necessary to an effective and thorough physical inspection.

[g] — Lock Out/Tag Out Update.

A NPRM is slated for July 2023. This rulemaking will address recent technological advancements that employ computer-based controls of hazardous energy that conflict with OSHA's existing lock-out/tag-out standard.

[3] — New Head of the Department of Labor.

Former Department of Labor Secretary Marty Walsh departed in March of 2023. As the first deputy, Deputy Secretary Julie Su became acting Secretary upon Walsh's departure. Ms. Su worked for more than a decade as an attorney with the Asian Pacific American Legal Center and became secretary of the California Labor and Workforce Development Agency, where she was instrumental in enforcing A.B. 5, the state's high-profile 2019 law presuming most workers were employees, as opposed to independent contractors.

Ms. Su likely would focus on issues surrounding wage and hour violations, contractor civil rights, and worker safety—particularly for low-wage workers—if she were to lead the agency. Ms. Su faced a contentious nomination hearing during her confirmation process for deputy labor secretary in 2021 and was peppered with questions on her management of California's unemployment insurance system. Odds are slim her confirmation would be blocked with Democrats' small electoral gains in the Senate during the midterms, despite GOP and business objections. With the way the Federal Vacancies Act is written, President Biden also could do nothing, leaving Ms. Su to assume power in an acting capacity and just continuing to do so as she was already confirmed by the Senate for the No. 2 spot.

[4] — OIRA Now Pro-Regulation.

The head of OSHA, Doug Parker, will be pressing forward in 2023 with their agenda, including new standards for COVID in healthcare and heat illness. The regulatory process will pick up the pace in 2023, in part, because the White House's Office of Information and Regulatory Affairs (OIRA) now has a new fully confirmed Administrator. Prof. Richard Revesz is a pro-government regulation expert in environmental issues and administrative law. OIRA is the last stop for proposed OSHA standards and Prof. Revesz has a long academic history of siding with government regulations. He favors an approach that strongly defers to bureaucratic determinations of costs and benefits if the business community does not have too much influence in the process. Prof. Revesz has been highly critical of prior administrations, including Democratic ones, that he believes listened too much to the business community about the practical effectiveness and benefits of proposed regulations. This means the pipeline of regulatory action should see an accelerated pace in 2023.

[5] — A New Urgency — Resorting to Regulatory Mode.

The mid-terms are over, and we are entering the second half of President Biden's first term. With the House and Senate split between the parties, the Administration's reliance upon regulatory moves becomes even more important. Look for OSHA to increase its reliance on administrative actions, such as proposed standards and national emphasis programs, and be particularly wary of the new Notice of Enforcement Policy (NEP) on OSHA's Severe Violator Enforcement Program (SVEP).

The Biden Administration feels the political urgency to get things done and executive agency/bureaucratic action is its best option considering the make-up of the Congress and the Supreme Court.

[6] — OSHA and Clouds in the Economic Horizon.

Even with looming economic challenges, the construction industry will likely continue facing a labor shortage. Employers will have to continue relying upon less experienced workers, temporary workers, and new subcontractors. OSHA knows this and is closely watching for improved safety training and compliance for workers in these categories who sometimes tragically get overlooked. Recently the Bureau of Labor Statistics and other data show fatalities are up (especially in construction and trenching). The agency's scrutiny of employers' actions (or inaction) considering this data will be reflected in how it targets industries and employers for inspections and aggressive citations.

[a] — The Heat Standard.

On October 27, 2021, OSHA issued an advanced notice of proposed rulemaking (ANPRM) beginning the rulemaking process to consider a heat-specific workplace standard.[36] The ANPRM requested employers the "regulated community" submit comments on whether or not it issue should issue a standard and regarding various issues, such as heat illness prevention plans and programs, engineering controls, administrative controls, and personal protective equipment, acclimatization, physiologic and exposure monitoring, planning and responding to heat illness emergencies, worker training and engagement, among others. The comment period closed on January 26, 2022. The question remains: when will OSHA take the next step and issue a NPRM?

[b] — OSHA Updates HazCom Standard.

OSHA issued Notice of Proposed Rulemaking back in 2021 to update its Hazard Communication Standard (HazCom) to align with Revision 7 of the UN's Globally Harmonized System of Classification and Labeling of Chemicals (GHS). Changes are broad and include:

- New classifications for Aerosols, Desensitized Explosives, and Flammable Gases
- New labeling provisions for "small" and "very-small" containers
- Updated several hazard and precautionary statements for clarity and precision
- Updated labeling requirements for packaged containers "released for shipment"
- Labels for bulk shipments of hazardous chemicals
- Trade secrets on SDSs (Safety Data Sheets) for chemical concentrations
- Section 2 of the SDS updated to list hazards not required on label
- Potential additions from GHS Revision 8

---

[36] Heat Injury and Illness Prevention in Outdoor and Indoor Work Settings (Advanced Notice of Proposed Rulemaking), 86 Fed. Reg. 59309 (proposed October 27, 2021).

§ 8.03   ENERGY & MINERAL LAW INSTITUTE

The Rule is expected to be finalized this year – the last change was made in 2012. The Rule will become effective 60 days after publication in the Federal Register. Chemical manufacturers, importers, and distributors evaluating substances must comply within one year from the effective date. Chemical manufacturers, importers, and distributors evaluating mixtures must comply within two years from the effective date.

[c] — OSHA Updates to the PSM Standard.

OSHA is considering expanding the scope of the PSM standard to include:

- Oil and Gas well drilling and servicing.
- More employee involvement.
- Stop work authority.
- Formal resolution of PHSA recommendations.
- Specific PHA considerations.
- Audits and emergency planning.

[d] — Healthcare COVID-19 Rule.

Worker and employer organizations alike are continuing to meet with White House officials over concerns that OSHA's proposed rule to protect health-care workers from Covid-19 will either be too broad or not strict enough. Meetings with the White House's Office of Information and Regulatory Affairs over the OSHA proposal are currently scheduled through at least January 6. OIRA's review is usually the last outside analysis of a rule before it's cleared for release, and the scheduled sessions are a last chance for advocates to make their case before that review is concluded. OSHA has not yet released the rule's proposed text, leaving advocates to guess what requirements will be included. Overall, it is expected to resemble OSHA's 2021 emergency temporary standard for health-care workers that OSHA stopped enforcing a year ago. OSHA officials have said the rule will not include a vaccination mandate.

[i] — Increasing Infections.

"The unions continue to advocate for strong OSHA protections in health care settings," said Rebecca Reindel, the AFL-CIO's director of safety and health.[37] The labor federation is advocating for methods to reduce the airborne spread of Covid, such as respiratory protections and ventilation systems that filter out the virus, Ms. Reindel told Bloomberg Law.[38] Unions are also concerned the OIRA review could last several weeks, while infections continue to increase during the winter. The regulatory office's analysis of the 2021 emergency temporary standard lasted about six weeks. "We will strongly be urging OIRA to expedite its review process so the final rule can be issued as soon as possible to ensure that nurses and other health care workers get the protection they need in this current surge of Covid, RSV, and influenza cases," said Ken Zinn, political director for National Nurses United.[39]

[ii] — Coverage Concerns.

Many business groups are concerned that the permanent standard will cover a broader range of health-care providers like retail pharmacies, dentist offices, and medical clinics inside factories, which were largely exempted from the temporary rule. The thrust of the temporary standard was to protect workers in facilities where Covid patients were likely to be treated. In March, OSHA announced that the agency "is considering whether the scope of the final standard should cover employers regardless of screening procedures for non-employees and/or vaccination status of employees."[40] The emergency rule could be read to only apply to workers who faced a "grave danger" from Covid, while by law the permanent rule must have the lower threshold of "significant risk," the agency said. A pharmacist might not be in "grave danger" from Covid but could face a "significant risk," OSHA reasoned.[41]

---

[37] Bruce Rolfson, *Union Slams Lack of Covid Rule in 2023 'Death on the Job' Report*, BLOOMBERG LAW (April 26, 2023), https://news.bloomberglaw.com/safety/union-slams-lack-of-covid-rule-in-2023-death-on-the-job-report.

[38] *Id.*

[39] *Id.*

[40] Occupational Exposure to COVID-19 in Healthcare Settings (Notice of limited reopening of comment period; notice of informal hearing), 87 Fed. Reg. 16426 (proposed March 23, 2022).

[41] *Id.*

[iii] — Potentially Illegal.

The American Hospital Association (AHA) declined to comment on what issues it will address at its meeting with OIRA but said concerns the organization raised earlier have not abated. In an April 22, 2022 letter to OSHA, the AHA said a permanent rule was not needed because the Centers for Medicare and Medicaid Services already require hospitals to follow Centers for Disease Control and Prevention recommendations.[42] The association also objected to OSHA getting involved in personnel decisions such as paid time off for vaccinations.[43]

The United States Chamber of Commerce maintains that the proposed permanent rule is not legal because OSHA needed to enact it a year ago because the OSH Act requires permanent rules to be enacted within six months of the temporary rule taking effect.[44]

A 2022 Congressional Research Service review of previous OSHA emergency rules found no clear federal court direction on whether a permanent rule would be enforceable if enacted outside the six-month window.[45]

[e] — A New Infectious Disease Standard.

OSHA stated that it is prioritizing resources on the COVID-19 health care standardm[46] but it is possible OSHA could then turn to the broader

---

[42] Letter from Stacey Hughes, Executive Vice President, American Hospital Association, to Douglas L. Parker, Assistant Secretary of Labor (April 22, 2022) (available at https://www.aha.org/lettercomment/2022-04-22-aha-urges-osha-not-finalize-covid-19-emergency-temporary-standard).

[43] *Id.*

[44] Marc Freedman, *Why is OSHA Still Pushing Emergency Covid Standards?*, U.S. Chamber (June 15, 2023), https://www.uschamber.com/employment-law/why-is-osha-still-pushing-emergency-covid-standards.

[45] *Occupational Safety and Health Administration (OSHA): COVID-19 Emergency Temporary Standards (ETS) on Health Care Employment and Vaccinations and Testing for Large Employers*, Congressional Research Service, November 10, 2021 (available at https://crsreports.congress.gov/product/pdf/R/R46288/32).

[46] *Statement on the Status of the OSHA COVID-19 Vaccination and Testing ETS*, Occupational Safety and Health Administration, January 25, 2022 (available at https://www.osha.gov/coronavirus/ets2#:~:text=The%20agency%20is%20prioritizing%20its,Disease%20(COVID%2D19).).

SAFETY ENFORCEMENT § 8.03

rule after. OSHA previously rebooted rulemaking for an infectious disease standard in high-risk environments like hospitals, labs, and prisons that would expressly cover COVID-19 along with other dangerous pathogens. OSHA announced a plan to create a standard regulation infectious diseases in the workplace (tuberculosis, chicken pox and shingles, measles, SARS, MRSA, and COVID-19).[47] This move was likely forced by the Supreme Court's decision to strike down the Emergency Temporary Standard.

[7] — Expect to Be Inspected.

Last Year (2023): OSHA conducted 34,221 inspections[48]
- 15,844 Programmed Inspections and 183,377 Unprogrammed Inspections were conducted in 2023
- OSHA Conducted 31,820 inspections in FY 2022
  - 14,081 Programmed Inspections and 17,739 Unprogrammed Inspections were conducted in 2022

OSHA's Top 10 Most Frequently Cited Standards for 2023[49]
1. Fall Protection—General Requirements (1926.501): **7,271 violations**
2. Hazard Communication (1910.1200): **3,213 violations**
3. Ladders (1926.1053): **2,978 violations**
4. Scaffolding (1926.451): **2,859 violations**
5. Powered Industrial Trucks (1910.178): **2,561 violations**
6. Lockout/Tagout (1910.147): **2,554 violations**
7. Respiratory Protection (1910.134): **2,481 violations**
8. Fall Protection—Training Requirements (1926.503): **2,112 violations**

---

[47] *Infectious Diseases*, Unified Agenda, Office of Information and Regulatory Affairs, RIN 1218-AC46, Fall 2023 (available at https://www.reginfo.gov/public/do/eAgendaViewRule?pubId=202310&RIN=1218-AC46).

[48] *OSHA Inspection Activity,* Occupational Safety and Health Administration (available at https://www.osha.gov/enforcement/current-enforcement-summary#:~:text=OSHA%20INSPECTION%20ACTIVITY,injuries%2Ffatalities%2C%20and%20referrals).

[49] *Top 10 Most Frequently Cited Standards,* Occupational Safety and Health Administration (available at https://www.osha.gov/top10citedstandards).

9. Personal Protective and Lifesaving Equipment—Eye and Face Protection (1926.102): **2,074 violations**
10. Machine Guarding (1910.212): **1,644 violations**

The OSHA budget for FY 2024 is $632.3 Million. This is unchanged from the previous year, which saw a 3.3% increase.[50]

- 2022: $612 Million
- 2023: $632.3 Million

Without an increase in the budget in 2024, the number of inspectors declined slightly in FY 2023, following an increase in OSHA inspector hiring in 2022. However, OSHA did boost field enforcement supervisor levels in FY 2023, with an additional 15 area directors and assistant directors at the end of the fiscal year.[51]

[a] — Instance-by-Instance Citations.

On January 26, 2023, the Department of Labor issued enforcement guidance on instance-by-instance citations. The accompanying press release explains "OSHA Regional Administrators and Area Directors now have the authority to cite certain types of violations as "instance-by-instance citations" for cases where the agency identifies "high gravity" serious violations of OSHA standards specific to certain conditions where the language of the rule supports a citation for each instance of non-compliance."[52] These conditions include: lockout/tagout, machine guarding, permit-required confined space, respiratory protection, falls, trenching and for cases with other-than-serious

---

[50] *Commonly Used Statistics,* Occupational Safety and Health Administration (available at https://www.osha.gov/data/commonstats).

[51] *Federal Workplace Safety Inspector Ranks Drop After Earlier Jump* (available at https://news.bloomberglaw.com/safety/federal-workplace-safety-inspector-ranks-drop-after-earlier-jump).

[52] Press Release, U.S. Dep't of Labor, Department of Labor announces enforcement guidance changes to save lives, target employers who put profit over safety (January 26, 2023) (available at https://www.osha.gov/news/newsreleases/national/01262023-0#:~:text=OSHA%20Regional%20Administrators%20and%20Area,of%20the%20rule%20supports%20a).

violations specific to record keeping.[53] The Department of Labor's press release states that the purpose of this change is to ensure that OSHA personnel are applying the "full" authority of the OSH Act where increased citations are needed to discourage non-compliance. According to the agency, a decision to use instance-by-instance citations should normally be based on consideration of one or more specific factors, which are:

- The employer has received a willful, repeat, or failure to abate violation within the past five years where that classification is current;
- The employer has failed to report a fatality, inpatient hospitalization, amputation, or loss of an eye pursuant to the requirements of 29 CFR 1904.39;
- The proposed citations are related to a fatality/catastrophe; and
- The proposed recordkeeping citations are related to injury or illness(es) that occurred as a result of a serious hazard.[54]

"OSHA's January 26 memorandum also provides that instance-by-instance citations may be applied when the text of the relevant standard allows (such as per machine, location, entry, or employee), and when the instances of violation cannot be abated by a single method of abatement. The memorandum further provides that agency inspectors should document each instance thoroughly when an inspection may result in instance-by-instance violations. It offers examples of this thoroughness: type of material being processed, equipment, facility conditions, human factors, personal protective equipment, et cetera."[55]

---

[53] *Id.*

[54] Memorandum from Amanda Edens, et al. (January 26, 2023) (available at https://www.osha.gov/memos/2023-01-26/application-of-instance-by-instance-penalty-adjustments).

[55] Phillip C. Bauknight, *OSHA Announces Aggressive Plan to Address Workplace Safety in 2023: 6 Tips for Employers*, Fisher Phillips, January 30, 2023, https://www.fisherphillips.com/en/news-insights/osha-announces-aggressive-plan-address-workplace-safety.html.

[i] — Grouping Will Be Discouraged.

"OSHA's memorandum also reminds Regional Administrations and Area Directors of their authority not to group citations. Rather, the agency suggests that employers can be more effectively "encouraged" to comply with the OSH Act through the issuance of separate citations. The memorandum also includes links to the existing guidance on instance-by-instance citations contained in OSHA's Field Operations Manual and CPL-02-00-080: "Handling of Cases to be Proposed for Violation-by-Violation Penalties." It provides that "violations, which are proposed as instance-by-instance citations, shall not normally be combined or grouped."[56]

[b] — The Fairfax Memo — Changes to Inspection Procedures.

OSHA recently proposed a rule revisiting and revitalizing the Obama Administration's Fairfax Memo.[57] This would include union-friendly changes to current OSHA inspection procedures and may allow non-employees to participate in inspections.

According to Bloomberg News, "OSHA is reviving a defunct enforcement policy by proposing a rule that would allow worker advocates to take part in inspections of nonunion workplaces, even if those advocates are not employees. The standard also may clarify union participation during inspections at worksites where workers are represented by organized labor. OSHA's proposed rule[58] could essentially reinstate policy OSHA adopted in 2013 during the Obama administration but was withdrawn by the Trump administration in 2017. The regulation exemplifies the Biden administration's commitment to organized labor in the workplace. OSHA set May as its target date for issuing a notice of proposed rulemaking, a step that requires the agency to explain options being considered for the standard and open a

---

[56] *Id.* (quoting Memorandum from Amanda Edens, et al. (January 26, 2023) (available at https://www.osha.gov/memos/2023-01-26/application-of-instance-by-instance-penalty-adjustments)).

[57] Worker Walkaround Representative Designation Process (Proposed rule, request for comments), 88 Fed. Reg. 59825 (proposed August 30, 2023).

[58] *Id.*

public comment period. The proposed rule if enacted seems certain to face a court battle."[59]

[i] — Revisiting 'Fairfax Memo'.

The original policy was detailed in a February 2013 interpretation letter sometimes called the "Fairfax Memo," which said that, if an inspector approves, "a person affiliated with a union" or "a community representative" can act on behalf of employees during the inspection so long as the individual is authorized by employees to be their representative.[60]

[ii] — Who Gets Say.

According to Steve Sallman, Director of Safety and Health for the United Steelworkers, this OSHA rule could clarify the role of union representatives during inspections. While employers generally understand that a local union member may be designated to participate in an inspection, problems have arisen when a national union office sends a staff person to participate. OSHA has sometimes sought a court order to allow the participation, which delays the inspection.[61]

Richard Fairfax, who signed the 2013 policy letter while serving as OSHA's deputy assistant secretary and is now a safety consultant in Frederick, Md., said he is concerned the proposed rule could put pressure on inspectors to determine whether someone, as the proposal says, is "reasonably necessary."[62] "They already have a tough job," Mr. Fairfax said. OSHA could consider involving OSHA supervisors in the decision, he added.[63]

---

[59] Bruce Rolfsen, *Biden OSHA Revives Union-, Worker-Friendly Inspection Rep Rule*, BLOOMBERG LAW, January 17, 2023, https://news.bloomberglaw.com/safety/biden-osha-revives-union-worker-friendly-inspection-rep-rule.

[60] Memorandum from Richard E. Fairfax, Deputy Assistant Secretary, Dep't of Labor, to Steve Sallman, Health and Safety Specialist, United Steelworkers (February 21, 2013) (available at https://www.osha.gov/laws-regs/standardinterpretations/2013-02-21).

[61] Bruce Rolfson, *Biden OSHA Revives Union-, Worker-Friendly Inspection Rep Rule*, BLOOMBERG LAW (January 17, 2023), https://news.bloomberglaw.com/safety/biden-osha-revives-union-worker-friendly-inspection-rep-rule.

[62] *Id.*

[63] *Id.*

[iii] — Defending the Policy.

The 2013 policy was challenged in at least two federal lawsuits. Nissan North America in 2016 contested OSHA's decision to allow employees who were union backers at the nonunion Nissan factory in Canton, Miss., to accompany an OSHA inspector. The case was settled when Nissan agreed to allow three union advocates to participate after they became members of the plant's safety committee.[64]

In the other case, the National Federation of Independent Business represented by the Pacific Legal Foundation challenged the policy on the grounds that it had the effect of a rule and therefore OSHA should have gone through the normal rulemaking process of notices and public comment periods. The Trump administration's decision to withdraw the letter in 2017 led to the case's closure.[65]

[c] — Beware Agency Sharing.

Biden Administration is using cross-agency partnerships to enhance enforcement. A recent example has been between the NLRB and DOL's Wage and Hour Division. We can expect the same for OSHA.

---

[64] In the Matter of the Establishment Inspection of: Nissan North America, Civil Action No. 3:16-MC-00692-HTW-LRA (S.D. Miss. Nov. 14, 2016).

[65] Nat'l Fed'n of Indep. Bus. v. Dougherty, Civil Action No. 3:16-CV-2568-D (N.D. Tex. Feb. 3, 2017).

OFFICERS AND EXECUTIVE COMMITTEE

Energy & Mineral Law Foundation
Officers and Executive Committee 2022-2023

President	R. Clay Larkin
Vice President and President-Elect	Britt A. Freund
Secretary	Travis L. Brannon
Treasurer	Stefanie L. Burt
Past President	Sheila Nolan Gartland
Past President	Kevin L. Colosimo
At Large	Nicole R. Snyder Bagnell
At Large	Armando F. Benincasa
At Large	Jessica Brisendine
At Large	Drew McCallister
At Large	Troy Nichols
At Large	Michelle Elmore Wooton

Foundation Staff

Anna Girard Fletcher	Executive Director
Dawn Law	Office and Web Administrator

ENERGY & MINERAL LAW INSTITUTE

Past Presidents

Samuel L. Douglass
President 1979-1981

Peter S. Wellington
President 1981-1982

J. Richard Emens
President 1982-1983

John L. McClaugherty*
President 1983-1984

Cyril A. Fox, jr.
President 1984-1985

James P. Holland*
President 1985-1986

Douglas J. Richards
President 1986-1987

William A. Pusey
President 1987-1988

Timothy J. Battaglia
President 1988-1989

Edward B. Weinberg
President 1989-1990

Sean Cassidy
President 1990-1991

Joseph P. Congleton
President 1991-1992

J. Thomas Lane
President 1992-1993

Thomas C. Means
President 1993-1994

Ronald E. Meisburg
President 1994-1995

Steven P. McGowan
President 1995-1996

Benita Kahn
President 1996-1997

Richard C. Ward*
President 1997-1998

Gregory B. Robertson
President 1998-1999

R. Neal Pierce
President 1999-2000

Edward M. Green
President 2000-2001

Robert G. McLusky
President 2001-2002

Joseph J. Zaluski
President 2002-2003

Thomas E. Meng
President 2003-2004

Timothy W. Gresham
President 2004-2005

David J. Laurent
President 2005-2006

Mary Sue Schulberg*
President 2006-2007

David G. Ries
President 2007-2008

Maureen D. Carman
President 2008-2009

C. David Morrison
President 2009-2010

Kirsten L. Nathanson
President 2010-2011

John T. Boyd II
President 2011-2012

Timothy M. Miller
President 2012-2013

Sharon O. Flanery
President 2013-2014

Kevin K. Douglass
President 2014-2015

G. Brian Wells
President 2015-2016

Daniel W. Wolff
President 2016-2017

Erin E. Magee
President 2017-2018

Natalie N. Jefferis
President 2018-2019

Timothy J. Hagerty
President 2019-2020

Kevin L. Colosimo
President 2020-2021

Sheila Nolan Gartland
President 2021-2022

*Deceased

Law Schools

**American University
Washington College of Law**
Professor Barlow Burke

Appalachian School of Law
Professor Buzz Belleville

**Louisiana State University
Law Center**
Professor Keith B. Hall

**Texas Tech University
School of Law**
Professor Bruce Kramer

**University of Kentucky
College of Law**
C. David Morrison

**University of Oklahoma
College of Law**
Professor Monika U. Ehrman

**University of Pittsburgh
School of Law**
Professor Kevin Abbott

University of Texas at Austin
Professor Owen L Anderson

**Washburn University
School of Law**
Professor Blake A. Klinker

**West Virginia University
College of Law**
Professor James Van Nostrand

Trustees-at-Large

Kevin C. Abbott
J. Tyler Adkins
Mark Adkins
Renee V. Anderson
Nicolle Snyder Bagnell
Stephen G. Barker
Kathy G. Becket
Armando F. Benincasa
Laura E. Beverage
Donald C. Bluedorn II
Richard J. Bolen
Travis L. Brannon
Jessica Brisendine
Matthew F. Burger
Stefanie L. Burt
David Carlson
James A. Carr III
Caroline Pitt Clark
Charles A. Compton
Daniel P. Craig
Bruce E. Cryder
Chauncey S. R. Curtz
Charles B. Dollison
Jonathan Ellis
Elizabeth B. Elmore
Stanton D. Ernest
Erik Fargo
David M. Flannery
Robert D. Fluharty
Sandra K. Fraley
Britt A. Freund

Bridget Furbee
Katherine Gafner
William T. Gorton, III
Richard L. Gottlieb
Karen J. Greenwell
Megan S. Haines
Keith B. Hall
Roger G. Hanshaw
Frank B. Harrington
M. Shane Harvey
Mark E. Heath
Guy W. Hensley
William M. Herlihy
Kara H. Herrnstein
Amber Nisbet Hodgdon
Stephen M. Hodges
James W. Kane
Clay K. Keller
Robert Kelly
Melanie J. Kilpatrick
Williams Kilpatrick
Kurt L. Krieger
Seth M. Land
R. Clay Larkin
W. Henry Lawrence
Alexandria D. Lay
Richard L. Lewis
Lucas Liben
M. Shaun Lundy
I. Bobby Majumder
Drew McCallister
Gary D. McCollum
Timothy B. McGranor
Leslie Miller-Stover
Michael J. Moore
R. Henry Moore
Kara Mundy
Todd Myers
Troy N. Nichol
Roger L. Nicholson
Patrick R. Northam
Gregory J. Ossi

Tammy J. Owen
Ashley C. Pack
Jesse M. Parrish
Jeffrey K. Phillips
R. Cordell Pierce
Nicholas S. Preservati
Ryan T. Purpura
Joseph E. Reinhart
John E. Rhine
John R. Rhorer, Jr.
F. Thomas Rubenstein
Gregory D. Russell
Thomas C. Ryan
Bridget Sasson
Tyson D. Schwerdtfeger
Michael J. Settineri
Andrew R. Smith
Barkley J. Sturgill
Benjamin M. Sullivan
Chad J. Sullivan
Joseph A. Tarantelli
Allyn G. Turner
James M. Van Nostrand
Jeffrey W. Wagner
Christopher B. Wallace
Justin Werner
Martha A. Wiegand
John Williams
William G. Williams
Kathryn S. Wilson
Arthur M. Wolfson
Michelle Elmore Wooton
Brian D. Zoeller

HONORARY TRUSTEES

Honorary Trustees

Bruce A. Americus*
John H. Armstrong
Cameron S. Bell
James A. Bibby, III
Timothy M. Biddle
Rex Burford
Steven M. Carpenter
Edward P. Clair
Anna M. Daily
James H. Davis, III*
R. Eberley Davis
W. Blaine Early, III
C. William Fechtig
Larry W. George
Vaughn R. Groves
John H. Henderson
John H. Heyer
Stephen M. Hopta
Robert G. Jones
Scott L. Kreutzer
John A. Macleod
Elizabeth A. McClanahan
Ronald E. Meisburg
Veryl N. Meyers
Bruce D. Reed
William Roy Rice*
Kendrick R. Riggs
Richard D. Rivers
Justin W. Ross
Arnold L. Schulberg
Brooks M. Smith
Robert F. Stauffer
Donald C. Supcoe
David H. Thomason
Donald H. Vish
Robert C. Williams
John R. Woodrum
Jeff A. Woods
Arthur J. Wright
Minturn T. Wright, III
Marvin O. Young

Deceased

ENERGY & MINERAL LAW INSTITUTE

Sustaining Members

Alliance Resource Partners, L.P.
Alpha Metallurgical Resources, Inc.
Antero Resources Corporation
Arch Resources, Inc.
Ascent Resources, LLC
Babst Calland
Blackhawk Mining, LLC
Bowles Rice LLP
Bricker Graydon LLP
Buchanan Ingersoll & Rooney PC
CNX Resources Corporation
CONSOL Energy Inc.
Dentons Bingham Greenebaum LLP
Dickie, McCamey & Chilcote, P.C.
Dinsmore & Shohl LLP
Diversified Oil & Gas Corporation
Equitrans Midstream Corporation
EQT Corporation
Fisher Phillips LLP
Flaherty Sensabaugh Bonasso PLLC
Frost Brown Todd LLC
Jackson Kelly PLLC
K&L Gates LLP
Kentucky River Properties LLC
Lewis Gianola PLLC
LG&E and KU Energy LLC
Ogletree, Deakins, Nash, Smoak & Stewart, P.C.
Peacock Keller, LLP
Penn, Stuart & Eskridge
Ramaco Resources
Reed Smith LLP
Robinson & McElwee PLLC
Spilman Thomas & Battle, PLLC
Steptoe & Johnson PLLC
Stites & Harbison, PLLC
VanAntwerp Attorneys, LLP

FOUNDATION MEMBERSHIP

Sustaining Members

Vorys, Sater, Seymour and Pease LLP
Williams Kilpatrick, PLLC
Wyatt, Tarrant & Combs, LLP

Supporting Members

Baird & Baird, P.S.C.
Cassidy, Anderson & Kane
Clark Hill PLC
Emens Wolper Jacobs & Jasin Law Firm, LPA
Faegre Drinker Biddle & Reath LLP
Greylock Energy
John T. Boyd Company
Kirkland & Ellis LLP
Krugliak Wilkins Griffiths & Dougherty Co., L.P.A.
Maynard, Cooper & Gale, P.C.
McGuireWoods LLP
Northeast Natural Energy LLC
Pardee Resources Company
Pennsylvania General Energy Co., L.L.C.
Perkins Coie LLP
Reminger Co., L.P.A.
Thompson & Knight LLP

Associations

American Association
  of Professional Landmen
Kentucky Coal Association
Kentucky Oil & Gas Association
National Mining Association
Ohio Coal Association
Ohio Oil & Gas Association
United States Energy Association
West Virginia Coal Association
Gas & Oil Association of West
  Virginia (GO-WV)

Law Schools

American University – Washington
  College of Law
Appalachian School of Law
Capital University Law School
Louisiana State University Law
  Center
Southern Methodist University –
  Dedman School of Law
Texas Tech University School
  of Law
University of Houston Law Center
University of Kentucky College
  of Law
University of Oklahoma College
  of Law
University of Pittsburgh School
  of Law
University of Texas School of Law
  at Austin
Washburn University School
  of Law
West Virginia University
  College of Law

FOUNDATION MEMBERSHIP

Individual Members

Aaron, Craig S.
Abbott, Kevin C.
Abel Jr., William C.
Adkins, J. Mark
Adkins, J. Tyler
Adkins, Jamie
Adkins, CPL, Richard D.
Adkins, Wendy G.
Aldridge, Evan
Alexander, Patricia M.
Allert, Jenae
Allevato, John F.
Alston, Brittany J.
Alter, Jr., Jason P.
Anderson, A. Dale
Anderson, Brian
Anderson, Jonathan L.
Anderson, Owen L.
Andre III, Robert J.
Andrews, Scott W.
Anson, Tom
Antonelli, Stephen A.
Appaya, Lia
Arbaugh, Tiffany
Armstrong, Amanda
Arnold, Janna D.
Atkinson, Nathan B.
Baber, Heather
Bagnell, Nicolle R. Snyder
Bailey, Melissa A.
Baird, Charles J.
Baird, David L.
Baird, John H.
Baker, Dudley D.
Ball, Robert
Balcar, F. Andrew
Banks, Ernest C.
Banse, Lee
Barack, Cory Roger
Baran, Raymond J.
Barfield, Mindy G.
Barissi, Matthew Vafa
Barker, Andrew
Barley, Kevin L.
Barnes, Brent A.
Barnette, Scott E.
Barret, Kendall S.
Barrett, Brandi C.
Barrett, Zachary H.
Barrette, Amy L.
Barton, April
Basdekis, Vivian H.
Basile, Michael J.
Bastien, Jonas S.
Batikov, Ilya
Battle III, H. Dill
Bauer, Stacey R.
Baxter, Vanessa A.
Bays, Robert L.
Beam, Gerilyn H.
Bean, Rodney L.
Beatty, Jr., Robert H.
Beckett, Kathy G.
Beckman, Jon C.
Beem, Shawn M.
Beeson, Craig S.
Beirne, Lydia M.
Bell, Robert A.
Belleville, Mark L.
Bender, Jack C.
Benincasa, Armando F.
Beverage, Laura E.
Bibikos, George A.
Billiter, Delbert D.
Binotto, Peter J.
Black, Sarah
Black, Terry R.
Black, IV, William J.
Blair, Christopher
Blalock, Joseph R.
Blank, Jonathan T.
Blankenship, Anne C.

Bloomstone, Ajaye
Bluedorn II, Donald C.
Boarman, Keeana Sajadi
Boggs, Curtis R.
Bolen, Richard J.
Booher, Kacie
Books, Nick
Borchers, Dylan F.
Borror, Nicholas O.
Bowers, Katrina N.
Bowman, Gregory W.
Boyd II, John T.
Boyd, Sydney
Boyer, Wayne
Bragg, Jeremy D.
Brandon, Coty
Branin, Melinda A.
Brannon, Travis L.
Breeding, Carl W.
Brennen, David A.
Brewster, Michael D.
Bridges, Max E.
Brisendine, Jessica Blake
Brock III, Samuel M.
Brouse, Matthew G.
Brown, Brooke
Brown, Carolyn M.
Brown, Jeffrey A.
Brown, Lyle B.
Brown, W. Rodes
Bruderly, Lisa M.
Bruggeman, Aaron M.
Brumley, Christina T.
Brumley, Christopher A.
Bryan, Jamie
Bryson, Marc C.
Buckley, Allison Grogan
Buckley, Evan
Bullock, Kenneth
Bunt, Jr., Walter A.
Burd, Charlie
Burger, Matthew F.

Burgess, Patricia
Burgett, Catherine
Burke, Laurel L.
Burns, Jr., Robert L.
Burt, Stefanie L.
Burton, J. Mark
Byrne, Sean
Bytner, Timothy S.
Caldera, Anthony
Callahan, Jay
Callas, Christopher L.
Callicotte, Harry D.
Canaday, Theresa A.
Capehart, Curtis R.A.
Capito, Katherine B.
Capito, Moore
Cappucci, Jim
Cardi, Michael C.
Carlson, David
Carman, Maureen D.
Carney, Edmund M.
Carr II, James A.
Carr, Kevin L.
Carroll, Gale E.
Carter, Stacie
Casper, Andrew
Cassidy, P. Sean
Castle, Janie
Casto, Matthew S.
Cather, III, Carl H.
Catsonis, John
Cave, Jennifer J.
Cave, Stan
Champeau, Michele
Chang, Steven A.
Chapman, Jamie D.
Chase, Matthew F.
Chincheck, Julia
Christenson, Roger
Christopher, Braden
Chumney, Andrew S.
Churchfield, Tia L.

FOUNDATION MEMBERSHIP

Cimino, Michael T.
Clapp, Ben
Clark, Brian J.
Clark, Briana
Clark, Caroline Pitt
Clark, Clifton B.
Clark, Mark D.
Claybourn, Joshua
Clegg, Whitney G.
Cobb, Tiffany Strelow
Cokeley, Bryan R.
Cole, Zyeda T.
Colley, Gary Lynn
Collier, Bryon D.
Colosimo, Kevin L.
Comas, Maria D.
Compston, Tyler
Compton, Charles A.
Conant, Douglas E.
Conard, Evan J.
Condaras, Steven M.
Condo, Kathy K.
Coneby, Brandon D.
Conley, Eric N.
Connor, Thomas M.
Cook, Kayla A.
Corbelli, James V.
Corcoran, Patrick R.
Cornett, John Gregory
Corwin, Jonathan P.
Cottle, Joshua A.
Cottrell, Jamie
Coyle, Casey
Coyle, Keith J.
Craft III, Joseph W.
Craig, Daniel P.
Cramer, Wesley
Cremonese, Michael J.
Cress, Jr., Lloyd R.
Crockett, John R.
Crockett, Jr., James S.
Crouse, Doug

Croyle, Kimberly Schmidt
Crow, Valerie
Culp, Tiffany A.
Cunningham, II, M. Edward
Curry, James
Curry, Mike
Curry, Stephen P.
Curtz, Chauncey S. R.
D'Antoni, Mark B.
Dague, Grace
Dailey, Anna M.
Dailey, CPL, Richard W.
Dale, Frank
Daniels, Craig
Daniels, Ryan R.
Dausch, Mark K.
Davis, Frank
Davis, James M.
Davis, K. Paul
Davis, R. Eberley
Dawkins, Lori A.
DeCesar, Thomas R.
DeJesus, Joel
Dellinger, Mark H.
Deniker, Susan L.
Dennison, Patrick W.
Desmond, Josh
Dettinger, G. Kurt
Detweiler, Jarred M.
Devinney, Craig
Dobbs, William F.
Doerfler, James M.
Dollison IV, Charles B.
Doman, Kourtney E.
Domike, Julie
Donovan, Daniel T.
Doran, Scott M.
Doran, William K.
Dorman, Andrew J.
Dotson, Christa A.
Douglass, Kevin K.
Drezewski, Anthony

Duncan, Robert F.
Dunlap, Lori A.
Dunnigan, Brady W.
Durst, Paula L.
Early, III, W. Blaine
Eaton, Kara S.
Eaton, Stephanie U. Roberts
Eckley, Travis H.
Edelstein, David M.
Edelstein, Lawrence A.
Edinger, Lisa M.
Eggerding, Matthew
Ehler, Anthony L.
Ehrler, Jr., Robert J.
Eisenberg, Ann
Eisermann, Jackie
Elliott, James D.
Elliott, Ryan D.
Ellis, Andrew J.
Ellis, Jonathan R.
Ellis, J. Kevin
Elmore, Elizabeth B.
Elsen, James
Elswick, Chris
Emch, Alvin L.
England, M. Ed., Becky
English, James
Ennis, Adam S.
Ernest, Stanton D.
Etheredge, Christopher S.
Everitt, Shelli
Fagan, Kevin
Falaschi, Gina
Farias, Sirissa Elizabeth
Farmakis, Christian A.
Farmer, Mark J.
Fazekas, Matt
Feczko, Mark D.
Feichtner, Douglas J.
Feinberg, Lee F.
Fendig, John
Ferretti, David P.

Fields, Joshua
Fields, Tyler H.
Finck, David E.
Fine, David R.
Finn, Amanda
Finnerty, David J.
Fisher, Justin L.
Fisher-Edwards, Suzanne
Flaherty, Thomas V.
Flanery, Sharon O.
Flanigan, Thomas
Flannery, David M.
Fletcher, Anna Girard
Flick, Gillian
Fluharty, Jr., Robert D.
Fluharty, Lucinda L.
Foley, Alice B.
Foley, Chantell
Foster, Michael D.
Fraley, Sandra K.
Frankovitch, W. Taylor
Freibert, David J.
Freund, Britt A.
Fridley, Tiffany L.
Friedmann, Joseph W.
Frye, Eric T.
Fullington, Mary L.
Funari, Brad A.
Funk, Joseph E.
Funk, Michael J.
Furbee, Bridget D.
Fusonie, Thomas H.
Gafner, Katherine M.
Gallagher, Richard W.
Gallagher, Shawn N.
Galligan, Thomas J.
Gandee, Stephen F.
Gann, Andrew
Gant, Kelli K.
Gao, Xiaoming
Garber, Kevin J.
Gardner, Tyson

FOUNDATION MEMBERSHIP

Garfinkel, Daniel C.
Garrison, Michael S.
Gartland, Sheila Nolan
Gasiorek, Austin L.
Gentile, Heather J.
George, Larry W.
Gevaudan, Denise
Gibeaut, Sarah A.
Gilkison, Olivia H.
Gilpin, Thomas H.
Gish, Jr., Kenneth J.
Giuliani, Anthony J.
Giunta, Greg
Glass, Michael D.
Goes, Kelley M.
Goins, Jace H.
Gold, Ronald E.
Gold, Sharon L.
Goldman, Kathleen Jones
Gonzalez-Lopez, Alexis
Gorton, III, William T.
Gottlieb, Max
Gottlieb, Richard L.
Graff, Jr., F. T.
Graham, Andrew S.
Graham, Heather Gale
Grattan, Edward J.
Gratton, Brian
Gray, James
Green, Caroline
Green, Steven M.
Greenwell, Karen J.
Gresham, Timothy W.
Griffith, Chad
Griffith, Craig M.
Griffith, Philip S.
Grimes, Marcia L.
Grimes, Melissa
Grundman, Carrie H.
Guzman, Kathleen
Hagedorn, Jennifer
Hagerty, Timothy J.
Haines, Megan
Hall, Christopher J.
Hall, J. R.
Hall, Jill E.
Hall, Jordon A.
Hall, Jr., W. Mitchell
Hall, Keith B.
Hall, Steven R.
Hallos, Jeffrey L.
Halter, Kevin M.
Hamoudi, Haider Ala
Hampton, Andrew B.
Hanna, William J.
Hannold, Joshua C.
Hanshaw, Roger G.
Harcar, Jesse A.
Hardman, Steven R.
Harkins, Clayton T.
Harrington, Frank B.
Harrison, Dale H.
Hartman, Barry M.
Hartsog, Gary
Harvey, M. Shane
Hatherill, Dustin J.
Hawkins, Lea Anne
Hawrot, Lisa M.
Hayes, Seth P.
Hayes, William D.
Hayhurst, Richard A.
Heal, Ben
Heath, Mark E.
Heflin, Stanley
Heidt, Mason E.
Heinz, Chelsea R.
Heiskell, Matthew P.
Hellerstedt, Jr., Carl H.
Henderson, John H.
Henderson, Scott A.
Hensley, Guy Wayne
Herder, Daniel
Herlihy, William M.
Herrnstein, Kara H.

Heyer, John H.
Hicks, Jennifer J.
Hicks, Jr., Ronald L.
Higgins, David K.
Higie, Jonathan G.
Hill, Keisa
Hill, Thomas A.
Hivick Jr., Kevin W.
Hobbs, Eric
Hodges, Stephen M.
Hoffman, Timothy D.
Hoffmann, Warren J.
Holbrook, Janet Smith
Holland, Gary D.
Holland, Lexy Gross
Holland, Mark
Holland, Nathaniel I.
Holliday, Jason L.
Holmes, III, John B.
Holtzman, Anthony
Honorable, Colette D.
Hopkins, Brian R.
Horneman, H. Carl
Hoskins, William A.
House, Brent
Hudkins, Marsha K.
Hudson, David R.
Huff, Pamela R.
Hughes, Charles R.
Hughes, Jennifer L.
Hunt, Dean K.
Hunter, Christopher M.
Hurst, Heather Blandford
Hutnick, Matthew W.
Hylton, Mark A.
Ingle, Jay E.
Irwin, Kate Koop
Irwin, Kerry O.
Iskra, Eric W.
Jackson, Helena
Jacobs, Bruce M.
Jacobs, Sean

Jamieson, Kristian
Jasko, Jason
Jefferis, Natalie
Jelsma, Franklin K.
Jenkins, Andrew G.
Jernigan, Jr., W. Henry
Jesko, Anthony W.
Jett, Brian P.
Jevicky, John E.
Joest, David R.
John, Brian
Johnson, Charles M.
Johnson, Jaslyn W.
Johnson, Jenell S.
Johnson, Kyle D.
Johnson, Reggie
Johnston, Karen L.
Jones, Christopher M.
Jones, Heather H.
Jones, Patricia
Jones, William H.
Jordan, Matthew S.
Jordan, Will
Junker, Robert Max
Kantos, Gina
Kearns, Kristin D.
Kegley, Adam R.
Keisling, Jennifer M.
Keller, Clay K.
Kelly, Emmett M.
Kelly II, Robert W.
Kennedy, Ellen Arvin
Kennedy, Rebecca E.
Kennington, Mike
Kent, Ryan J.
Kerns, Whitney R.
Ketron, Westley A.
Kidd, Misty A.
Killion, Michael T.
Kilpatrick, Melanie J.
Kimbel, Ericson
Kimble, Jeffrey A.

FOUNDATION MEMBERSHIP

Kinder, Eric E.
Kingery, Matthew P.
Kinney, Clifford F.
Klein, Rosemary
Knezevic, Christopher
Koch, Nicholas J.
Konrad, Daniel J.
Kontul, Philip K.
Koop Irwin, Kate
Kopp, Ryan
Koppitch, Matthew R.
Kothmann, Paula
Krasnow, Melissa
Krassen, Glenn S.
Kratzer, Dallas
Kreutzer, Scott
Krieger, Kurt L.
Krupliski, Kylie
Kulander, Christopher S.
Kurdock, Brianne K.
Kush, Victoria B.
LaFramboise, Leah R.
Land, Seth M.
Landa, Victoria L.
Landon, Lee M.
Lane, J. Thomas
Lannan II, Robert E.
Larch, CPL, S. Diane
Larkin, R. Clay
LaRocco, Chris
Latherow, Leigh Gross
Latimer, Derek
Laurent, David J.
Lawrence, W. Henry
Lay, Alexandria D.
Leahey, Michael P.
Lemley, Gregg M.
Lentz, Gaye W.
Leonelli, Justin
Leonoro, Joseph U.
Lewis, Richard L.
Liben, Lucas

Liberati, David K.
Light, Randall C.
Lincecum, Gideon
Lintal, Alison Flowers
Little, Barbara D.
Little, David R.
Loeb, Jr., Charles W.
Logsdon, Todd B.
Lonier, Arbre M.
Lopez, Margaret S.
Lord, Elizabeth O.
Lovejoy, II, Roger R.
Lowe, John S.
Lowe, Timothy K.
Lucas, Blaine A.
Lund, Kenneth
Lundy, M. Shaun
Lusenhop, Peter A.
Lusk, Neva G.
Lutz, Douglas
Macfarlan, Tad J.
Macia, Alexander
MacIntyre, Jr., Grant
Magee, Erin E.
Mahfood, Alex G.
Mairs, John A.
Majumder, I. Bobby
Malcho, Matthew J.
Malecki, Donald E.
Malhouitre, Chacey R.
Marling, Ramonda C.
Marsh, Judith L.
Martin, J. Breckenridge
Martin, Breck
Martin, Kaelyn S.
Martinez, Anna
Martinez McCracken, Staci
Mason, Jr., A. George
Massie, Wade W.
Masterson, Robert S.
Mattes, William M.
Matthews, Michelle

Mattingly, Bryan
Mattingly, Patrick W.
Mattingly, William S.
Mazezka, Jared A.
McArthy, Matthew L.
McCallister, Andrew B.
McCann, Kimberly S.
McClanahan, Elizabeth A.
McCollum, Gary D.
McComis, Lance E.
McCoy, Charlotte Turner
McCreary, Jr., John A.
McDowell, Derrick W.
McElroy, Alexander T.
McElwee, Douglas C.
McFadden, Angela
McFarland, Benjamin M.
McGinley, Patrick C.
McGinty, Sean B.
McGovern, Sean M.
McGranor, Timothy B.
McGrath, V. Brandon
McGraw, Dan F.
McGuire, Kevin M.
McIntyre, L. Jill
McKeen, Timothy M.
McKernan, Scott K.
McKinney, Benjamin C.
McKinney, Emily C.
McLaughlin, Erin J.
McLaughlin, Jim G.
McLusky, Robert G.
McManus, Lisa C.
McMaster, Esq., Lori E.
McMillan, Stuart A.
McPeak, David
McQuaid, Janet L.
McQueen, Aaron E.
Meadows, John J.
Meder, Richard C.
Melick, John Philip
Merrill, Frank L.

Mersing, Jennifer
Mettler, Fara
Michaels, Gregory C.
Michelmore, Daniel R.
Midler, Evan D.
Miller, Brant T.
Miller, George J.
Miller, Matthew R.
Miller, Timothy M.
Miller-Stover, Leslie
Mitchell, Daniel K.
Monferdini, Gary W.
Monroe, Katie L.
Monroe, Philip C.
Monteleone, Marc A.
Moody, Kevin J.
Mooney II, Nicholas P.
Mooney, Tim
Moore, Angel R.
Moore, Benjamin N.
Moore, Brian J.
Moore, Edward
Moore, Michael J.
Moore, R. Henry
Moore, Stephen M.
Moran, John
Moran, Sean W.
Morgan, Grahmn N.
Morgan, Nicole
Morgan, Ryan J.
Morley, Brian D.
Morrison, C. David
Moses, Matthew I.
Mosites, Jean M.
Mott, W. Gregory
Mounts, Ricky B.
Mulhall, Alexander S.
Mullin, Daniel
Mullins, Chuck
Mullins, Emily M.
Mundy, Kara M.
Mungai, Evan M.

FOUNDATION MEMBERSHIP

Munson, Melissa
Murphy, Ashley
Murphy, Jr., Daniel P.
Murphy, Katie Elizabeth
Murray, Daniel A.
Myers, Todd C.
Nadeau, Danielle J.
Nahley, Christopher
Naidu, B. David
Naresh, Ragan
Naum, Barry A.
Naumann, Mary Elisabeth
Negaard, Joseph
Nelson, Jeffrey N.
Nett, Cody E.
Nicholas, Elizabeth E.
Nichols, Troy N.
Nicholson, Roger L.
Noble, Stephanie
Normane, Todd
Normil, Sydney Rochelle
Norris, Melanie Morgan
Northam, Patrick R.
Nortz, Marissa G.
Nowlin, Jack Wade
Nunez, Jacinto A.
Nunley, Jonathon P.
Nutzman, Jason M.
O'Brien, William J.
O'Neill, M. Beth
O'Neill, Thomas J.
O'Rourke, Sean E.
O'Toole Jr., James
Oakley, K. Bradley
Oehler, Kathiejane
Oelrich, Lauren
Ofsa, Joyce Fleming
Oki, Kensuke
Olson, Victoria
Onest, Matthew
Orr, James
Osborne, Colin B.

Ossi, Gregory J.
Owen, Tammy J.
Pachowicz, Mark R.
Pack, Ashley C.
Palk, Roy M.
Palmer IV, John C.
Palmer, Jordan
Palmore, Austin R.
Palumbo, Corey L.
Park, Jennifer Sun
Parrish, Jesse M.
Parsons, Colton C.
Patsakis, Peter T.
Paternostro, Erin Anderson
Patterson, III, George A.
Patton, Jeffrey D.
Paul, Niall A.
Pechin, Tim W.
Peck, Alison
Pennington, James C.
Pepe, Raymond P.
Perdue, Cynthia D.
Persinger, III, Howard M.
Petersen, Terri
Peterson, Christopher G.
Petricoff, Nicholas
Petrucci, Gretchen
Phillips, Earl
Phillips, Jeffrey K.
Phillips, Kathleen R.
Phillips, William L.
Pichardo, Robert
Pierce, Jesse R.
Pierce, R. Cordell
Pierce, Robert Neal
Pifer, Ross H.
Pinson, John N.
Pizatella, Jason C.
Plybon, Christopher J.
Polinsky, Matthew
Potter, Sharon L.
Povilaitis, John F.

Powell, Jennifer
Power, Christopher B. (Kip)
Preservati, Nicholas S.
Presley, Nicklaus
Price, Joseph M.
Prozinski, Jennifer G.
Pulito, Brian J.
Purpura, Ryan T.
Puz, Rodger L.
Rabbitt, Chris
Rams, Filip M.
Ramsay, Ashlyn M.
Raney, William B.
Raphael, David J.
Ray, Jay
Reale, II, Philip A.
Receski, Edward A.
Rech, Steven R.
Rector, Larry J.
Reer, Michael K.
Reinhart, Joseph K.
Reyes, Alexander J.
Rhein, Mitchell J.
Rhine, John E.
Rhodes, Steven A.
Rhorer, Jr., John R.
Rich, Jr., Peter R.
Richards, Douglas J.
Richardson, Pierce
Richner, Amber M.
Rickman, Jennifer
Ries, David G.
Riggs, Susan J.
Riley, Steven Patrick
Ritchie, Alex
Ritter, Karsten H.
Roberts, Jeffrey D.
Robertson, David L.
Robertson, W. Craig
Robinson, Heath
Robinson, William E.
Roeder III, George E.

Rogers, Austin D.
Rogers II, Fon
Rogers, Christopher W.
Rogers, David A.
Rogier, Rachel
Roles, Forrest H.
Romito, John
Roncevich, Pat
Rorabaugh, Roger R.
Rose IV, H. Hampton
Rossi, Ellen
Rounds, Timothy R.
Rubenstein, F. Thomas
Rubenstein, Justin A.
Rudoy, Bruce F.
Ruffin, Karia
Rush, Donald
Rush, Michael L.
Russell, Gregory D.
Ryan, Thomas C.
Sadd, Mark A.
Saffer, Charles F. W.
Samford, Courtney Ross
Sanyal, Anna
Sasson, Bridget K.
Sayre, Floyd McKinley
Scarr, Thomas E.
Schaefer, Joseph V.
Scheller, Walter Jennings
Schirra, Christine R.
Schlimmer, Philip A.
Schmitt, Lisa M.
Schock, Andrew N.
Schock, Marnie S.
Schoonover, Timothy A.
Schulberg, Arnold L.
Schuler, Ronald W.
Schultz, Chelsea
Schultz, Josie
Schultz, Yvette
Schulz, Mychal S.
Schuster, Timothy D.

FOUNDATION MEMBERSHIP

Schwabenbauer, Andrew K.
Schwabenbauer, Stephanie
Schwallie, Dennis
Schwerdtfeger, Tyson D.
Seabourne, Clare
Sebok, Al F.
Secret, Michael
Seeds, John R.
Seiler, Raymond
Selent, John
Seltzer, Alan M.
Sennett, Lance A.
Sergent Walls, Claire
Sersen, Jonathan
Sesek, Christian E.
Settineri, Michael J.
Sexton, J. Scott
Shain, Alex
Sheely, Sommer
Sheets, Sam
Sheets, Scott
Shillingstad, Hal A.
Shuck, Jakeb H.
Shum, Nicholas N.
Shuman, Grant H.
Siepman, Kenneth B.
Silkwood, Eric L.
Silverman, Steven B.
Simmons, Brittany Given
Simon, Corinne
Simon, Jennifer
Sims, Jason B.
Skelton, Madeline
Skrzysowski, Larry
Slagel, Gary E.
Slagle, Christopher N.
Slaughter, Christopher L.
Slavensky, Roy
Smith, Amy M.
Smith, Andrew R.
Smith, Candace B.
Smith, Cody R.
Smith, Dennise R.
Smith, Ernest E.
Smith, Nelva J.
Smith, Shannon P.
Smith, William H.
Smock, Thomas A.
Snyder, James R.
Snyder, Joshua S.
Sourgens, Frederic G.
Southworth, Louis S.
Spitz, Arie M.
Staiger, Carl F.
Stallard, W. Patrick
Standish, Arthur M.
Starcher, Ann R.
Steinbauer, Gary
Steptoe, Jr., Robert M.
Stewart, Madison
Stobbe, Nicholas A. R.
Stockman, Paul K.
Stoller, Samuel J.
Stone III, Darrell C.
Stonestreet, Robert M.
Strait, Bradley
Strnad, Barbara Y.
Sturgeon, Allyson K.
Sturgill, Jr., Barkley J.
Sullivan, Benjamin M.
Sturm, Kerri C.
Sullivan, Benjamin M.
Sullivan, Chad J.
Sullivan, Paul E.
Surma, John D.
Svirnovskiy, Simon Y.
Tannon, Elizabeth M.
Tatro, Brian
Tawney, Kenneth E.
Tennant, Linda K.
Terek, Christina S.
Thomas, Elizabeth
Thomerson, Robin B.
Thompson, Glenn A.W.

Thompson, Jim
Thompson, Teresa Ann
Tiblets, Elizabeth L.
Titus, III, Gerald M.
Tobias, Mitchell A.
Travis, Thomas E.
Trent, Paige
Trogdon, Holly
Truss, Marty
Turner, Allyn G.
Turner, James W.
Turner, Lauren K.
Turzai, Michael C.
Tynes, Jared
Tyree, Matthew S.
Tysiak, Nikolas E.
Underwood, Seth
Unger, Joseph
Unick, Mark A.
Valencia, Reynaldo
Valentine, Casey
Van Bever, G. Christopher
Vanneman, Julie
Varnado, Lauren
Veltri, Melissa Dodd
Veltri, Peter J.
Vennum, Michael K.
Verney, Benjamin
Very, Dennis R.
Vissing, Jacob
Vorys, Webb I.
Vuljanic, Erin R.
Wade, Charles K.
Wade, Suzanne
Wagner, Jeffrey W.
Wahoff, William J.
Wakefield, Jeffrey M.
Wallace, Christopher B.
Wallace II, William D.
Wallin, Anne Barret
Walls, Claire Sergent
Walls, James A.

Walston, David B.
Ward, Joseph
Warran, Jason R.
Watt, Kristin L.
Watt, Whitney Frazier
Watts, Gregory W.
Watts, Ryan
Webb, A.J.
Webster, Mickey T.
Weeks, Josh P.
Wein, Howard J.
Weingart, Karin L.
Weiss, Emily C.
Wells, Bret
Wells, G. Brian
Werner, Justin H.
West, J. Kevin
Westbrook, Margaret R.
Westbrook, Paul B.
Weston, R. Timothy
Whipkey, John
White, Alan Matthew
White, David E.
White, Hunter
White, J. Tyler
White, Kristin R.B.
Whitt, Sean M.
Wiegand, Martha A.
Williams, Allison B.
Williams, Christopher R.
Williams, Daniel L.
Williams, John M.
Williams, Sierra R. M.
Williamson, Derrick Price
Williamson, Rod E.
Willis, Paul
Wills, Kevin T.
Wilmoth, William D.
Wilson, C. Seth
Wilson, Craig P.
Winek, Michael H.
Wissinger, Chad

FOUNDATION MEMBERSHIP

Witcher, R. Lance
Witt, Jason D.
Witzel, Kenneth J.
Wochner, David L.
Wolfe, Emma
Wolfe, Katie
Wolfson, Arthur M.
Wood, J. Nelson
Woodrum, John R.
Woody, Charles L.
Wooton, Michelle Elmore
Woyt, Elia O.
Wright, Anna
Yan, Celine
Yarborough, M. Caroline

Yaussy, David L.
Yocius, Stephanie M.
Yost, Jeffrey J.
Young, Randel R.
Zabela, Keith A.
Zemke, Megan
Zentmeyer, Brooke N.
Zerrusen, Sandra K.
Ziance, Scott J.
Ziegler, John David
Zirillo, Jesse J.
Zoeller, Brian D.
Zukowsky, Philip A.
Zurakowski, Scott M.

Table of Reported Cases

A Adams v. All Coast, L.L.C., 15 F.4th 365 (5th Cir. 2021) 48-50

Apache Corp. v. Castex Offshore, Inc., 626 S.W.3d 371 ... 86, 107 (Tex. App.—Houston [14th Dist.] 2021, pet. denied)

Appalachian Resources West Virginia WEVA 2022-0301 and WEVA 2022-428 159

B Bachtell Enterprises, LLC v. Ankor E&P Holdings Corporation, ...113-114
651 S.W.3d 514 (Tex. App.—Houston [14th Dist.] 2022, no pet.)

Barhight v. Terra Oilfield Servs.,
No. MO:19-CV-00214-DC, ...55-56
2021 U.S. Dist. LEXIS 111251 (W.D. Tex. Mar. 2, 2021)

Bernstein v. Buckeye, Inc., No. MO:18-CV-97-DC, ... 51-52
2020 U.S. Dist. LEXIS 262830 (W.D. Tex. Sep. 23, 2020)

Bluestone Oil, WEVA 2022-0176 158-159

Bradford Energy Capital, LLC v. SWEPI LP,
No. 17-1231, ... 111-112
2020 WL 5747841 (W.D. Pa. Sept. 25, 2020)

Brown v. Cont'l Res., Inc., 2021 U.S. Dist.
LEXIS 252396, *17 141

C Chartier v. Rice Drilling D LLC, 2023 Ohio 272, 206 N.E.3d 755 (Ohio Ct. App. 2023) 9-10

Chesapeake Operating, Inc. v. Sanchez Oil & Gas Corp., No. H-11-1890, ... 109-110
2012 WL 2133554, at *3 (S.D. Tex. June 12, 2012)

City of Kenai v. Cook Inlet Nat. Gas Storage Alaska, LLC, ... 141
373 P.3d 473, 484 (Alaska 2016)

TABLE OF REPORTED CASES

I-ii

Columbia Gas Transmission Corp. v. Smail, ...142-143
1986 U.S. Dist. LEXIS 22580, *13 (N.D. Ohio July 18, 1986)

Consol of Pennsylvania Company LLC PENN 2021-0108 159

Copley v. Evolution Well Servs. Operating, LLC, No. 2:20-CV-1442-CCW, ...54-55
2022 U.S. Dist. LEXIS 17266 (W.D. Pa. Jan. 31, 2022)

Corder v. Antero Res. Corp. 57 F.4th 384 (4th Cir. 2023) 11-12

County Line Stone Co. YORK 2022-0003 159

Crimson Exploration Operating, Inc. v. BPX Operating Co., ...110-112
No. 14-20-00070-CV, 2021 WL 786541
(Tex. App.—Houston [1st Dist.] Mar. 2, 2021, pet. denied)

D Dressler Family, LP v. PennEnergy Res., 2022 Pa. Super. 77 ...12
(Pa. Super. Ct. 2022)

Earp v. Mid-Continent Petroleum Corp., 27 P.2d 855
(Okla. 1933) 86-87

E Emeny v. United States, 412 F.2d 1319 (Ct. Cl. 1969) 145-146

G Ganci v. MBF Insp. Servs., 323 F.R.D. 249 (S.D. Ohio 2017) 44

Ganci v. MBF Insp. Servs., No. 2:15-cv-2959, 2019 U.S. Dist. LEXIS 207645 44
(S.D. Ohio Dec. 3, 2019)

Genesis Alkali, WEST 2022-0189 ALJ 159

Gentry v. Hamilton-Ryker IT Sol., LLC,
No. 3:19-cv-00320, ...36-37
2022 U.S. Dist. LEXIS 38398 (S.D. Tex. Mar. 4, 2022)

GPA Midstream Ass'n v. United States Dep't
of Transportation, ... 124-125
67 F.4th at 1199

Greenbrier Minerals, LLC., WEVA 2022-0294 158-159

Guyton v. Legacy Pressure Control, No. 5:15-cv-1075-RCL, 39, 41
2017 U.S. Dist. LEXIS 7836, (W.D. Tex. Jan. 18, 2017)

H Hargrave v. AIM Directional Servs., L.L.C., No. 21-40496, ... 52
(5th Cir. May 11, 2022)

Helix Energy Sols. Grp., Inc. v. Hewitt, 143 S. Ct.
677, 682 (2023) 31-36

Hernandez v. Helix Energy Sols. Grp., Inc., No. H-18-1588, 48, 50
2021 U.S. Dist. LEXIS 82107 (S.D. Tex. Apr. 29, 2021)

Hobbs v. EVO Inc., 7 F.4th 241 (5th Cir. 2021) 44-45

K KC Transport v. Secretary of Labor, MSHA, 77 F.4th 1022 (Aug.
1, 2023), ... 163
(Rehearing denied, 2023 W.L. 6466441 (Oct. 3, 2023)

Knight Hawk Coal, LAKE 2021-0160 158-159

L Last v. M-I, L.L.C., No. 1:20-cv-01205-ADA-EPG, ... 45
2022 U.S. Dist. LEXIS 232167 (E.D. Cal. Dec. 27, 2022)

Little v. Technical Specialty Prod., No. 4:11-cv-717, ... 57
2012 U.S. Dist. LEXIS 152041 (E.D. Tex. Oct. 23, 2013)

M Mapco, Inc. v. Carter, 808 S.W.2d 262 (Tex. App.) 145-146

Martin v. Rush, LLC, No. 6:20-CV-00005-JDL, ... 37-38
2021 U.S. Dist. LEXIS 12602 (E.D. Tex. Jan. 22, 2021)

TABLE OF REPORTED CASES

Maxxim Rebuild Co. v. Fed. Mine Safety & Health Review Comm'n, ... 162-163
848 F.3d 737 (6th Cir. 2017)

Mondeck v. LineQuest, LLC, No. MO:19-CV-221-DC, ... 46
2021 U.S. Dist. LEXIS 218651 (W.D. Tex. Aug. 28, 2021)

Myers-Woodward, LLC v. Underground Servs. Markham, LLC, ...145
2022 Tex. App. LEXIS 4082

P

Palace Exploration Co. v. Petroleum Development Co., ... 104
374 F.3d 951 (10th Cir. 2004)

Peppertree Farms, L.L.C., et al. v. Thonen et al., ... 8
167 Ohio St.3d 52, 2022-Ohio-395

Perry County Resources, KENT 2022-0024 159

Pomposini v. T.W. Phillips Gas & Oil Co., ... 144
580 A.2d 776 (Pa. Super. Ct. 1990)

R

Ramaco Resources LLC, WEVA 2022-0260 159

Raptis v. DPS Land Servs., LLC, No. 2:19-CV-01262-CRE, ...45-46
2020 U.S. Dist. LEXIS 89407 (W.D. Pa. May 21, 2020)

Rulon Harper Coal, WEST 2022-0249 and 0250 159

S

Sackett v. Environmental Protection Agency, No. 21-454 4-5

Scott v. Antero Res. Corp., 540 F. Supp. 3d 1039
(D. Colo. 2021) 33-34

Stine v. Marathon Oil Co., 976 F.2d 254, 261
(5th Cir. 1992)...106

U U.S. Steel Corp. v. Hoge, 468 A.2d 1380 (Pa. 1983) 143-144

V Venable v. Schlumberger Ltd., No. 6:16-CV-00241, ... 47-48
2022 U.S. Dist. LEXIS 55389 (W.D. La. Mar. 24, 2022)

W W. Va. et al. v. EPA, 985 F. 3d 914 (2022) 5-6

Wimberley v. Beast Energy Servs.,
No. 3:19-cv-00096, ...39, 43-44, 56
2022 U.S. Dist. LEXIS 38392 (S.D. Tex. Mar. 4, 2022)

Major Topic Index

A Administrative Agencies
    Environmental Protection Agency 4-6, 130
    Mine Safety and Health Administration 152-162
    Occupational Health and Safety Administration 165-178
    Pipeline and Hazardous Material Safety
    Administration 125-135
    United States Department of Transportation 65, 125-126, 135

Alternative Dispute Resolution 76-77

Arbitration 76-77

C Carbon Capture and Sequestration 6, 137-147

Clean Air Act 3

Clean Water Act 3, 4

Climate Change 3, 4, 7

Coal Leases 12-13

Coal Mining Operations 149-165

D Damages 23, 30-31, 57-59, 76

Due Diligence 93-94, 114

E Ethics 15-24

F Fair Labor Standards Act 27, 31-32, 59,

I Implied Covenants 13, 94

Intellectual Property 68-80

J Joint Operating Agreements 84-121

	Jurisdiction 98, 100-102, 163-164
L	Labor & Employment 29-66
	Landmen 84-121
	Liability 59-60, 120-121
M	Mine Safety & Health 151-164

Model Rules of Professional Conduct
    Model Rule 3.1.   Meritorious Claims and Contentions........17
    Model Rule 3.6.   Trial Publicity 17-18
    Model Rule 4.1.   Truthfulness in Statements to Others ..18-19
    Model Rule 4.4.   Respect for Rights of Third Persons...19, 22
    Model Rule 8.4.   Misconduct... 20

O	Ohio Marketable Title Act...7-8
P	Property Law Issues 137-148
	Protecting Our Infrastructure of Pipelines and Enhancing Safety (2020 PIPES Act) 128-130
R	Royalty Issues 10-13, 85-86, 146
T	Title Issues ....7-9, -138-139, 140, 143-146

Made in the USA
Middletown, DE
30 October 2024